SOUTH TYNESIDE PUBS

EILEEN BURNETT

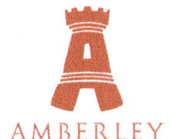

First published 2018

Amberley Publishing
The Hill, Stroud
Gloucestershire, GL5 4EP

www.amberley-books.com

Copyright © Eileen Burnett, 2018
Maps contain Ordnance Survey data.
Crown Copyright and database right, 2018

The right of Eileen Burnett to be identified as the Author of this work has been asserted in accordance with the Copyrights, Designs and Patents Act 1988.

ISBN 978 1 445 6 7801 6 (print)
ISBN 978 1 445 6 7802 3 (ebook)

All rights reserved. No part of this book may be reprinted or reproduced or utilised in any form or by any electronic, mechanical or other means, now known or hereafter invented, including photocopying and recording, or in any information storage or retrieval system, without the permission in writing from the Publishers.

British Library Cataloguing in Publication Data.
A catalogue record for this book is available from the British Library.

Origination by Amberley Publishing.
Printed in the UK.

Contents

Introduction 4
Key 6
Map 8
Acknowledgements 96

Introduction

I knew very little about the hotels, inns and taverns of South Tyneside until I started researching for this book. I have spent many hours trawling through directories in The Word, South Shields and Newcastle Library looking for the tenants, landlords, owners or licensees of those establishments. The oldest directory available is from 1822, but unfortunately it does not cover much of South Tyneside – only South Shields and Gateshead – and the oldest periodical is the *Courant* from 1726.

This book is about the hotels, inns and tavern in the old parochial parishes of Whitburn, Boldon and Jarrow taken from the old directories of the area. Unfortunately, unlike Sunderland, South Shields and Gateshead some areas covered in this book are not as well documented.

Whitburn parish covered both Whitburn and Cleadon, Whitburn village being 3½ miles north of Sunderland and 5 miles south of South Shields. In 1873 it was described as 2½ miles from Cleadon Lane station, which was on the North Eastern line. Cleadon village was 3½ miles from both Sunderland and South Shields. By 1873 both Whitburn and Cleadon had three public houses. Although Whitburn had a post office in 1873, letters were delivered each day from Sunderland. There is no mention of any coaches or carriers going through the village, although many would have.

In 1834 Boldon was comprised of two townships, east and west, and was within the union of South Shields. East Boldon station at Cleadon Lane saw carriers passing through the village on Tuesday, Thursday and Saturday, with letters being delivered by messenger every morning at nine o'clock. West Boldon was described as 'pleasantly situated in a rocky eminence, about 4½ miles north west of Sunderland'. West Boldon also had a station on a branch of the North Eastern Railways South Shields line but this was for goods only. White Mare Pool came under the parish of Boldon in 1841 and 1851 census.

The year 1870 saw the opening of a new colliery at Boldon New Winning. Around 3 miles from South Shields, this is what became Boldon Colliery and is known today as Boldon New Town.

In 1828 Jarrow was a village 3 miles south-west by west of South Shields and 6 miles east of Newcastle on the south side of the River Tyne. Jarrow parochial parish was much larger, taking in the townships and small hamlets along the River Tyne, which included Nether Heworth, Friar's Goose, Felling Shore, Low Felling, High Felling, Carr Hill, Windy Nook, Heworth Colliery, Heworth Lane, Heworth Shore, Bill Quay and Pelaw.

Hebburn was only a colliery village in the township of Monkton; Hebburn also belonged to Jarrow Monastery.

Jarrow covered a much larger area including parts of Tyne Dock, which was East Jarrow, Harton and Simonside.

Key

Cleadon
1. The Cottage Tavern, Shields Road, Cleadon village
2. The Britannia, Shields Road, Cleadon village
3. The Old Ship Inn, Front Street, Cleadon village

Whitburn
1. The Grey Horse Inn, North Guard, Whitburn village
2. The Jolly Sailor, East Street, Whitburn village
3. The Highlander Front Street, Whitburn village

Heworth, Felling, Pelaw and Bill Quay
1. The Swan, Sunderland Road Villas, Heworth
2. The Cumberland Arms, Sunderland Road, Heworth
3. Blink Bonny Inn, Sunderland Road, Felling
4. Green Mandolin, Collingwood Street, Felling
5. Oddfellows Arms, Davison Street, Felling
6. Beeswing Hotel, High Street and Sunderland Road, Felling
7. Halfway House, High Street, Felling
8. Blue Bell Inn, High Street, Felling
9. Victoria Jubilee, Split Crow Road, Felling
10. Bay Horse, Windy Nook
11. Black House Inn, Windy Nook
12. Bay Horse Inn, Coldwell Lane, Felling
13. The Portland Arms, Split Crow Road, Felling
14. Pear Tree Inn, Sunderland Road, Felling
15. The Mallard, Gosforth Street, Felling
16. Lord Collingwood Hotel, Collingwood Street, Felling
17. Mulberry Inn, Mulberry Street, Felling
18. Old Fox, Carlisle Street, Felling
19. The Wheat Sheaf and Malting House, Carlisle Street, Felling
20. The Pelaw Inn, Shields Road, Pelaw
21. The Albion Inn, Reay Street, Bill Quay
22. The Cricketers' Arms, Joel Terrace, Bill Quay
23. The Wardley, Brack Terrace, Bill Quay

South Tyneside

1. Grey Horse, Front Street, East Boldon
2. Black Bull, Front Street, East Boldon
3. Red Lion, Redcar Terrace, West Boldon
4. Travelling Man, Newcastle Road, West Boldon
5. Wheatsheaf, No. 5 St Nicholas Road, West Boldon
6. Black Horse, Rectory Bank, West Boldon
7. Flat Tops, North Road, Boldon Colliery
8. The Colliery, Hedworth Lane, Boldon Colliery
9. The Crown, Hedworth Lane, Boldon Colliery
10. The Grey Hound, Hedworth Lane, Hedworth
11. The Robin, Roman Road, Hedworth
12. The Prince of Wales, Calf Close, Hedworth
13. Lord Nelson, Monkton Village
14. The Lakeside Inn, East Fellgate Farm, Leam Lane, Fellgate
15. The Green, White Mare Pool, South Wardley
16. Argyle Hotel, Victoria Road, Hebburn
17. Station Hotel, Station Road, Hebburn
18. Mambo II (originally County Hotel), Station Road, Hebburn
19. Wardles Wine Bar, Albert Terrace, Hebburn
20. The Clock, Victoria Road, Hebburn
21. The Caladonian, Lyon Street
22. Banks of the Tyne, Hebburn
23. White Lead, Blackett Street, Hebburn
24. Western Hotel, Western Road, Jarrow
25. Rolling Mill, Western Road, Jarrow
26. Queen's Hotel, Western Road, Jarrow
27. North Eastern, Clayton Street and Wear Street, Jarrow
28. Ben Lomond Hotel, Ellison Street, Jarrow
29. Station Hotel, Ellison Street, Jarrow
30. Ellison Arms Hotel, No. 1 Western Road, Jarrow
31. Royal Oak, Grange Road and Staple Road, Jarrow
32. Bell Rock Hotel, Nixon Street, Jarrow
33. McConnell's Gin House, Walter Street, Jarrow
34. Golden Lion, Ellison Place and Walter Street, Jarrow
35. The Queens, Union Street, Jarrow
36. The Royal Hotel, Market Place, Jarrow
37. Gas Light, Commercial Road and Tyne Street, Jarrow
38. Prince of Wales, Commercial Road and Tyne Street, Jarrow
39. Globe Hotel, Buddle Street and Princes Street, Jarrow
40. Crown and Anchor, Chapel Road, Jarrow
41. Alexander Hotel, High Street, Jarrow
42. East Ferry Inn, Jarrow Quay,
43. Bridge Inn, Jarrow Church
44. Allison Arms, Straker Street, East Jarrow
45. Alkali Hotel, Swinburne Street, East Jarrow

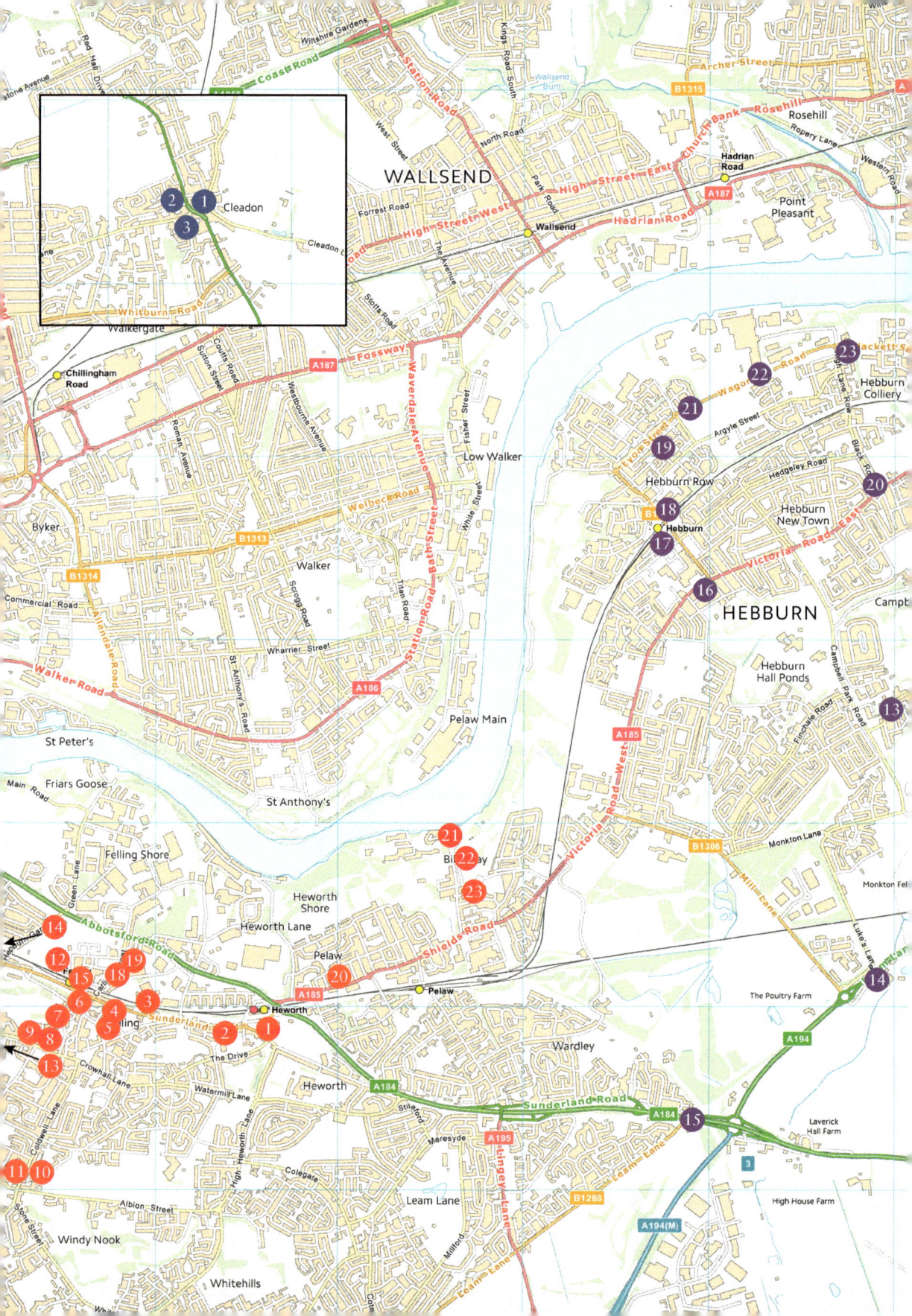

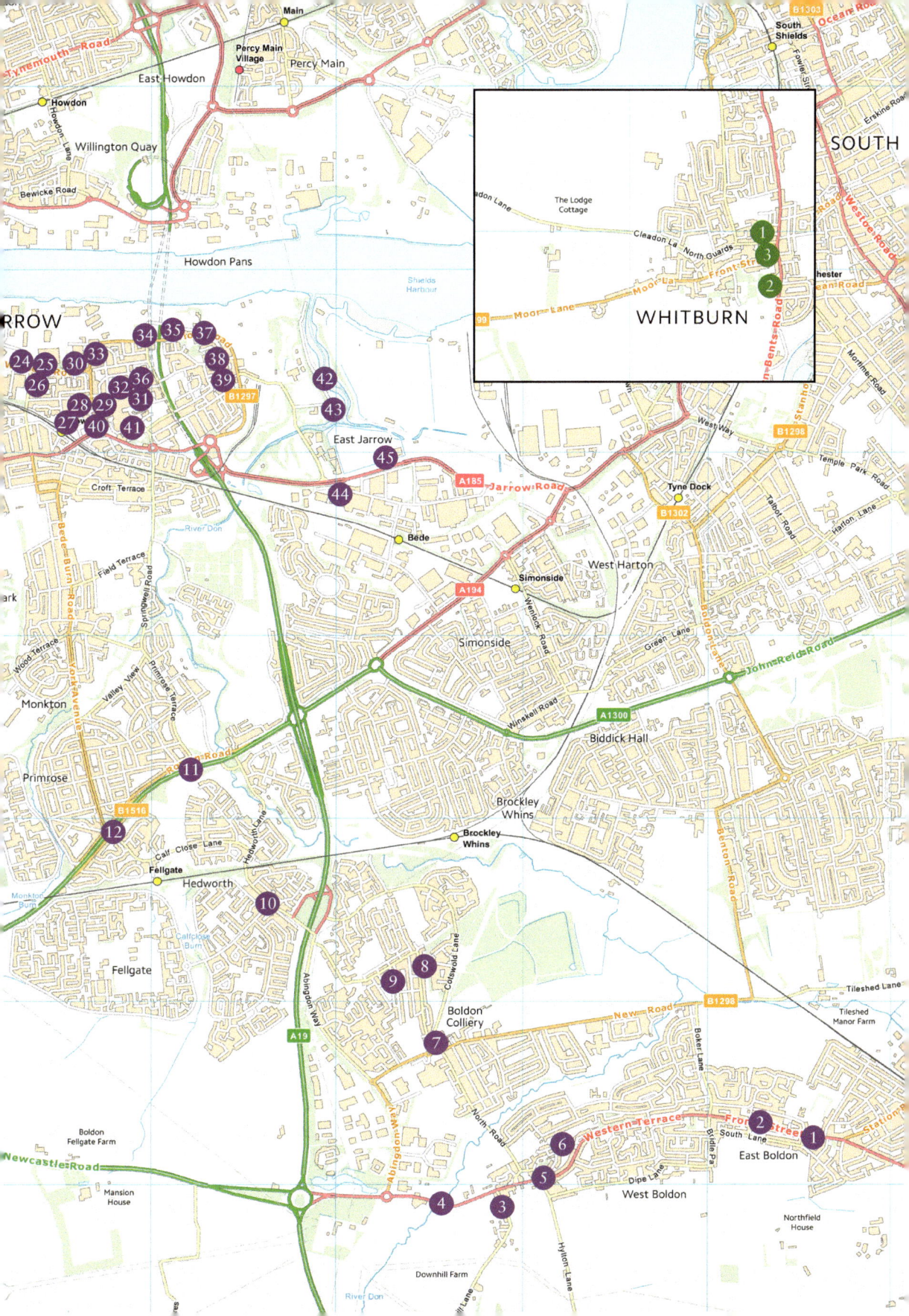

The Grey Horse Inn

The Grey Horse Inn, Whitburn village, is an impressive building that was no more than a farmhouse before becoming an inn. First advertised by Henry Merriman in 1834, it stayed in the Merriman family until William Holmes became the licensee in 1881. Today the Grey Horse is a Greene King pub and its prominent corner position shows it off to its best advantage. Not only does it have a public bar, which is excellent for a quiet drink or playing pub games, but it also has a large lounge with a warm comfortable environment to meet and catch up with friends. A raised dining area that serves both lunch and evening meals is popular, although you can eat anywhere you choose. Outside is a large pub garden for those warm summer days where you can take the family or your dog and relax and enjoy a pint of real ale, two of which are regular ales – Moreland Old Speckled Hen and Greene King Abbott – as well as traditional beer. It is also Cask Marque accredited (the cask ale on sale is kept to a required standard, temperature, taste, appearance and aroma, all checked by an unannounced assessor). In addition there is a car park at the rear and also a smoking area. As well as the local clientele Whitburn has many summer visitors coming to visit this tranquil village, and with a bus stop only yards away, you can enjoy a good night out without worrying and catch a bus home.

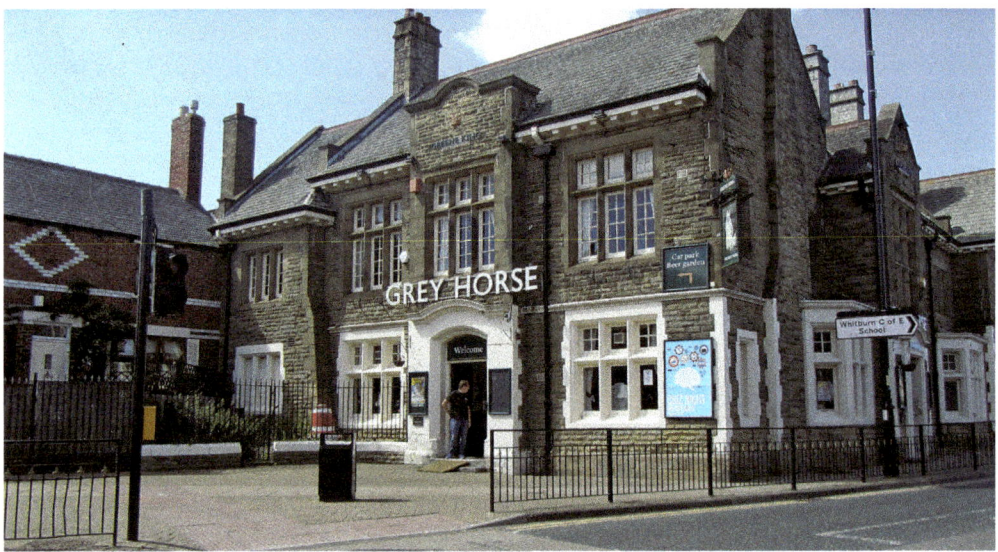

Grey Horse, Whitburn village.

The Jolly Sailor

The Jolly Sailor, Whitburn, was first advertised by Cuthbert Hutchinson in Pigot's 1828 directory, then by John Young in 1834. By 1839 Cuthbert Hutchinson was again the licensee. At that time it was on the sea path (East Street) connecting Whitburn to Whitburn Bents, a nearby hamlet, and Marsden. The pub was in the hands of the Punch Tavern Group as a beer-only public house before being sold in 2007 when the company

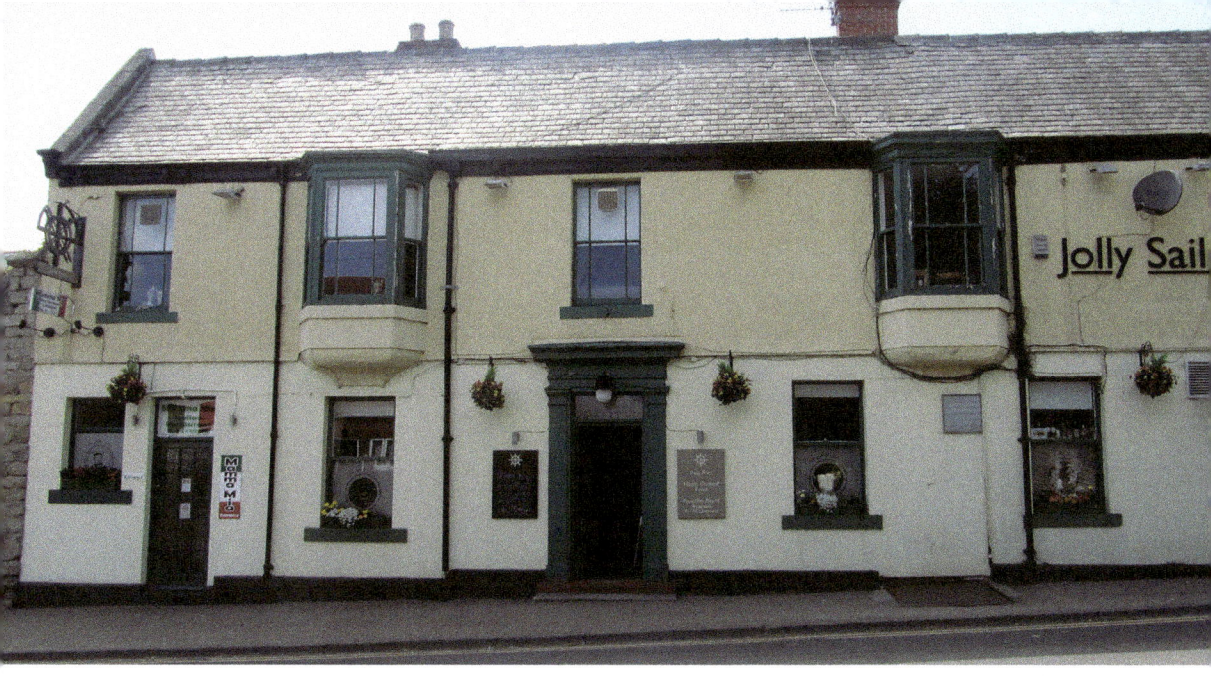

Jolly Sailor, Whitburn village.

started struggling and needed to sell 2,600 pubs. The new owner fully refurbished the pub and it now has two rooms: the Captain's Cabin where they usually serve food Thursday to Sunday and a quaint bar, which is the smallest room. They also converted part of the upstairs into a Mamma Mia Italian restaurant. Today the Jolly Sailor sells real ale as well as traditional beers – Courage Director is its regular beer. There is also a dog-friendly pub garden, and you can also borrow a newspaper to read while you enjoy your favourite tipple. Being close to bus stops that will take you to both Sunderland and South Shields by three different routes, you can enjoy a good night out.

The Highlander

This old photograph of the Highlander, Front Street, Whitburn, was taken around 1916 with Mrs Corfield standing in the doorway. Built in 1762, the Highlander was first advertised in 1828 by Elizabeth Swan, a licensed victualler (licensed to sell spirits as well as ale). By 1834 John Longstaff, licensed victualler and farmer, became the landlord, staying until in 1854 George Theaker Kirton, licensed victualler, became the licence holder. Cuthbert Story took over the Highlander in 1865, but in 1871 his wife Mary had become the licensee and the last person to advertise the Highlander in 1884. The Highlander was unfortunately demolished for the widening of Front Street in 1937.

Whitburn's other public houses, the Coble, Whitburn Bents, which was advertised in 1839 by Elizabeth Purvis, was advertised in 1846 and 1847 by William Purvis as the Board (a public house with no name). The next year William reverted back to calling it the Coble, giving the address as Whitburn Bent. In 1850 he again renamed the public house the Board Inn. When Henry Purvis became the licence holder in 1856, it was once again the Board, a name it kept. In 1865 William Purvis once again became the licence holder. The inn was not advertised again.

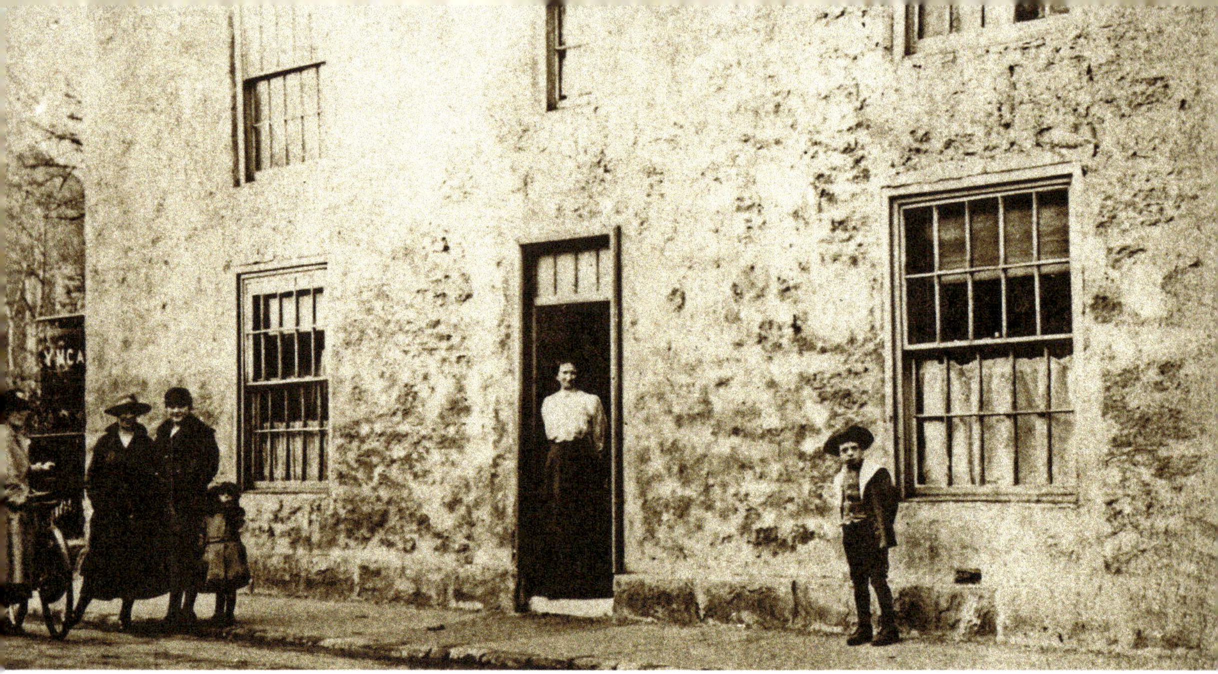

Highlander, Front Street, Whitburn village.

The Cottage Tavern
The Cottage Tavern, Cleadon village, was a private house before becoming a tavern more than 150 years ago – it is thought to have been a rope works before that. First advertised by John Shepherd in 1873, he could only sell ale and porter but no spirits.

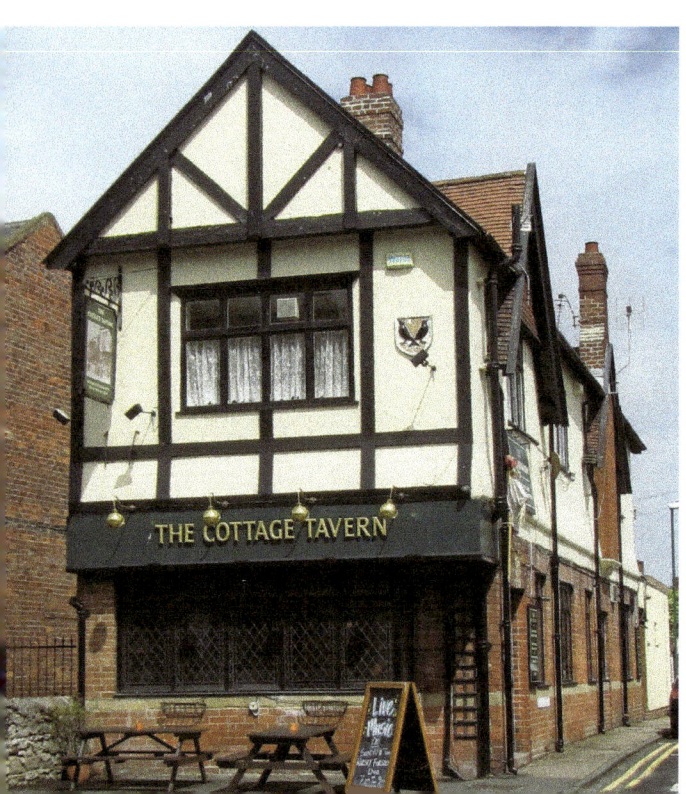

The Cottage, Shields Road, Cleadon village.

By 1881 John Weldon had become the innkeeper, possibly staying until Joe Hern took over the licence in 1910. The tavern has changed little over the years. With its single long room it has a nice friendly atmosphere, with a busker night every two weeks on a Wednesday and live music on a Sunday. The Cottage is on the list of CAMRA public house serving real ale and cider, as well as traditional beer. Traditional pub games are also played with quizzes being held every Monday and Thursday. It is also dog friendly and has a small pub garden. Although parking is available across the road, the Cottage is close to the bus stops in the village, with buses going to Sunderland, Boldon and South Shields.

Britannia Inn

Britannia Inn, Cleadon village, was first advertised in 1828 by Jane Hall. By 1834 William Merriman was the landlord, having moved from the Ship Inn across the road. The inn, originally a house, was much smaller than the present one. It is thought to have been built around 1675 and occupied by Michael and Isabel Matthews. This was once a coaching inn, like many in country villages, during the eighteenth and nineteenth centuries. Situated on the main route to South Shields from Leeds, passing coaches commuting from the south through Sunderland going both north and west would stop here. In 1825 The Royal Pilot Co. advertised an elegant 'Light Post-Coach' (four inside with guard throughout) commencing at five o'clock in the morning from the Golden Lion, South Shields, to Leeds, Manchester and Liverpool. It would leave South Shields travelling south through Cleadon village to Sunderland, then on to Castle Eden, Stockton on Tees, Yarm, Tontine Inn, Thirsk, Borough Bridge, Knaresborough and Harrogate, finally reaching the Bull & Mouth in Leeds. This was a daily service except for Sundays. On 20 August 1857 an auction held on behalf of the late Mr Wood sold the crops of Sunniside Farm, Cleadon. On 18 June 1877 the inn held the first monthly sale of cattle, horses, pigs and farming implements. On 20 August 1878 the 'away going crops' (a crop planted by a tenant that matures after the expiration of the tenancy and is rightfully the tenant's to harvest) from both Hill Top Farm and the Undercliffe estate were up for

Britannia, Boldon Lane, Cleadon village.

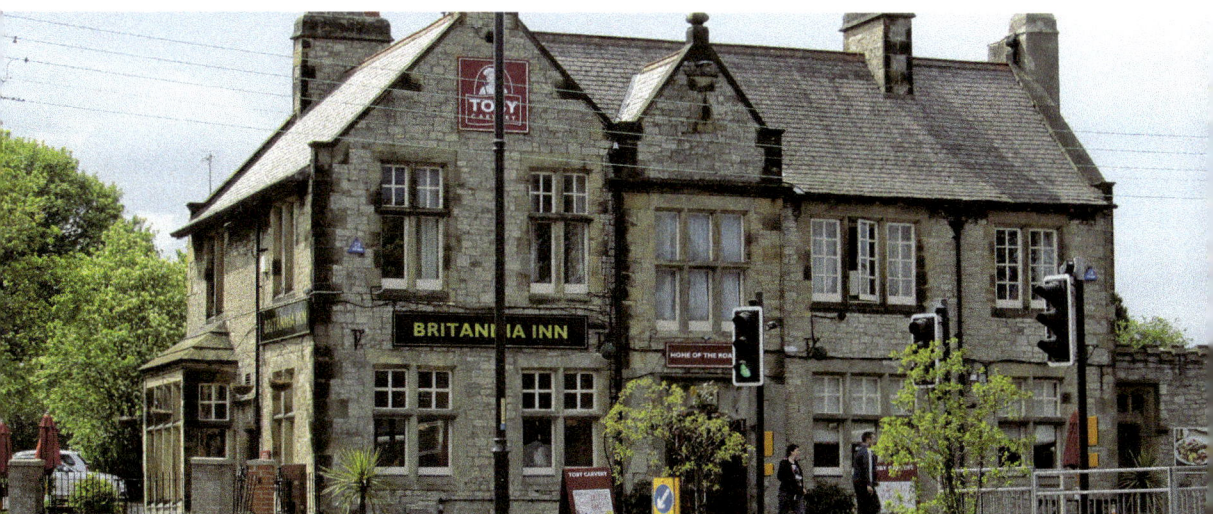

auction. The old Britannia was demolished around 1890 to make way for the present inn, which was built in 1894, becoming bigger and more modern as the village was growing fast. Today the Britannia is a very popular Toby Carvery selling real cask ale and is Cask Marque accredited. It has a good friendly atmosphere and is both dog and family friendly with disability access. Meals are served both at lunchtime and in the evening in both the restaurant and the bar area. Although there is a car park the buses run past the inn for those who like to socialise with friends.

The Ship Inn

The Ship Inn, Cleadon village, possibly dates back to the 1600s when it was a farmhouse before then becoming the first coaching inn for the village. When being demolished workmen found four coins dating back to 1702 beneath the old bar floor. The inn was first advertised by William Merriman, blacksmith, in 1828. Mary Merriman took over in 1834. At that time the inn was on the route coaches took journeying from the Sunderland to South Shields, each choosing their own taverns to stop at along the way. In 1806 the Royal Mail coach started running a daily service from the Golden Lion, South Shields, to York to catch the London Mail. Leaving South Shields it followed the same route as the Royal Pilot as far as Thirsk, then branching west joining the Great North Road for York. There it connected with the mail coaches going to London, Manchester or Liverpool, staying overnight at several inns along the way. Depending on your destination you would buy your ticket at the inns where the

Ship Inn, Sunderland Road, Cleadon village.

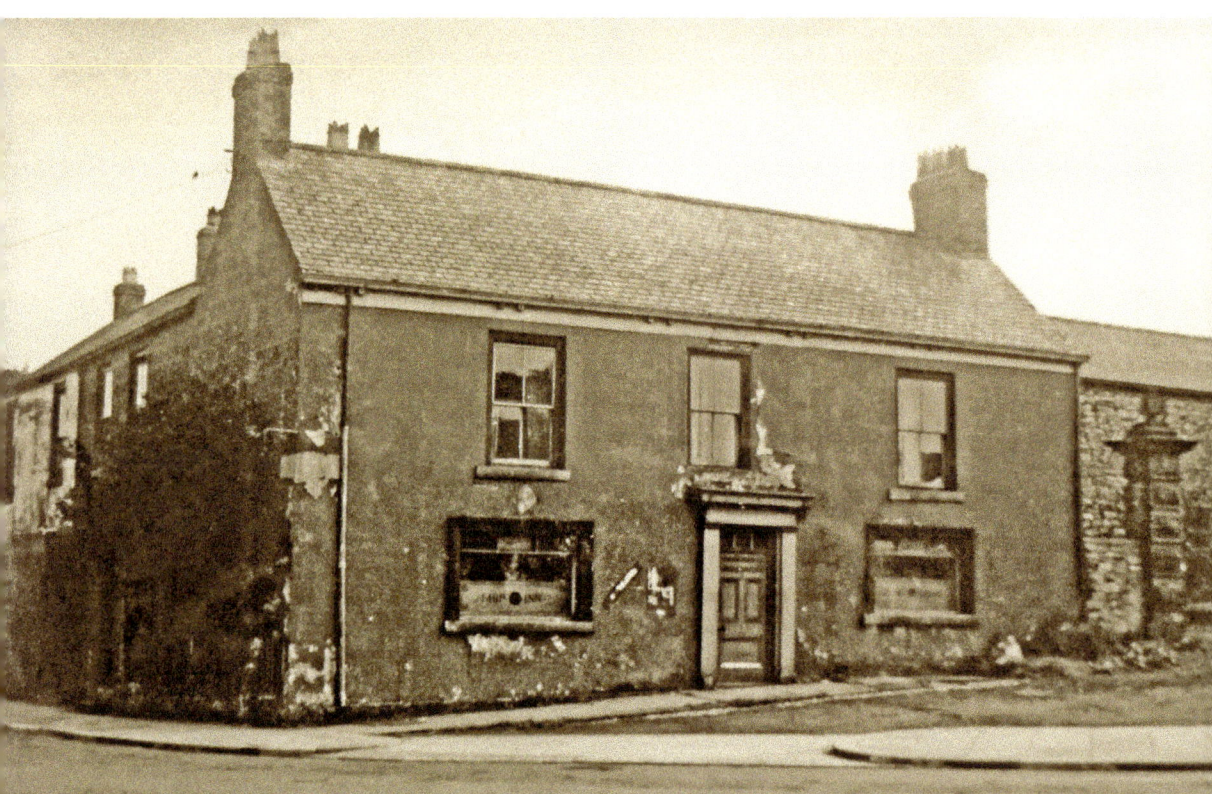

coach would stop at to pick you up. The Ship would see passengers only too happy to stop and stretch their legs and possibly refresh themselves, before enduring the long arduous ride across the hills to South Shields. The Old Ship licence was transferred to the New Ship in 1940. It was then used by the Home Guard during the Second World War, before being demolished for the widening of Sunderland Road in the 1950s.

The Grey Horse

The Grey Horse, Front Street, East Boldon, dates back to the beginning of the 1800s and was on the main coaching routes between Sunderland and Newcastle. I had heard that Dick Turpin once slept there but have found no evidence of this. In 1834 George Merriman, a blacksmith, advertised the inn and in 1853 it was in the hands of Henry Merriman. An auction held at the inn on Wednesday 27 April 1853 for the sale of two cottages states Mr Newman as the licence holder – many auctions were held there during his time as landlord. When William Corry took over the inn auctions continued to be held, these mainly being farmers selling their away going crops. In 1983 the Grey Horse, under the management of Albert and Brenda Coombes, won the Vaux Breweries Urban Pub of the Year title having competed against 453 other public houses. Albert and Brenda Coombes' masterstroke seems to have come from them opening a restaurant, which gave the pub that extra personal touch that Vaux had been looking out for. Today it is a traditional pub catering to a wide variety of clientele. It has a family-friendly atmosphere and caters for both lunchtime and evening meals, and with a real fire for those cold winter nights. There is a car park to the rear of the premises with disabled access at the front. Besides traditional beers, a selection of cask ales are also on offer and it is Cask Marque accredited. There is live sports TV and Wi-Fi is available. The Grey Horse is close to local transport with buses passing to South Shields, Sunderland, Jarrow and Newcastle.

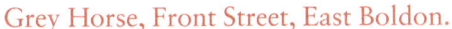

Grey Horse, Front Street, East Boldon.

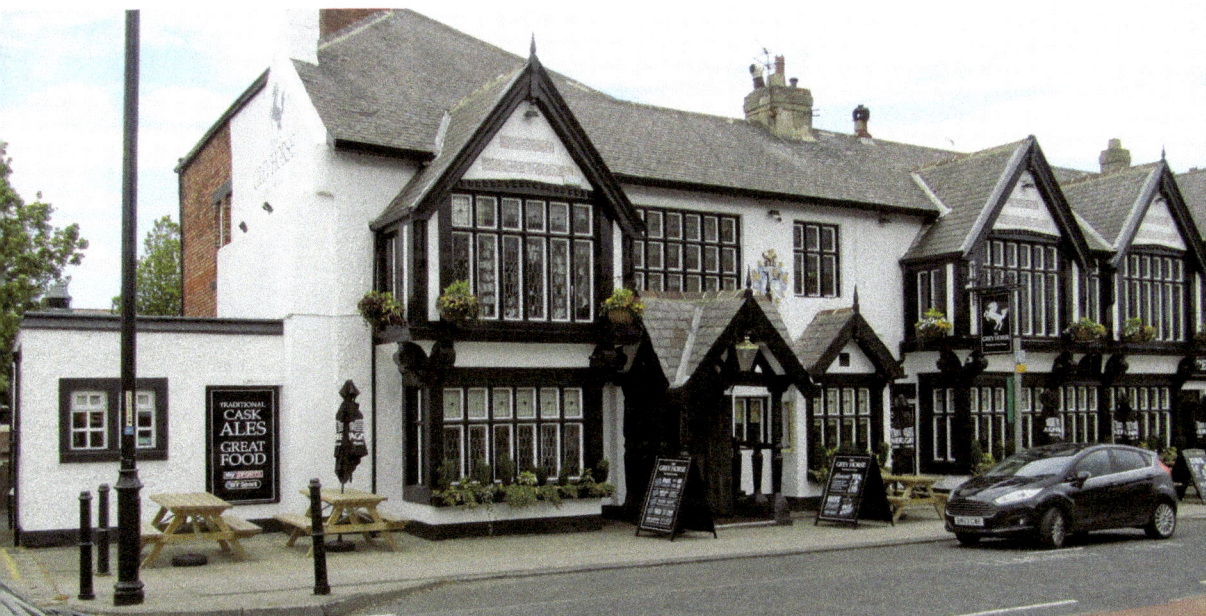

The Black Bull

The Black Bull, Front Street, East Boldon, was first advertised in 1834 by landlord Ralph Edward Robson. Mary Robson took over the licence in 1854 upon the death of her husband. Like other inns in the area, many auctions were held for the sale of the away going crops. On 20 July 1869 two 'substantial and well-built copy hold dwelling houses' were up for auction, these being Nos 4 and 6 Middle Boldon. These cottages were advertised as having no ground rent and 'many qualifications for Town's People being in close proximity to Cleadon Lane Station and free of the Heavy Taxation of the town'. They also boasted to having a flower garden to the front and a kitchen garden to the rear. Built at the end of the 1700s, this quaint old pub had a substantial investment of £100,000 spent on refurbishment and was reopened on 20 March 1987. Vaux Breweries added some new features to this popular pub, which included a beer garden with an access through its new conservatory. Inside there is a Victorian aspect with old-fashioned prints on the walls and other 'olde worlde' fittings. The kitchen had also been fully equipped, making it easier to cook more homemade traditional fare with the landlady cooking tasty bar lunches, early evening meals and traditional Sunday lunches. Children are made welcome. The car park was also enlarged to accommodate more clientele enjoying a night out in a more homely pub.

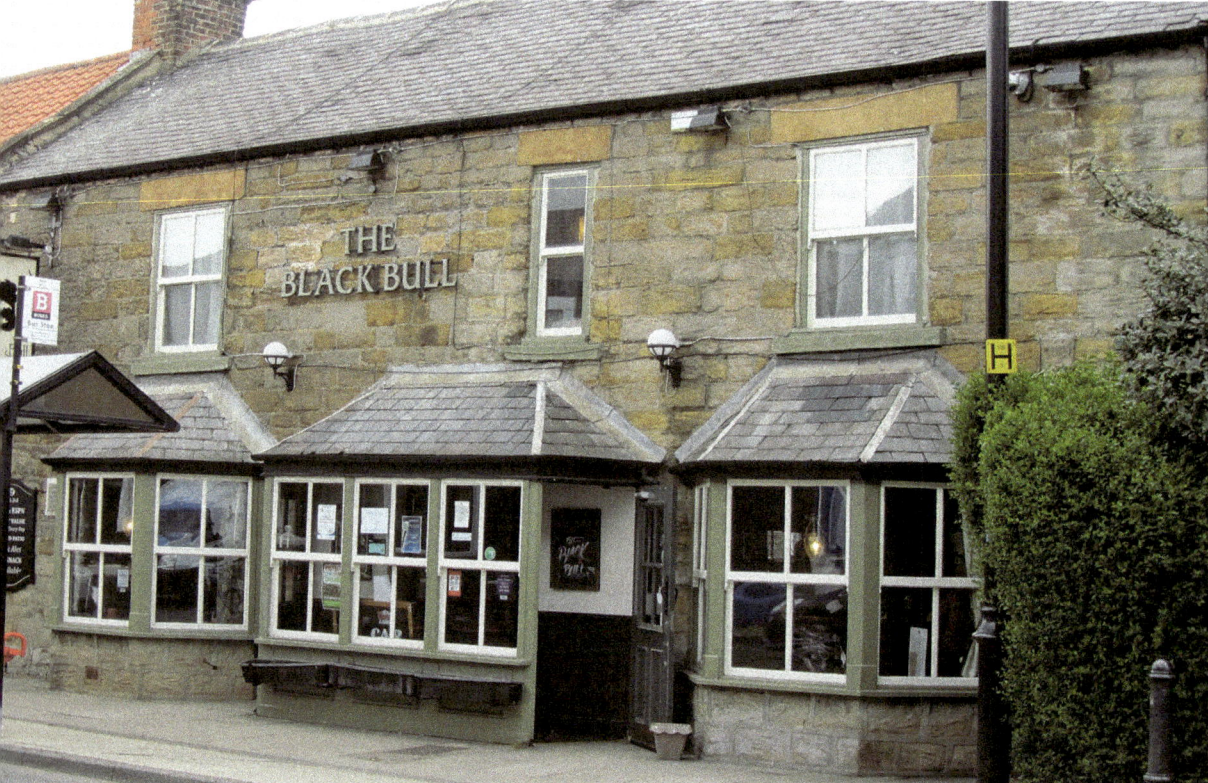

The Black Bull, Front Street, East Boldon.

The Red Lion Inn

The Red Lion Inn, Redcar Terrace, West Boldon, was originally called the Lion Inn when first advertised by Elizabeth Cowling in 1884. In 1899 the inn came up for sale and was bought by Joseph Horn, who was licensee of the Norfolk Hotel, Sunderland, at that time. Situated just before the turnoff into Downhill Lane leading to Hylton Bridge, Washington, then south to Chester Le Street and Durham, it was an ideal coaching inn for the weary traveller. In March 1903 Joseph Hern applied for a full licence as it was beer only. In February 1908 Arthur Ross also applied for a full licence or alternatively for wine on or off, explaining there was already an off-licence for the premises. He reasoned that although there were two licensed premises near people coming from Washington and going in the direction of Boldon Colliery, they would have to climb the hill if they desired spirits. The licence was dully granted. In March 1954 landlord Joseph Muckian and has wife Margaret were injured. Walter Lapsien, a twenty-six-year-old labourer of Boldon Colliery, threw a pint glass at Margaret that struck her on the face; he also struck Joseph on the head. Walter Lapsien was charged with unlawful wounding and demanding money with menaces. Today the Red Lion is both dog and family friendly with disability access. The bar and snug face onto the main Sunderland–Newcastle road. Behind these are the eating area, which includes a conservatory, with meals being served both at lunchtime and in the evening with a bar menu available. At the Red Lion you can have a pint of real ale with three regular beers being served: Black Sheep best bitter, Greene King IPA and Mortland Old Golden Hen. There is a pub garden and a car park to the rear.

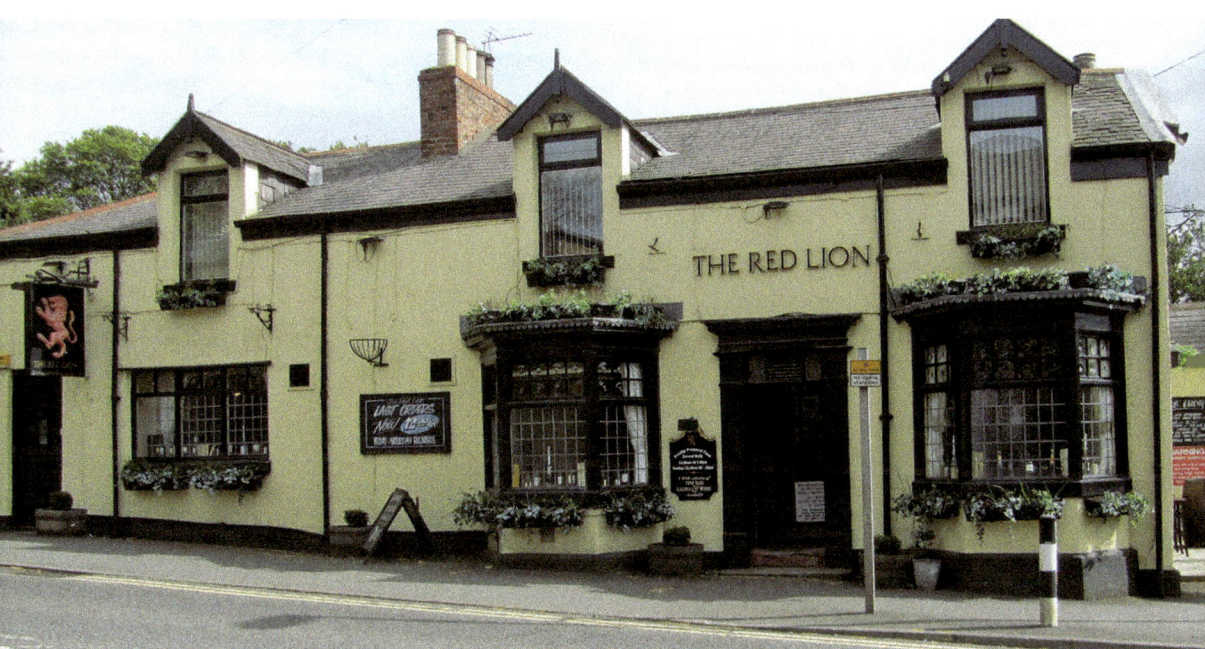

The Red Lion, Redcar Terrace, West Boldon.

Railway Tavern

This old photograph of the Railway Tavern, West Boldon, shows a house to one side and an off-licence on the other. In 1834 Michael Shaw, a licensed victualler, gave the address as Mount Pleasant. The tavern possibly took its name from the close-by colliery lines (between the A19 and Abington Way) that ran from Annfield Plain and Houghton Le Spring to Harton Staiths or Tyne Dock. Although a station was not far away, it was goods only; however this roadside tavern on the main Sunderland–Newcastle road was a handy stopping place for carriers picking up or dropping off parcels at the station. In January 1891 George Price, landlord, was up before South Shields Petty Sessions for illegally firing a gun on the highway. 'P. C. Wood stated that on New Year's Day, between one and two o'clock, he saw the defendant come out of his house onto the highway, and discharge a gun. Defendant said he did not wish to keep a loaded gun in the house. He drew the charge and fired the powder. The chairman said horses or people might have been frightened by defendant's conduct.' The case was dismissed on defendant paying costs. In August 1954 George Bell Smith, manager, the oldest licensee in Boldon, died aged eighty-three. He first became the licensee in 1936. On the outbreak of war he had gone back to sea at the age of sixty-nine, returning to the tavern afterwards. Today it is the Travelling Man, the shop and off-licence giving way to a much larger interior. It has held TripAdvisor Certificate of Excellence since 2014

Railway Tavern, Newcastle Road, West Boldon.

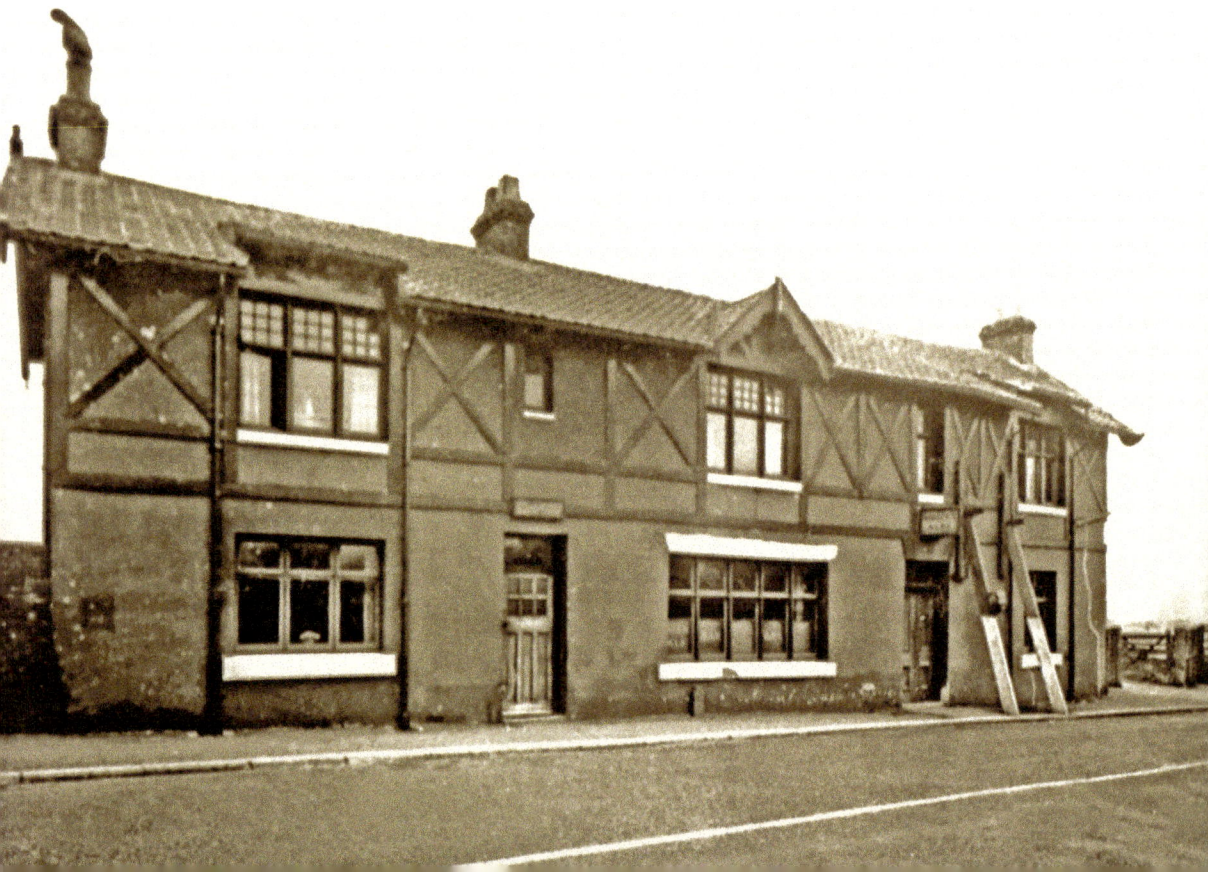

with a reputation for home-cooked food and a warm relaxing atmosphere. Selling real ale as well as the normal larger and beer, it caters for both lunchtime and evening meals. Outside there is pub garden for those warm summer days and modern disabled entrance for easy access to the pub, which is entered from the car park at the rear. This family-friendly pub has live music and on Sunday evenings there is a quiz and card bingo with a free buffet.

The Wheatsheaf

The Wheatsheaf, No. 5 St Nicholas Road, West Boldon, was first advertised by Thomas Leonard, licensed victualler, in 1828 but was taken over in 1834 by Margaret Ayre, licensed victualler. Margaret stayed until 1854 when Thomas Newburn, a butcher, became the licensee. On 20 September 1904 a presentation was held here for Mr Nathanial Brown, sexton of the parish church, on his retirement after forty years' service. A splendid gold watch, suitably inscribed, was given to him. It was attended by members of the parish council and parishioners alike. After the presentation a programme of vocal and instrumental music was rendered. In 1908, while George Ranson was the landlord, a young girl of six, Jessica Ann Hargreaves, was abused and murdered. Apparently Joseph Lawrence, a barman, was the murderer. Suzanne Hadwin, a psychic, claims they had as many as thirty-seven spirits roaming the pub, many of them children. At this time it was voted the most haunted public house in the UK. Today, with the spirits gone, there is a more tranquil atmosphere. The Wheatsheaf serves breakfast, lunch, coffee and drinks with table service and has outdoor seating. Food is also delivered or you can take it away. Children are welcome and you can also book parties there. There is a car park but with a bus stop not far away, you can have a good night out with friends and family.

The Wheatsheaf, No. 5 St Nicholas Road, West Boldon.

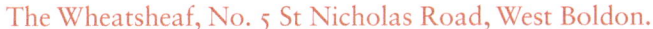

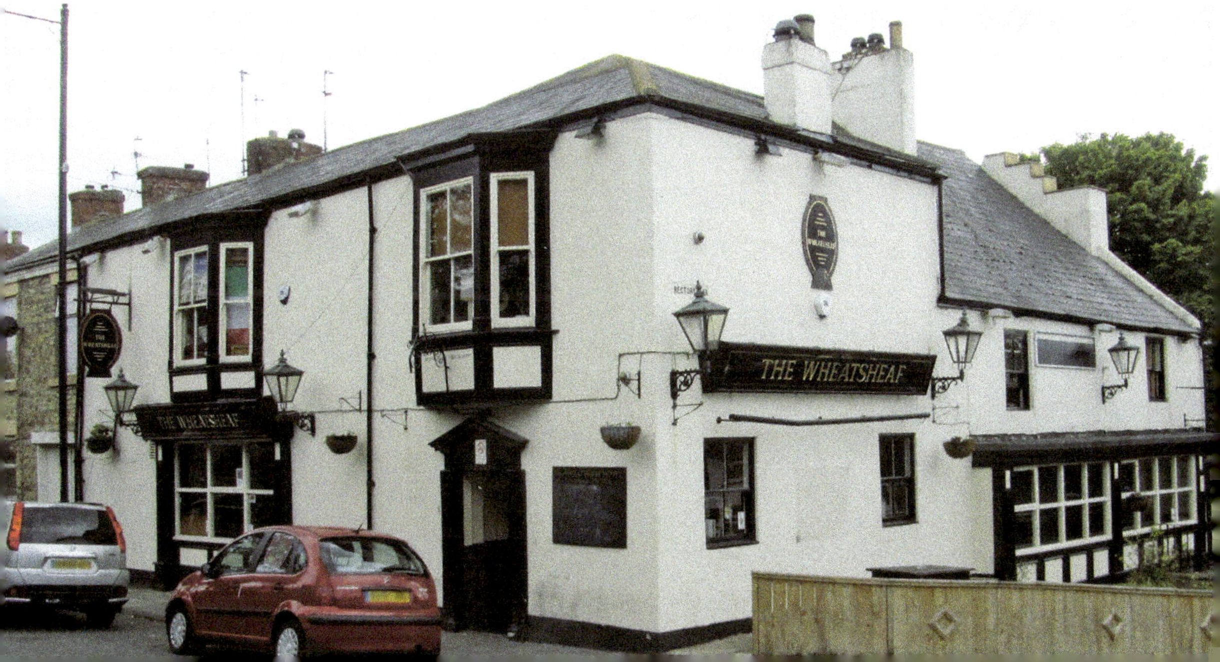

Black Horse

Dating back to at least the early 1700s but possibly earlier, the Black Horse, Rectory Bank, West Boldon, is steeped in history. A much earlier farmhouse dating from the 1300s may have once stood on this site. It is one of the oldest coaching inns in the area. During the battle of Boldon Hill where the Cavaliers and Roundheads fought, it is claimed Oliver Cromwell stayed there. John Merriman, a blacksmith like the previous generations of his family, was the landlord/owner in 1828, the premises having been in the family for four consecutive generations of John Merrimans. At that time there was his son and grandson, both John Merriman, to carry on the inn for the future. In 1871 William Davy became the landlord, causing speculation that the John Merriman name no longer existed. According to Pigot's Directory of 1828 the 'Wellington' coach (four inside) would leave Newcastle at eight o'clock in the morning, passing through Boldon and calling at the Black Horse, taking one hour, then travelling on to Sunderland, taking another half hour, and then returning to Newcastle at five in the afternoon. The Newcastle to Sunderland carriers would pass along the same route Tuesdays, Thursdays and Saturdays, returning the same evening. In September 1987 Whitbread started a major redevelopment scheme that cost £60,000 and would see the inn return to how it may have looked in its former days, ensuring it could accommodate the future trends of its clientele. As well as having the usual pool, dominoes and darts teams, it also had a football team. In the drinks department it had a good selection of beer, lager, wine and spirits and a hand-pulled ale. Besides the traditional Sunday lunch, lunches were served from Monday to Saturday and evening meals on Wednesday to Saturday.

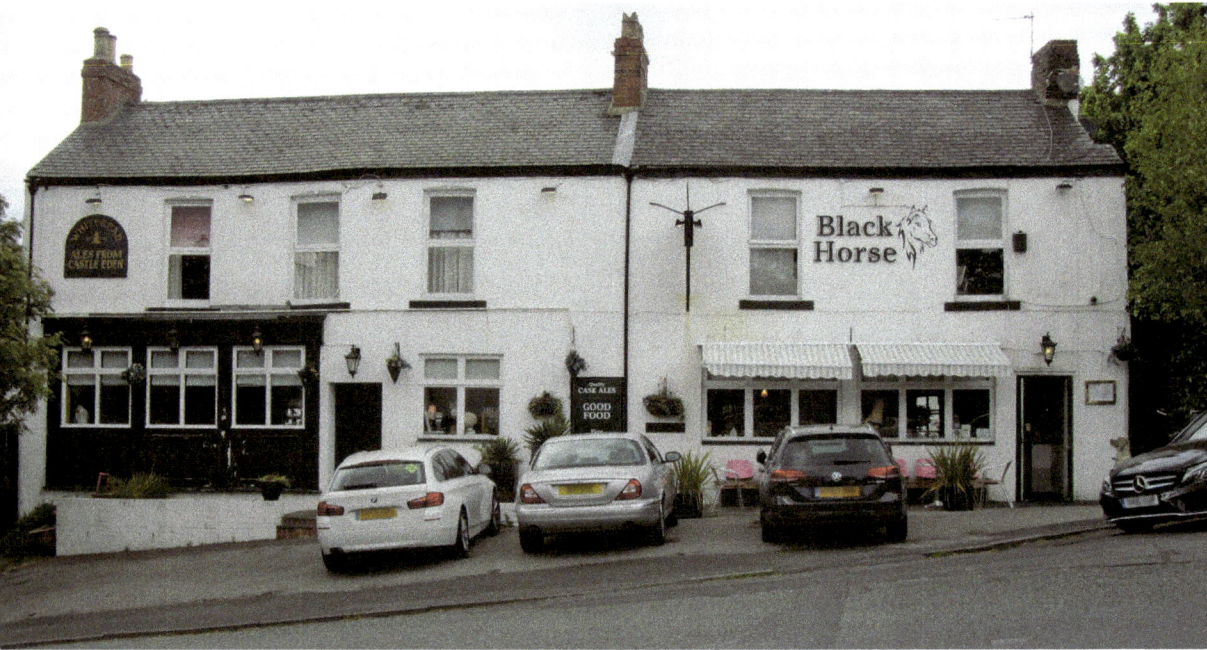

Black Horse, Rectory Bank, West Boldon.

The Flat Tops

The Flat Tops, North Road, Boldon Colliery, which was originally the Queen's Head Inn, was first advertised by Thomas Fenwick in 1871 but he had been there since at least 1867 when his wife gave birth to their son on 13 May that year. January 1879 R. S. and D. Crossthwaite, brewers who owned the inn, advertised it to let, with John Collins becoming the licensee. In December 1887 John was brought before the South Shields Sessions for being drunk on his premises on 28 November and fined 10s, plus costs. This was not the first time as he had been before the Sessions on three previous occasions. In January 1891 John Patterson was licensee. Fredrick Rowe was ordered out of the inn for being drunk. Rowe then threw a glass of spirits at Patterson's sister, later returning with a brick in his hand. South Shields County Petty Sessions fined him 29s and costs. On Saturday 21 February 1891 the Sunderland District of the Loyal William Browell lodge, Independent Order of Oddfellows, held their annual dinner at the inn where upward of forty members and friends sat down to an excellent repast served by Mrs Patterson. On Saturday and Sunday 10 and 11 October 1936, an open pot leek show was held there. Entry was 1s for two pot leeks (6 inches tight button). First prize was £1, second prize 10s and third prize 5s. The building was damaged during the war and the licence was temporarily transferred to premises 16 feet to the rear in November 1954 while the hotel was being rebuilt.

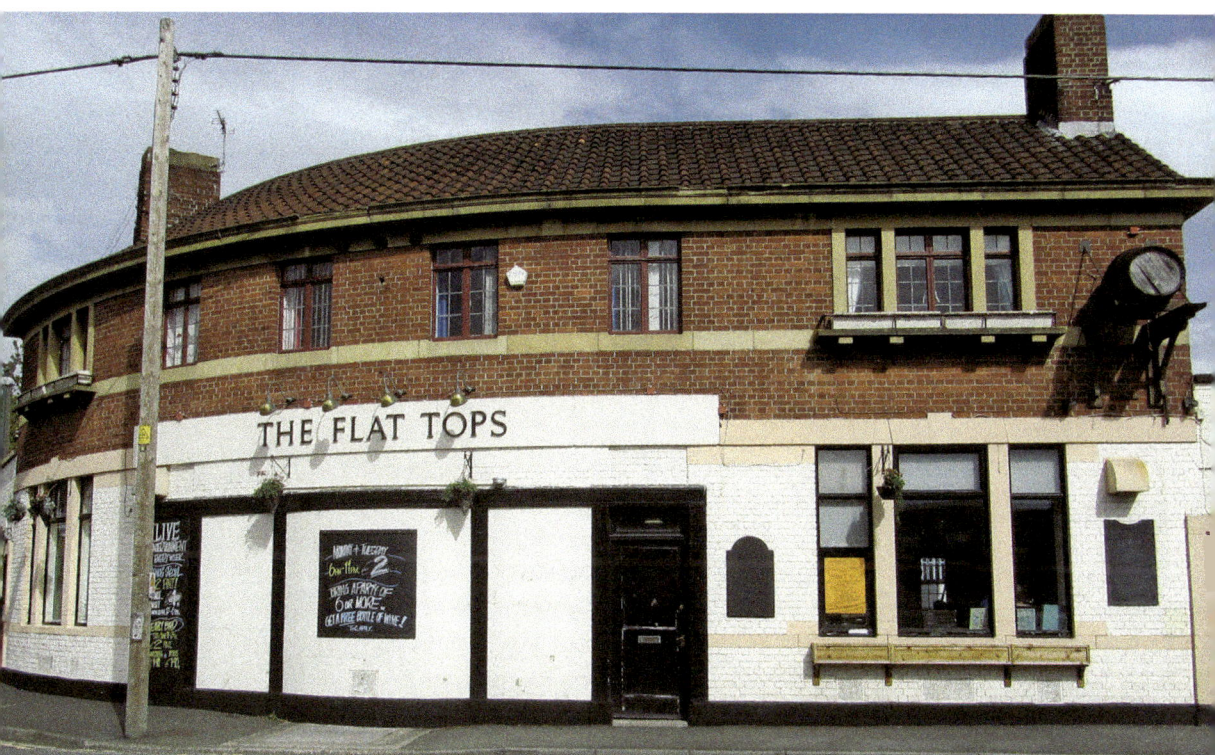

The Flat Tops (formerly the Queen's Head), North Road, Boldon Colliery.

The Colliery Tavern

The Colliery Tavern, Hedworth Lane, Boldon Colliery, was advertised in the *Sunderland Echo* on 10 December 1867 stating 'Colliery Inn, Brockley Whins, near West Boldon. George Smith, late of Seaton Delaval begs to inform his Friends and the Public that he has opened the above Inn. Tradesmen, Contractors and Parties visiting the new Colliery will find every accommodation and comfort. It is only five minutes' walk from Brockley Whins Station, Wine, Spirits, and Ales of the finest quality. Dinners and Luncheon on short notice. Good Stabling.' The *Newcastle Courant* on Friday 16 June 1871 called it the Collie Inn (possibly a typing error) house of Mr Smith, Boldon New Winning, Brockley Whins, when an inquest was held there into the death of Catherine Walker. In 1873 when Mrs Ann Smith advertised the inn it was in Boldon Colliery. Robert Simpson, the licensee in 1879, was brought before the court at South Shields for permitting drunkenness and boisterous conduct on his premises on 13 September; it appeared that on the day in question both a flower show and a cricket match had been held on the inn's premises. Police officers stated 'that the public house was full of people who had been more or less intoxicated from 2 p.m. until 11 p.m. and several fights had broken out'. Robert Simpson was fined 20s and his licence was endorsed. Today the Colliery Tavern has theme nights: Monday – Jackpot Joker; Tuesday – Chillout; Wednesday – quiz night; Thursday – karaoke; Friday – disco; Saturday – there is a live band; and Sunday – from five o'clock is an acoustic evening. All are welcome.

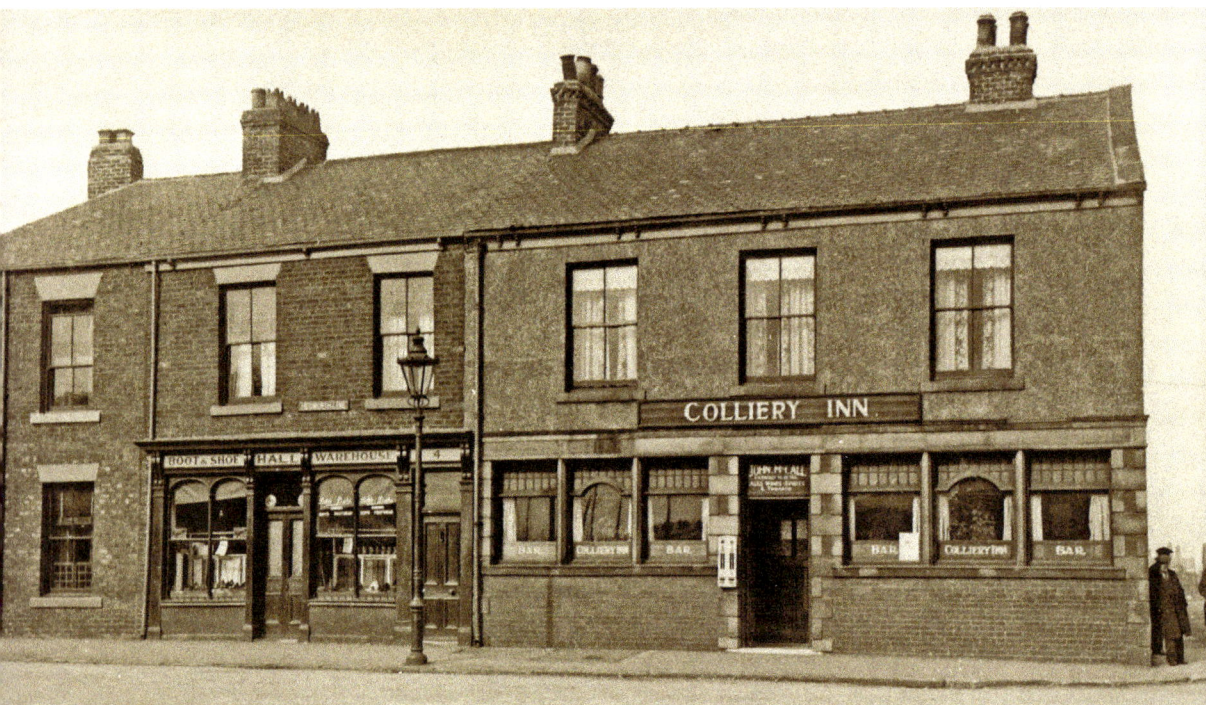

Colliery Inn, Hedworth Lane, Boldon Colliery.

The Crown

The Crown, Boldon Colliery, is the newest public house. In December 1896 the building of the hotel on Hedworth Lane was put out to tender and completed in 1897. John Dryden, a wine and spirit merchant, first advertised the hotel in 1899. In July 1904 Coroner Graham conducted an inquest here into the death of John Reah, aged seventy-seven. Mr J. W. Campbell stated that on 3 June he had been driving a trap with John Reah, the occupant, when the girth broke, causing Mr Reah to be thrown to the ground. When he was picked up he was found to have fractured his thigh. John Reah died at his son-in-law's house on 5 June. The verdict after medical testimony of Dr O'Kelly, 'That the deceased had died from shock, caused by being thrown from the trap, and his thigh fractured', was accidental death. In March 1939 the Boldon branch of the National Union of General and Municipal Workers held their Jubilee Super and social at the Crown. Councillor R. Ewart, the district organiser for South Shields, paid tribute to the pioneers of the movement. In May 1949 the annual meeting of Boldon Operatic Society was held in the hotel. After a report that 'The Mikado', which had been presented in March, had been a success and the local charity would be given the balance left over, it was decided to produce 'The Gondoliers' in 1950. Now known locally as the Dyke, the Crown serves traditional brewed ales as well as a good selection of beer, wines and spirits, and has weekly entertainment and you can watch Sky Sports live.

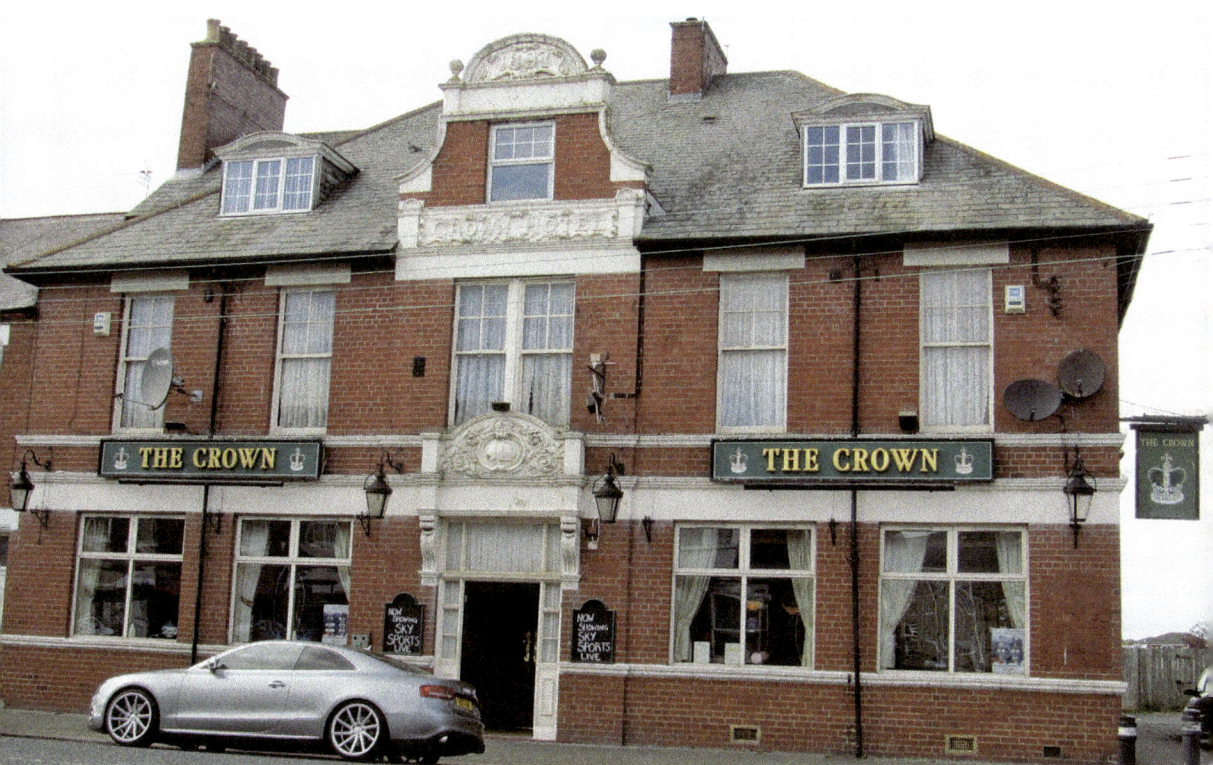

The Crown Hotel, Hedworth Lane, Boldon Colliery.

The Greyhound

The Greyhound, Hedworth Lane, Hedworth, was first advertised by Thomas Robinson in 1828. In 1850 Thomas Robinson was also a cartwright, which meant he could make new or repair any carts or wagons needing attention. The Greyhound, a converted farmhouse, sat among rolling countryside with the Calf Close Burn running beside it. In 1865 Edward Scott became the licensee but only stayed until 1873 when Thomas Hedley became the new publican. On 29 July 1885 Thomas Hedley committed suicide by hanging. He had been found suspended by the neck in the stable near the house. An inquest held by Coroner Graham on Wednesday 4 August heard from Dr Grant that he had been called in but life had already been extinct. The jury's verdict was that 'the deceased committed suicide in an unsound state of mind'. Saturday 5 October 1895 saw members of the Hedworth Leek and Vegetable Club hold their first show at the inn. Forty exhibits of first-class quality were on show.

The Greyhound is now a modern public house with a newly refurbished function room to the right, which you can book for those special occasions and can be opened up to accommodate the largest of parties.

Looking from the dining area through to the refurbished function room.

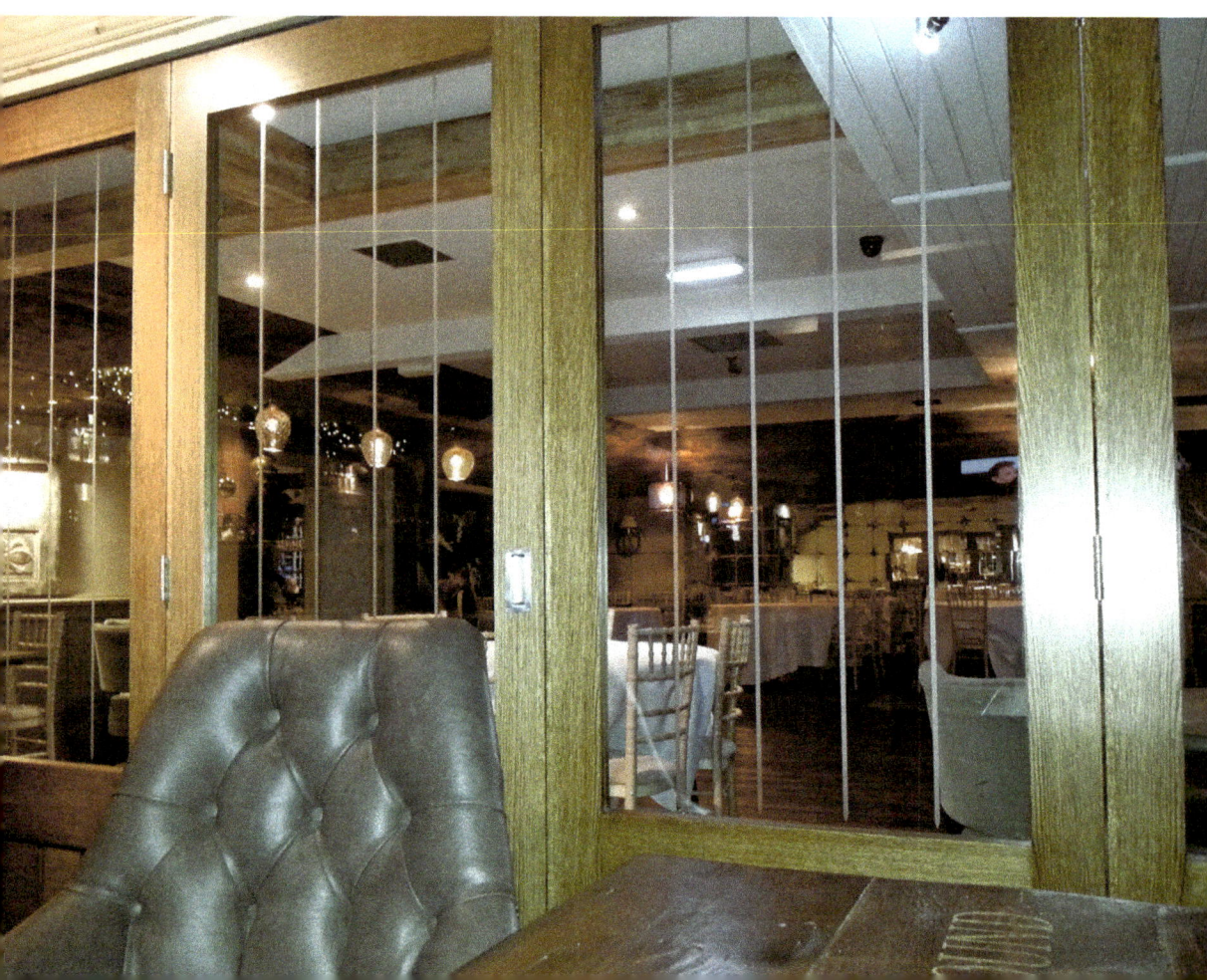

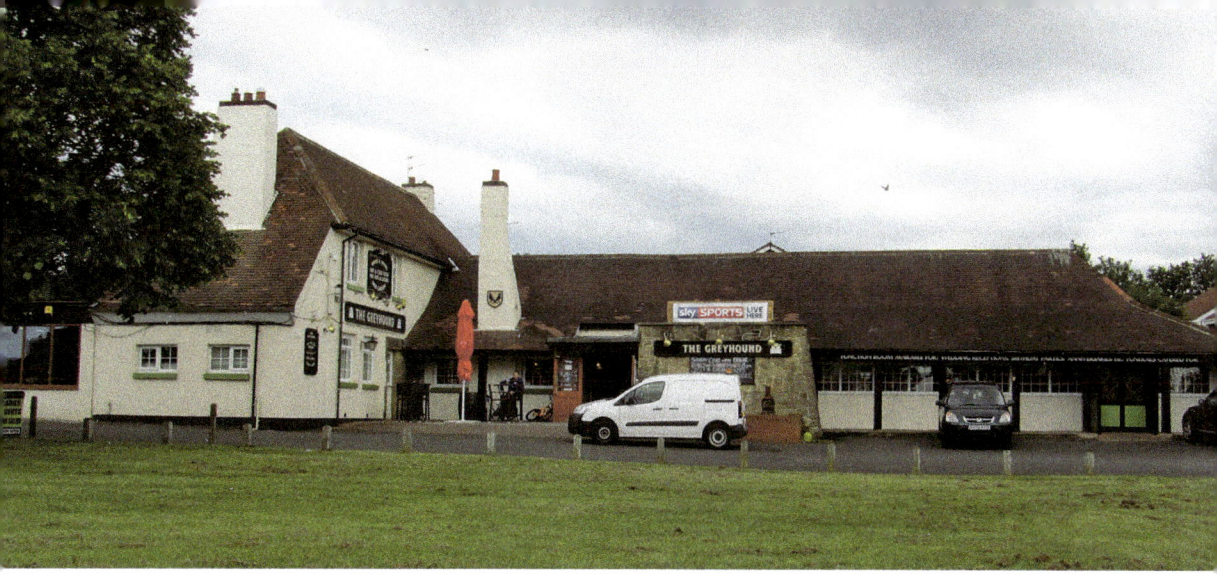

Above: The Greyhound, Hedworth Lane, Hedworth.

Below: The pool room with its beautiful ornate ceiling.

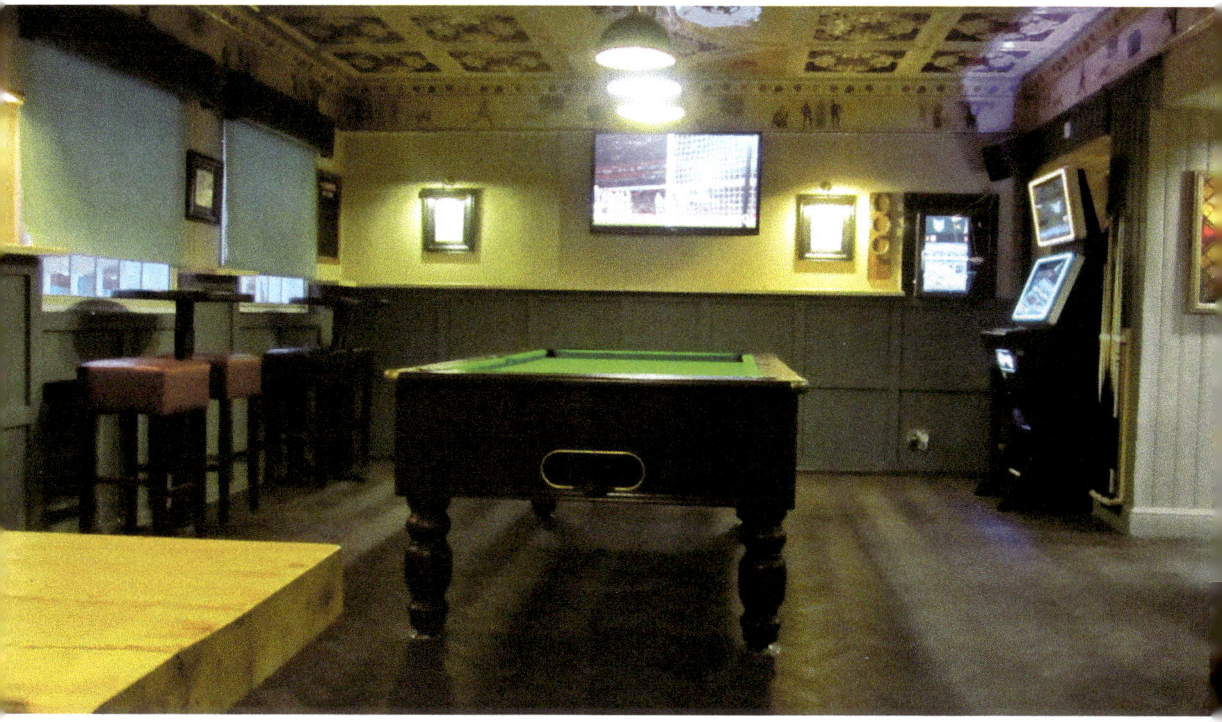

    The pool room to the left has a pool table, darts board and a big-screen television. The ceiling in this room is well worth a look as is thought to have been plastered by Italian prisoners of war who were camped nearby. There is also free Wi-Fi, an outside sitting area and car park. With buses stopping not far away you can have a pleasant evening leaving the car at home.

The Robin Beer House and Brewery

The Robin Beer House and Brewery, Primrose Hill, Hedworth, was first advertised as the Robin Hood in 1828 by John Rowe. By 1839 Joseph Walker, the licensee, had renamed the tavern Robin Hood and Little John, which was possibly a coaching inn standing at the bottom of Primrose Hill, a convenient place to change horses before climbing the hill and heading towards South Shields to the east, Gateshead to the west or south to Durham. In October 1844 when it came up for let, it was described as having a field around 14 acres and a well-stocked around 1½ acres garden. Applicants were to apply to Mr J. Jackson, King Street Brewery, South Shields. In 1850 James Purvis, a market gardener, took over the inn but on Tuesday 28 July 1853 the Robin Hood came up for auction, being described as having four rooms and a cellar, with stables and large gardens. Ralph Corner was the tenant at the time. In 1860 Isaac Humphreys became the landlord and stayed for around ten years until Robert Riccalton took over. Robert, a wine and spirit merchant, changed the name to the Archers Arms in 1875 but by 1879 it was the Old Robin Hood. In 2002 the Robin Hood was derelict when it

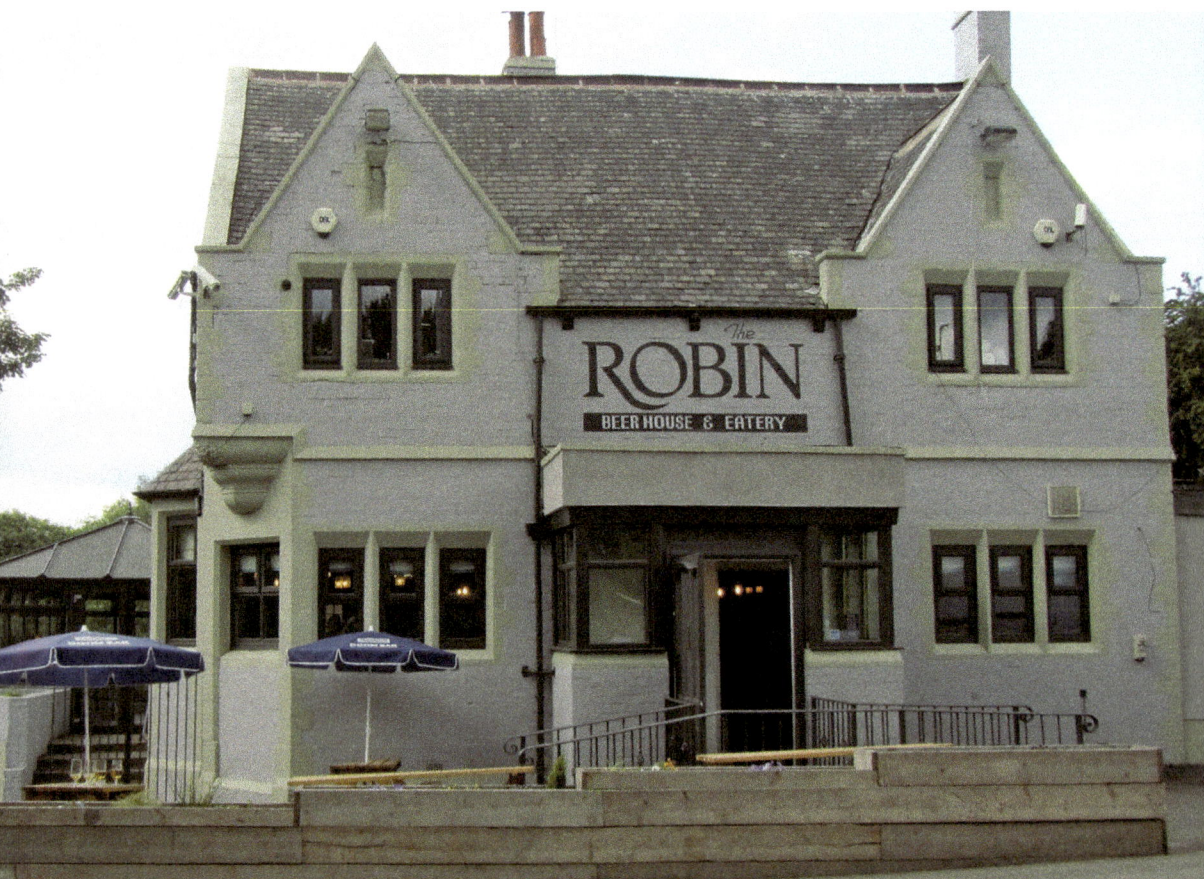

The Robin Hood, Primrose Hill, Hedworth.

was taken on by Jess McConnell and his wife. The Robin Hood also became a brewery, brewing many fine ales under the name of Jarrow Brewery.

The Prince of Wales

The Prince of Wales, Calf Close, Hedworth, is a modern public house. On Thursday 6 April 1939 Jarrow magistrates confirmed an application by Newcastle Breweries Ltd for the removal of the licence from the Prince of Wales, Commercial Road, Jarrow, to a new hotel to be built at the junction of Newcastle Road and South Shields Road at York Avenue. At the same time the brewery offered the licences of the Staith House, Tyne Street, and the Bell Rock Hotel, Nixon Street, to be surrendered, which the bench accepted. A census carried out in the neighbourhood on behalf of the brewery for the proposed new hotel showed of the 904 forms issued, 573 voted in favour, 55 against and 105 people were not interested. Redesigned in the late 1990s from the old traditional style of several rooms, it now has an open-plan design. It is part of the Flaming Grill chain with the emphasis on lunch and evening meals. You can get two meals for £8.99 all day Monday to Friday with a good selection of meals to choose from. A large area is set aside for a pool table and a darts board, television screens and a large screen for watching football or your favourite sport. To the front of the pub is a seating area for those warm days, a car park to the side and rear, and for those wishing to enjoy a good night out there is a bus stop in Calf Close Lane.

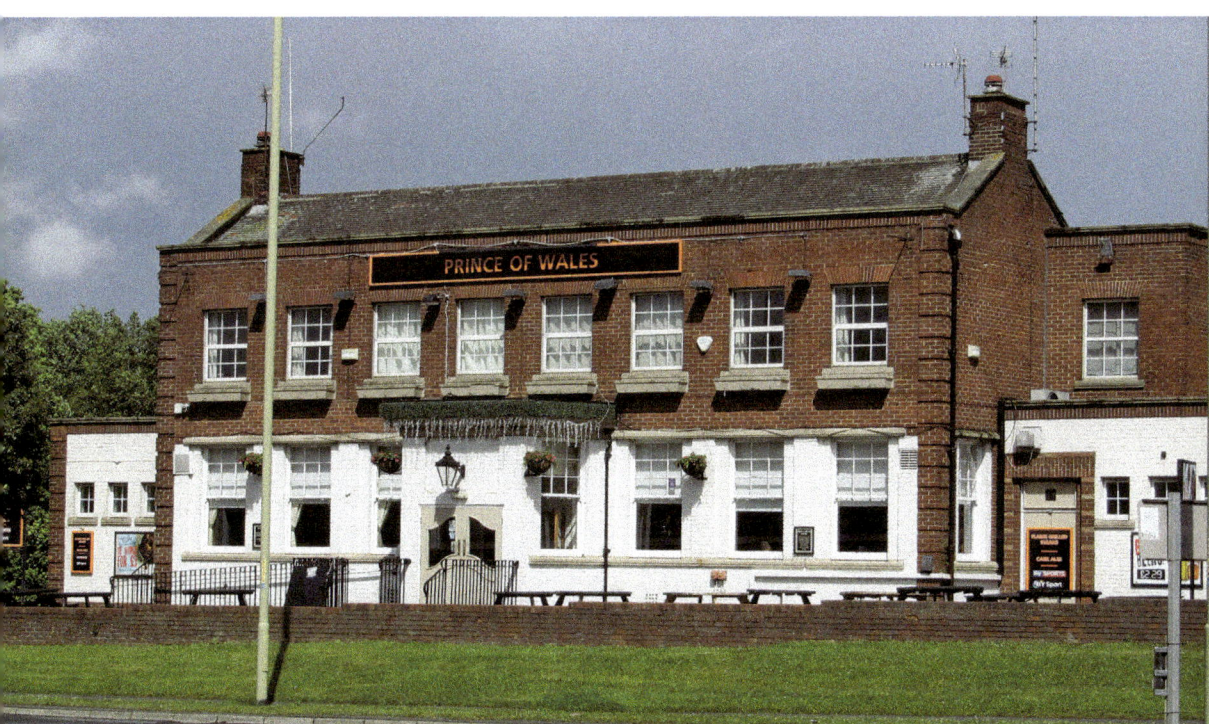

Prince of Wales, Calf Close, Hedworth.

The Lord Nelson

This lovely photograph of Monkton village shows the Lord Nelson left of centre. Possibly the oldest of Jarrow's public houses, it was converted from a cottage. Jacob Moses, a blacksmith, first advertised it in 1828. In 1839 Jacob changed the name to the Admiral Nelson, before changing it back a few years later. On 11 August 1882 a dinner and presentation for Mr John O'Neil, representative of Leyland's Company, Liverpool, and the officers of SS *Venetian* was given by the platers employed at the Jarrow shipyard. The dinner was served up in excellent style by the landlord Joseph Thompson. In 1945 former boxer Benny Shields became the licensee and leaseholder for the Scottish and Newcastle Breweries house. In 1956 Benny was joined by his son, John, a former bricklayer. When Benny retired in 1969 due to ill health, John not only took over the licence but also the lease. In the mid-1980s The Lord Nelson underwent major alterations. The once cosy old green room and select room, which the women were only allowed to use, became more open plan in design. Unfortunately John Shields suffered a heart attack in 1990 and had to retire, leaving his son Michael to take over the running of the pub. In October 1993 Michael decided to leave town for Bellingham to take over a general dealers. At that time John Shields still held the lease. Today the Lord Nelson is a family-friendly public house with a pub garden and car parking. Real ale is available with two changing beers that are hand pulled. Both lunchtime and evening meals are served. Live music can be heard on both Friday and Saturday nights and bank holidays. Wi-Fi is available and traditional pub games are played.

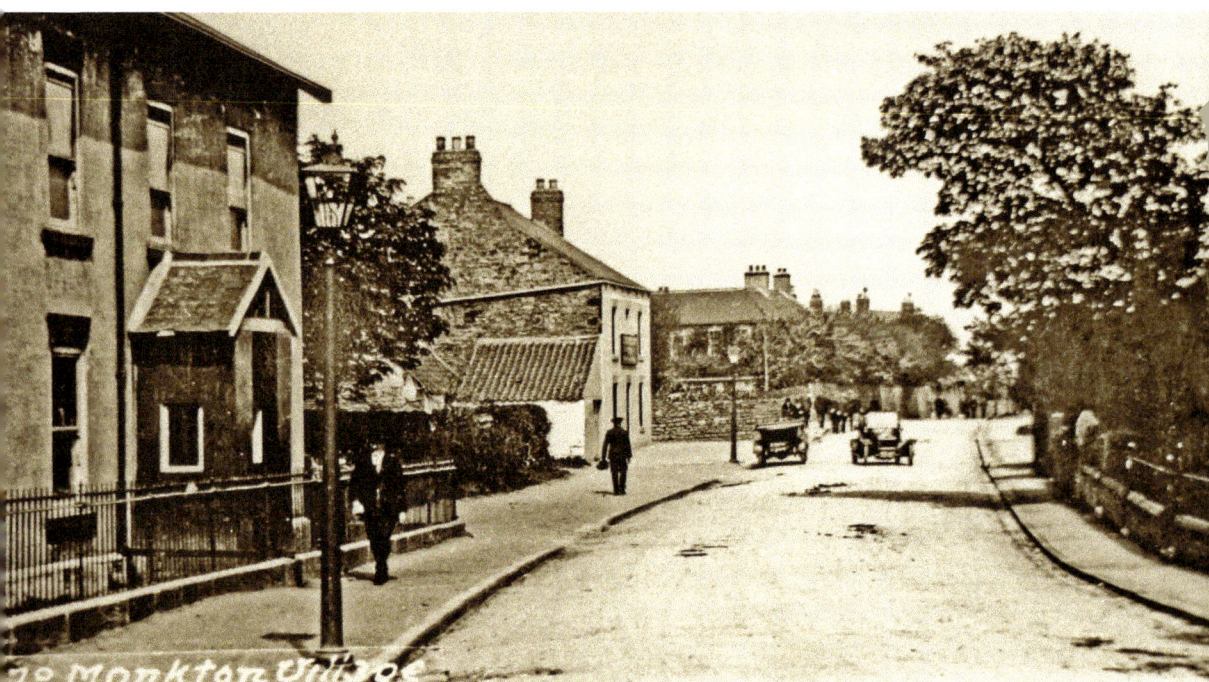

The Lord Nelson, Monkton village.

The Lakeside Inn

This former trout farmhouse, which I remember passing while travelling from South Shields to Newcastle on my way to work, once stood in rural tranquillity. The Lakeside Inn, East Fellgate Farm, Leam Lane, now lies off the busy duel carriageway and is accessible via a short road off the roundabout as you travel along Leam Lane. This was an immensely popular restaurant. In 1991 after only four and a half years, the inn was completely refurbished. The long building was divided into three areas. First the lounge, a quiet area for meeting friends for a catch up, was refurbished. Muted tones of green wallpaper with contrasting border, green upholstery and warm brown furniture, which blended excellently with the wallcovering and the carpet, was used. In the central area the bar also underwent complete reorganisation, forming a very pleasant place to relax with a drink. The conservatory, which is part of the central area, was carpeted to match, which creates a light airy space for those who like to sit and relax in brighter surroundings. The third and last area of this intriguing farmhouse fulfils a duel function: a restaurant during the day with an extensive and appetising menu at lunchtime, and in the evening tables and chairs would be moved to the sides giving a larger standing area. Having reopened around two years ago the Lakeside is a family-friendly roadside inn, well signposted off the A184 roundabout. The emphasis is upon food with both lunch and evening meals being served. With three hand pulls, drinks are not being neglected and real ale is available. There is a pub garden with disabled access and a car park. When I was there a marquee was being used for a wedding reception.

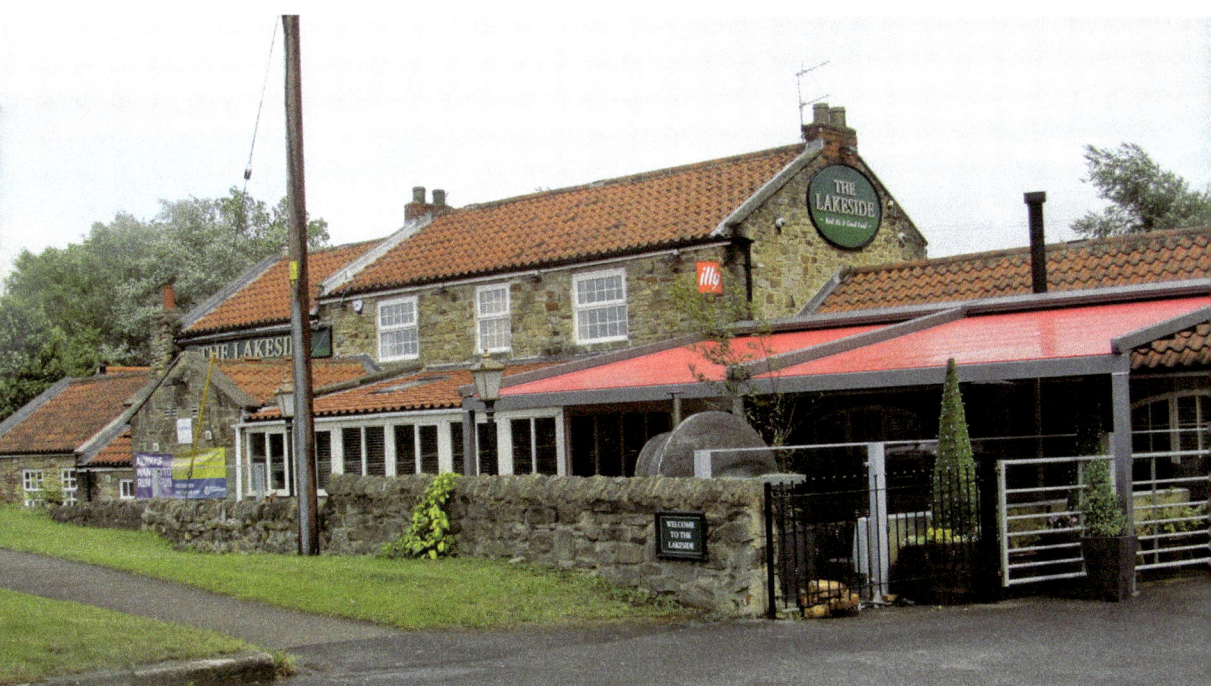

The Lakeside, Leam Lane, Fellgate.

The Green Bar & Brasserie

The Green Bar & Brasserie is where the White Mare Pool Hotel once stood. The White Mare Pool was built near the site of a stagnant pond tinged white by the soluble magnesian limestone common in the area at the time. Legend relates to a merchant going missing, presumed murdered, in 1753 while travelling from South Shields to Sunderland. Left standing at the side of the pool was his horse, a white mare. It was ideally situated for a coaching inn, being on the crossroads for many coaches going to all point north, south, east and west, especially coaches heading up Leam Lane to the A1 road to change horses before continuing to Chester-Le-Street and Durham. It was first advertised by John Hedley in 1829 but is older than this as in March 1803 it was to let, occupied by Ralph Shorter at the time. Taken over by John Forster in 1834, by 1839 John White Middlemas was the licensee. In 1841 John Middlemas was a blacksmith and John Foster Hedley was the new licensee. After Andrew Scott, a blacksmith, advertised the inn in 1855, it was not advertised again until William Duncan in 1879. Around 1970 the White Mare Pool Hotel became the Dixie Landers Music Hall run by a group of comedians of the same name, featuring stars such as the duo Bobby Hooper and Billy Martin, and comedians Bobby Thompson and Bobby Knoxall. The music hall was pulled down and rebuilt after builders found something was wrong when they started work on an extension to the Dixie Landers. Now The Green is a stylish brasserie and bar serving a range of meals that will satisfy anyone's cravings. It is open on Monday to Thursday from 11.00 to 23.00, Friday and Saturday from 11.00 until midnight and Sunday 11.00 until 22.30. This family-friendly pub also has a function area, free Wi-Fi, a big-screen television for Sky Sports and a large car park.

The Green, White Mare Pool, South Wardley.

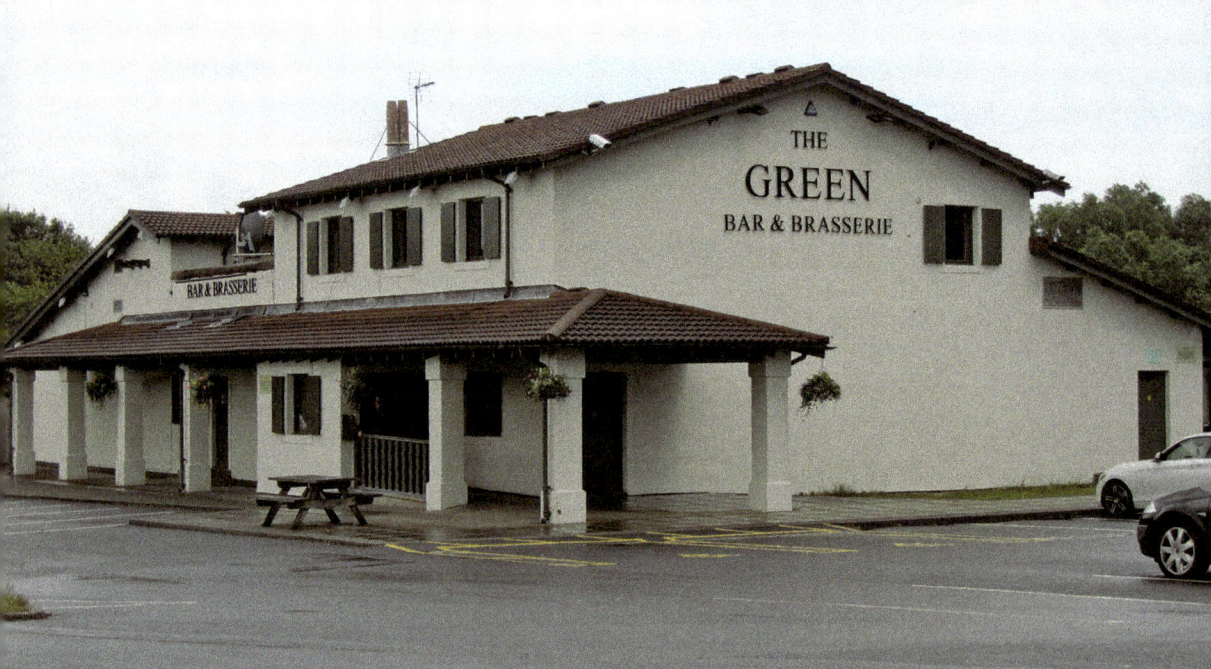

The Swan Inn

The Swan Inn, Sunderland Road Villas, was first advertised by James Butterwick Maxwell in 1854. William Hindmarsh took over the Swan in 1855, giving the address as Nether (Low) Heworth. When Ord Coxon, a licensed victualler, advertised the Swan in 1865, he gave the address as Heworth Lane End. In September 1893 Heworth Derby Leek Club held its annual competition and the licensee was John Styles Roy. In the leek class there were thirty-two competitors. On 7 January 1962 landlady Stella Rylance gave a party for the children of her staff. Although it was a small party, she decided to include twenty children from Nazareth House Orphanage in Newcastle. Stella Rylance thought it would be a good idea to invite some needy children and also wrote to some of the local businesses asking for donations of small presents. On 28 June 2012 the Swan was flooded, with the cars in the car park under water with only the tops visible. The next day a big clean-up operation began and the Swan was counting the cost of the damage.

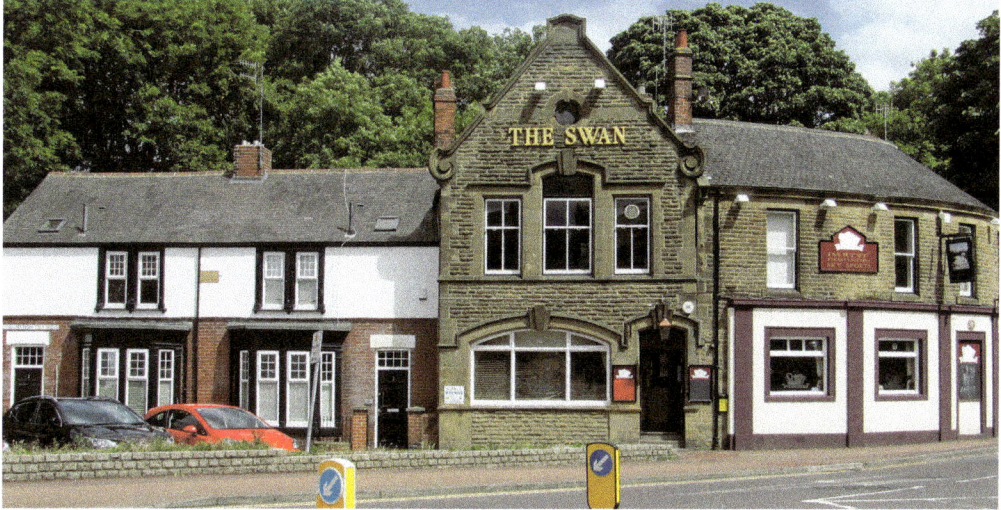

The Swan, Sunderland Road, Heworth.

The Duke of Cumberland

The Duke of Cumberland, Sunderland Road, Felling, was originally built at Heworth Colliery and first advertised by Luke Morris in 1828 as being in Upper Heworth. William Coward, a blacksmith, owned the Duke of Cumberland in 1841; William had his smithy adjoining the inn. In 1843 the first of many Gooseberry Shows were held at the inn, the first prize that year going to Richard Musgrove. The Gooseberry Show continued each year with at least four varieties on show: 'Green Thumper', 'London', 'Snowdrop' and 'Freedom'. Auctions were also held in there, especially for farmers' away going crops, and one held on 6 September 1853 was for crops from High Heworth Farm. In 1895 the Duke of Cumberland was rebuilt at the bottom of Holly Hill on Sunderland Road.

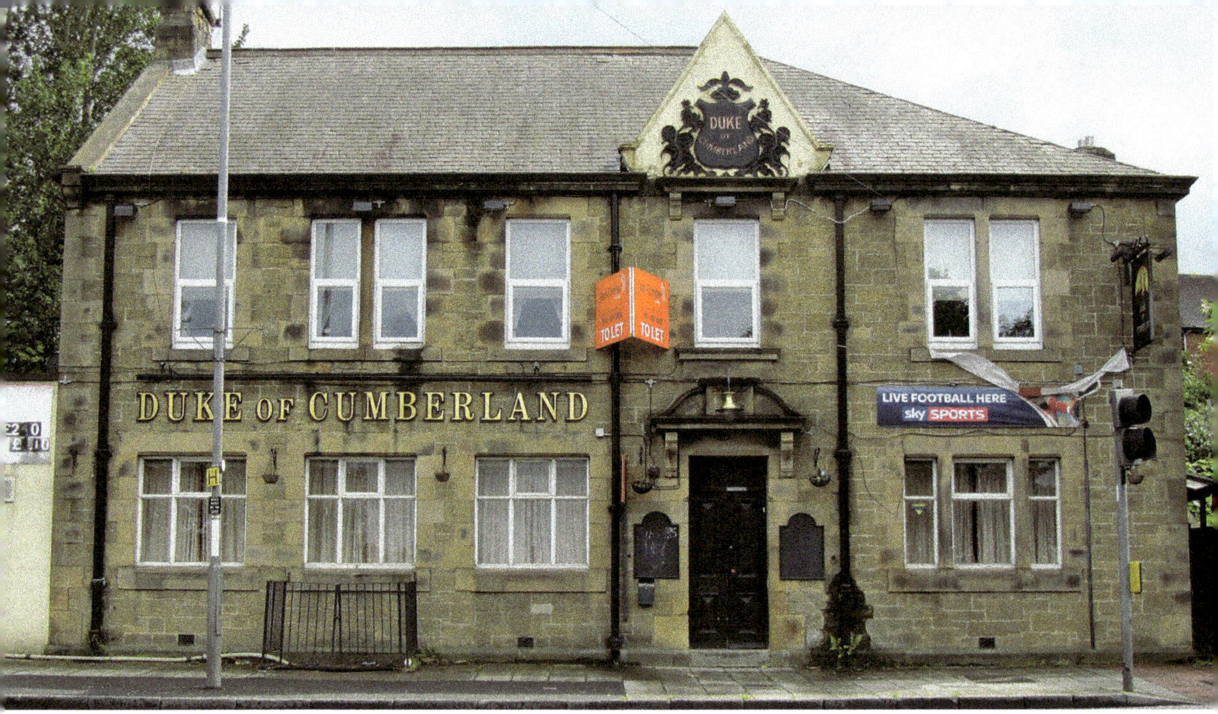

Duke of Cumberland, Sunderland Road, Heworth, originally stood next to the old Upper Heworth Waggon Way.

The Blink Bonny Inn

The Blink Bonny Inn, Sunderland Road, Felling, was named after a British thoroughbred racehorse and brood mare who won fourteen races in her two-year career including the Gimcrack Stakes at York in 1856, the Epsom Derby, Epsom Oaks, the Lancaster Oaks

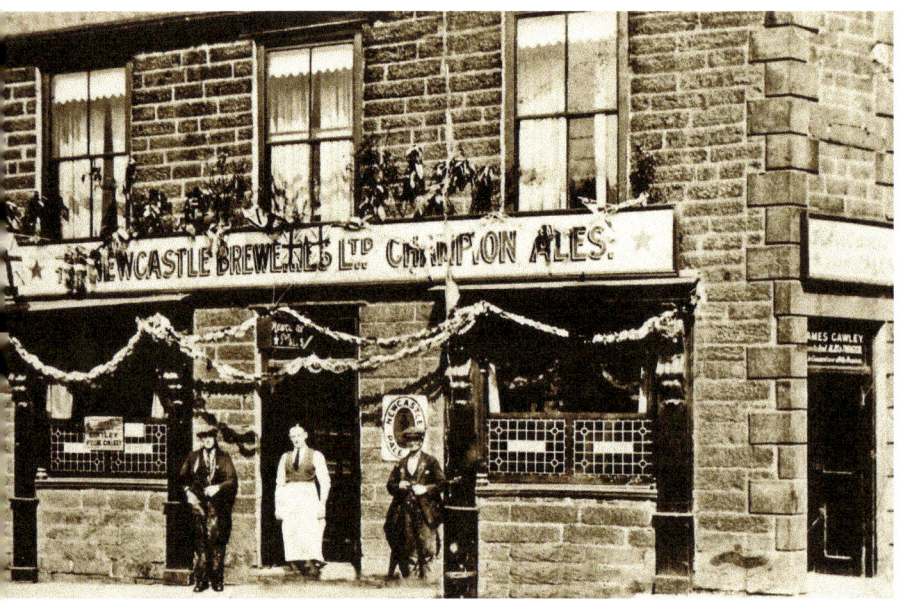

The Blink Bonny Inn, Ridley Terrace, Felling. James Cawley, the manager, is standing at the front door.

and the Park Hill Stakes in 1857. On 27 August 1870 Michael Carden, the licensee, applied for a full licence but was refused. He applied again on 27 August 1873 and was refused again after deliberation by the magistrates as he was on the blacklist for a breach of his licence. In February 1888 William Coverdale, the licensee, was fined £1 and costs for keeping his premises open during prohibited hours on the 9th of the month. Gabriel Williamson, Elizabeth Williamson, Francis Stein and Robert Carson, who were found on the premises at the same time, were each fined 2s and 6d. In April 1916 Charles Longstaff, the licensee, was fined £5 for having ill-fitted blinds in the windows – it was a requirement by law that everyone must have blinds properly fitted so no light could be seen through them at night on account of the war. On 24 September 1937 Durham County Licensing Committee offered the owners of the Blink Bonny £2,100, although the claim had been for £2,950. The owners had until 30 October to inform the clerk of the peace whether they accepted the offer stated. A supplementary meeting was fixed on 26 November. The Blink Bonny was closed and later demolished.

The Green Mandolin

The Green Mandolin, Collingwood Street, Felling, which was originally named the Turf Hotel, stands out not only because of the colour but the combination of a tower with a large corner oriel window and deep semicircular windows. First advertised in

The Turf Hotel, now the Green Mandolin, Collingwood Street, Felling.

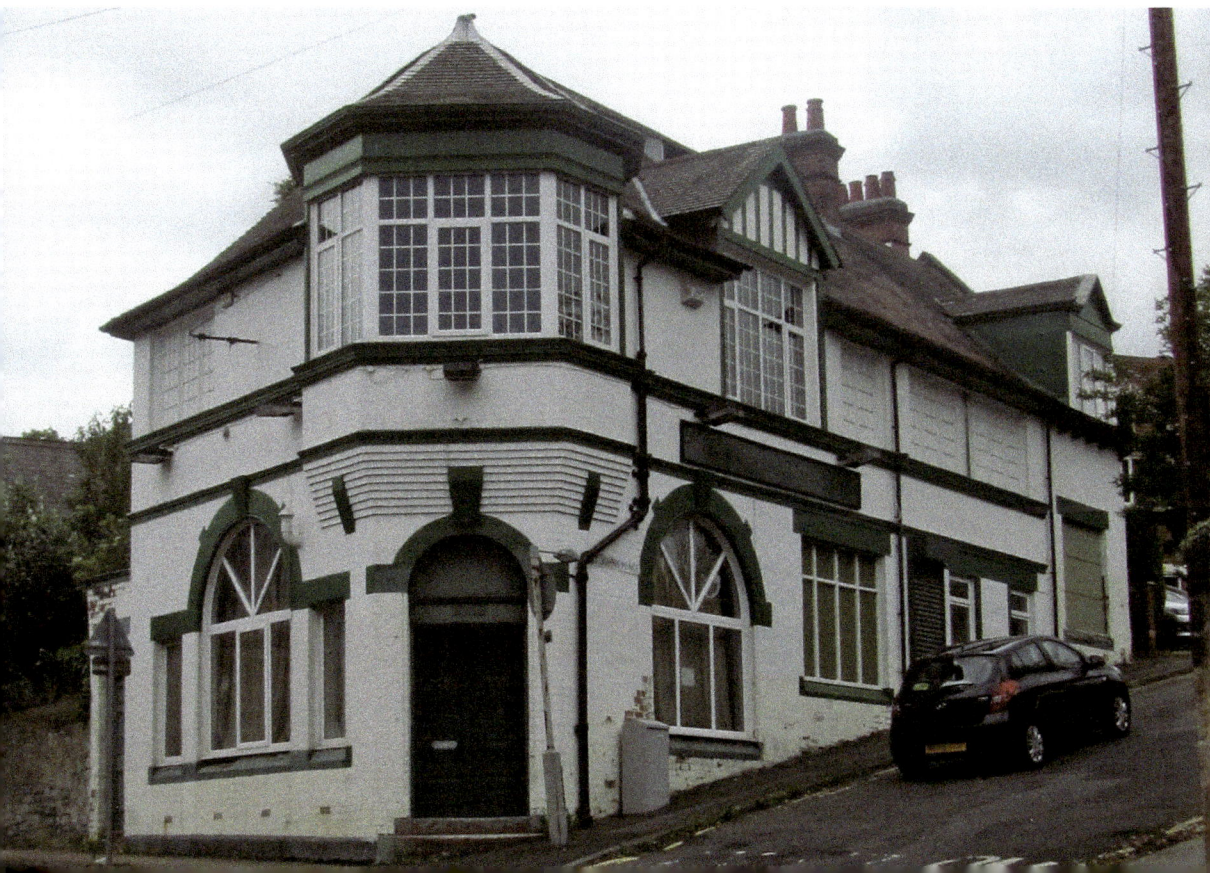

1892 by John Brown Makepeace, a mineral water manufacturer of Victoria Square, it is possibly older. In October 1892 the local leek show was held at the hotel with twenty-one stands of excellent-quality produce. At the Brewster Sessions held in Gateshead in August 1893 Mr Johnson Boyd applied for a full licence for the Royal Turf Hotel as it was then called, the owner being Messrs F. Deuchar & Co. from Newcastle. In February 1914 Thomas Jefferson, licensee, was up before Gateshead magistrates for having, on 3 February, permitted drunkenness on the premises and was fined £2 with costs. In August 1942 clubs interested in the Heddon Home Charity Cup that were within a radius of 6 miles from Newcastle were invited to meet at the hotel on Tuesday 1 September. Unfortunately it is now closed.

The Oddfellows Arms Inn

The Oddfellows Arms Inn, Davison Street, Felling, was first advertised by Thomas Laws in 1859. On Saturday 29 September 1860 the Independent Order of Oddfellows, M. U. Loyal Operative Lodge of the Newcastle District, celebrated their twenty-first anniversary there when 120 members and friends sat down to an excellent repast. Mrs Margaret Armstrong took over the inn in 1865, and by 1871 John Scott had become the licensee. A dinner for around 200 poor of the parish of Heworth took place at the inn on Wednesday 16 January; roast beef with beer and plum pudding was much appreciated by the folk and on leaving each received a quarter pound of tea, a pound of sugar and

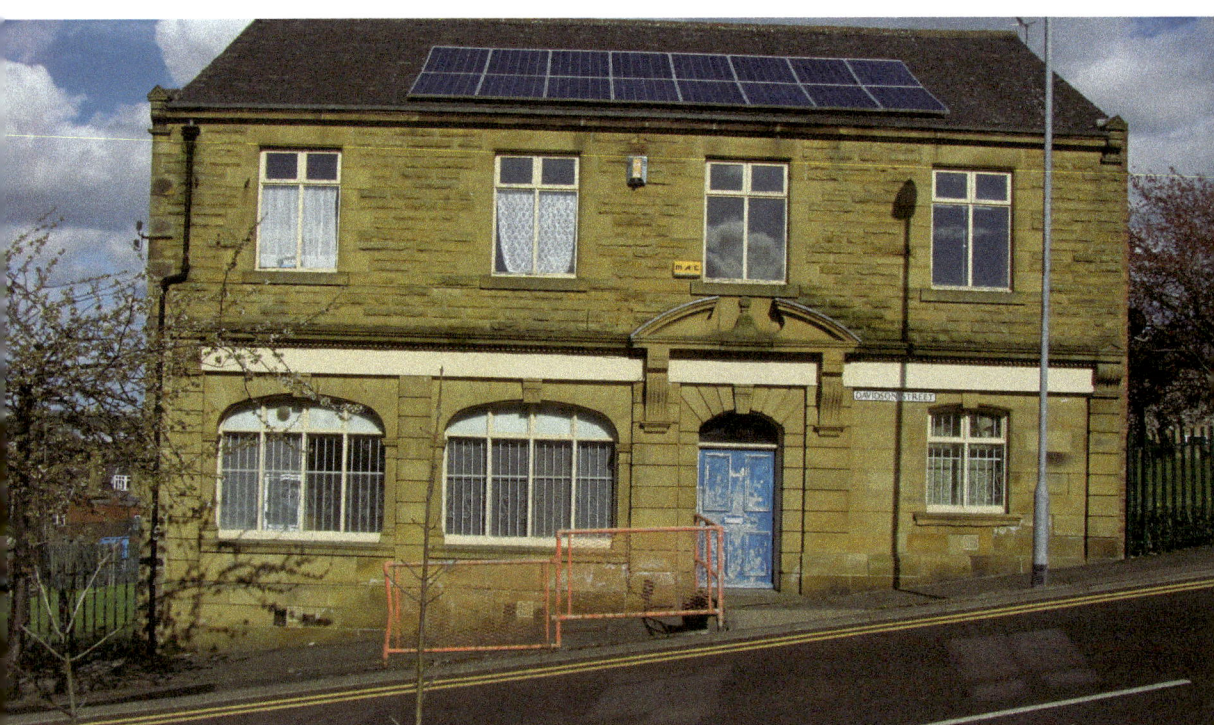

The Oddfellows Arms Inn, Davidson Street, Felling.

a bun. On 25 August 1883 the *London Gazette* reported John, who also owned the Druids' Brewery in Newcastle, had gone into liquidation. Patrick Bennet became the licensee in 1891, succeeded by his daughter in 1897. On Saturday 27 June 1908 a large number of ambulance men and friends assembled to pay tribute to Dr Miller and Mr W. Handyside, two of the chief officers of the ambulance brigade, which was then in its third year. Left isolated by the demolition of the surrounding streets it closed, becoming the Felling UDC Rates Office, and then the Social Services offices.

The Beeswing Hotel

The Beeswing Hotel on the corner of Sunderland Road and High Street, Felling, was first advertised as the Bee's Wing Inn by Andrew Oliver in 1848. The Beeswing is named after a racehorse. Beeswing, nicknamed 'the Pitmen's Horse', won fifty-one races including the Ascot Gold Cub in 1842, the Newcastle St Ledger, the Newcastle Gold Cup six out of seven times, the Doncaster Cup four times and many more besides in her eight-year racing history. On Wednesday 10 July 1872 the auction of the Felling Hall estate was held at the inn by Mr Samuel Donkin under appointment from the court of Chancery. John Stephenson became the licensee in 1860 and his son George took over the licence in 1878. On 24 December 1880 Felling Ornithological Society

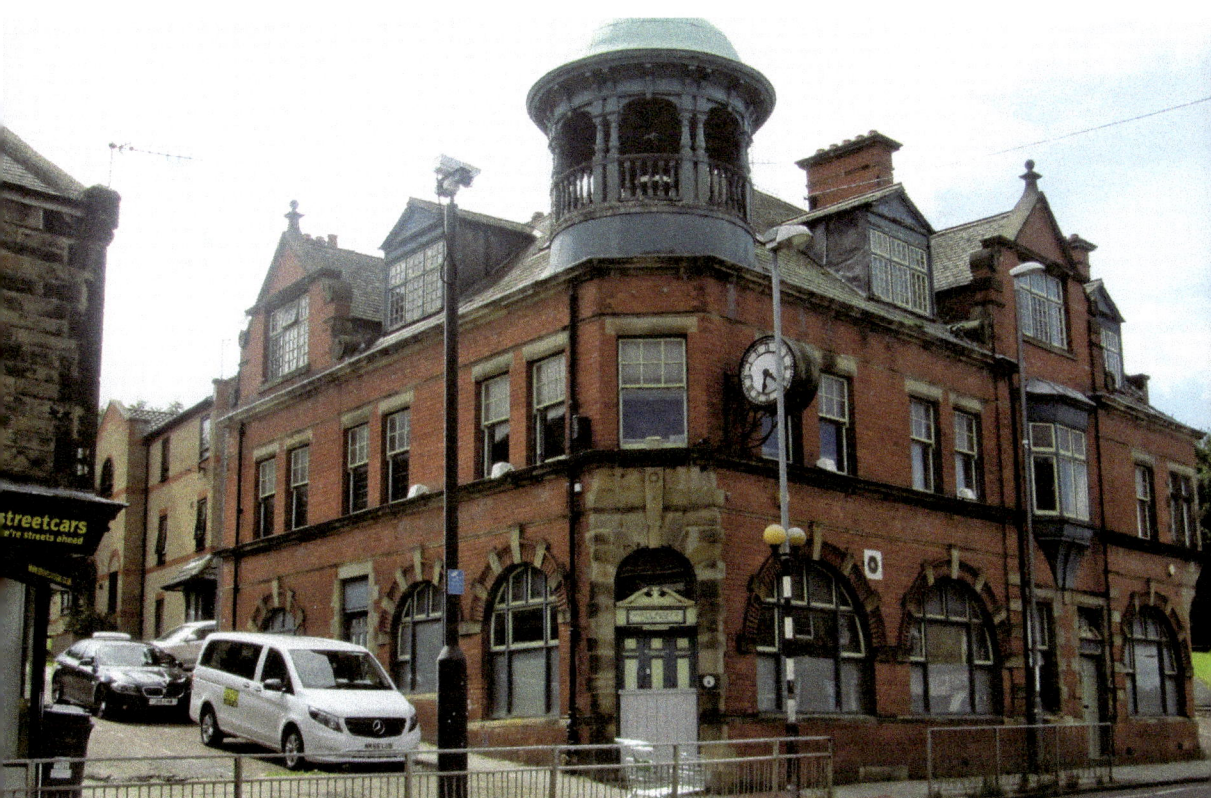

The Beeswing Hotel on the corner of High Street and Sunderland Road.

held its annual show in the large room where there were over 300 birds on show. These ranged from Yellow Belgian Canaries, Yellow Glasgow Canaries and various other types of canaries, linnets and goldfinch. In 1899 Robert Deuchar & Co. had the inn rebuilt into the splendid building that you see today. The Beeswing later became Dirty Nelly's Irish Pub before finally closing its doors.

Halfway House Inn

This old Monarch postcard of Felling High Street shows the Halfway House Inn standing around halfway up the High Street to the centre right. Although first advertised by John Simpson in 1854, it was older. In January 1850 the Loyal Operative Lodge of Oddfellows, MU, held their tenth anniversary there with around seventy members and guests sitting down for dinner. By 1856 James Morgan was the licensee when the 'Alma Quadrille Party' held their annual dress ball there on Friday 8 February. Sadly on 29 April 1863, Mr G. Cairns was holding an auction on the premises for all the furniture, which included tables, chairs, measures pots, glasses, etc., of the late Mrs Morgan, an innkeeper. Thomas Laws, a licensed victualler, took over the premises. On 31 March 1900 Messrs Atkinson and Garland sold the Halfway House, two shops and two houses together with a piece of land to Mr Weatherett for £5,020. The Halfway House has now been converted into housing.

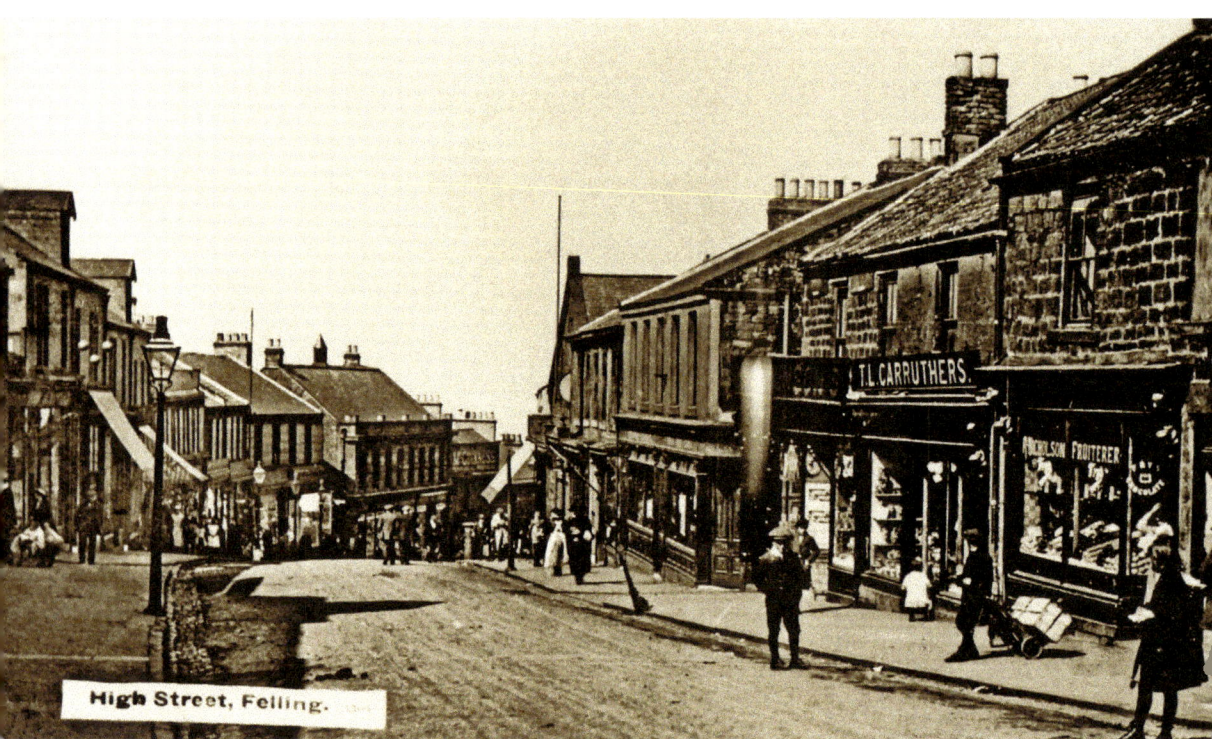

Felling High Street, with the Halfway House Inn shown as third premised down on the left-hand side.

The Blue Bell

The Blue Bell, High Street, Felling, was first advertised by William Robson in 1834 as High Felling. On Saturday 15 April 1848 the inn was described as having 'yard and gardens attached, containing kitchen, cellar, tap room, club room occupied by William Robinson, let to Gateshead Brewery at an annual rent of £20, when auctioned by Mr William Cook Auctioneer of Newcastle'. In 1853 John and Robert Anderson were the leaseholders; Robert became the licence holder with many auctions being held in the long room over the years. On Tuesday 7 August 1867 Robert Anderson was before Gateshead County Police Court for selling an eighth of a pint of wine without a licence on 22 June. Robert had been suspected of selling wine on previous occasions, so on the day in question Mr Cole, an excise officer, had gone into the inn to purchase the wine. Robert Anderson pleaded guilty, and was fined £12 10s. On Friday 20 April 1888 Robert was again in court, this time

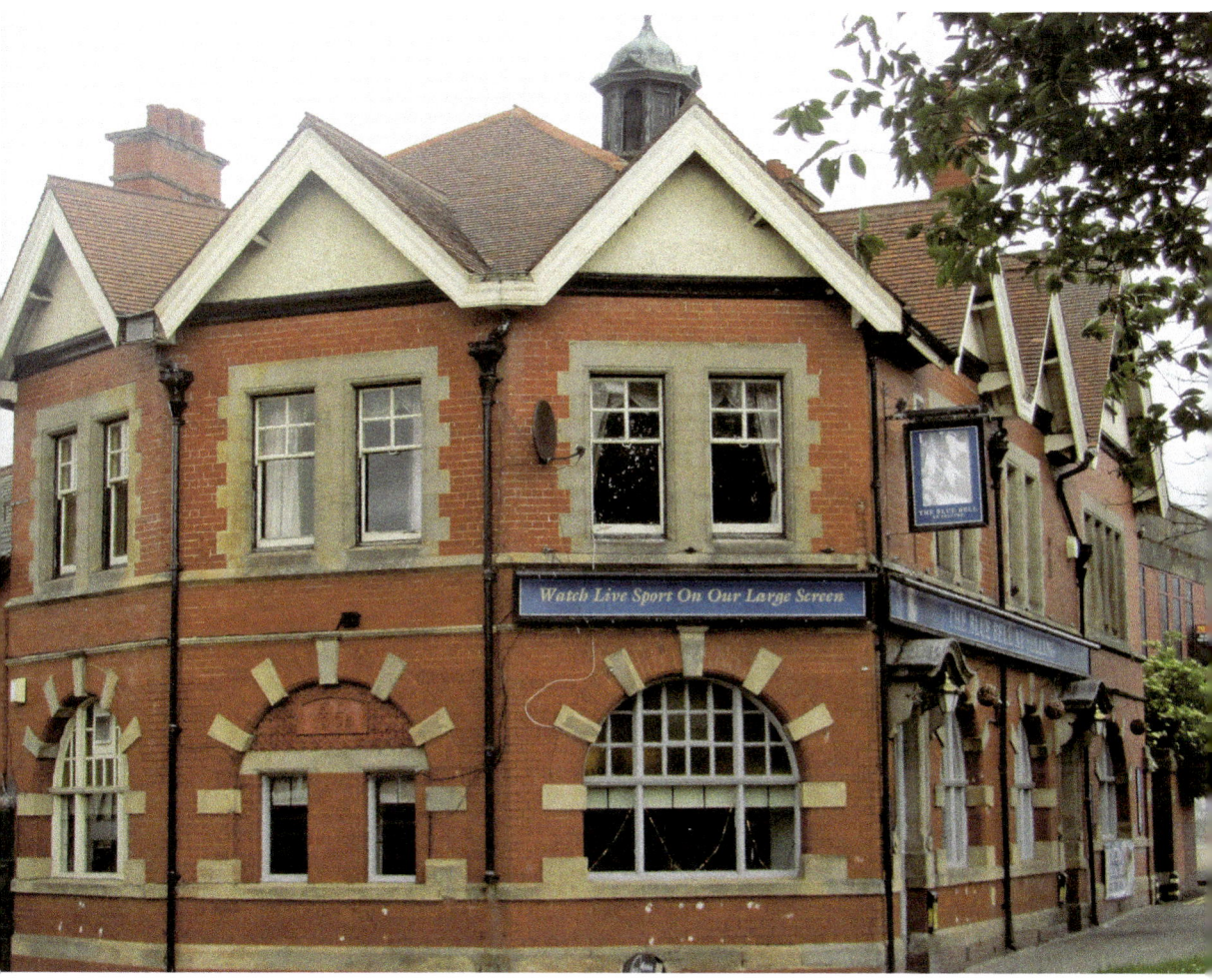

The Blue Bell Inn, High Street, Felling.

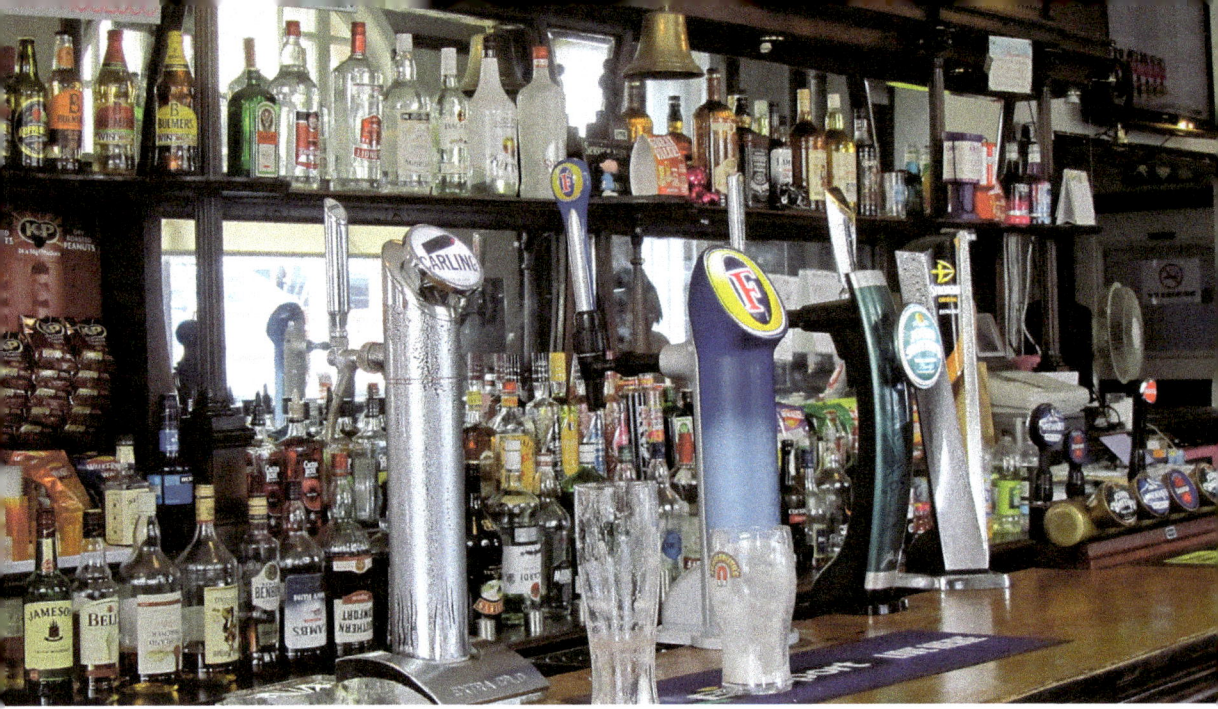

The bar is thought to be the original one from 1905.

for keeping the inn open during prohibited hours on Sunday 8th and for the sale of intoxicating liquor. Police Constable Hogg proved the case and Robert was fined 40s and costs. The Felling Hopping's were once held in the yard of the old inn on Whit Mondays as well as in the square. By 1904 rides included roundabouts and gondolas with a pole also being erected. Newcastle Breweries obtained planning permission to rebuild the old Blue Bell and a plaque above the second ground-floor window in the High Street gives the date as 1905. The well-stocked bar is thought to be the original bar from 1905.

The Victoria Jubilee

The Victoria Jubilee split Crow Road and Victoria Square and was originally the Barley Mow Inn first advertised by Thomas Dixon in 1848, before then being taken over by Margaret Laverick in 1854. Margaret did not keep the inn long as by 1859 Robert Wallace was the licensee. In the 1866 Brewster Sessions Robert Wallace was one of many licensees on the blacklist for keeping an unruly house, but he kept the inn until 1878 when Elizabeth Wallace became the licensee, who stayed until John White became the landlord in 1888. In May 1879 Coroner Graham held an inquest into the deaths of James Prudham and John Little, employees of Messrs Nickolson and Paton, the oil-cloth manufacturers of Crow Hall Lane. The men had been hoisting a roll of floor cloth when one of the hook ends broke. James Prudham was killed when the roll fell on him and John Little when the block struck his head. The verdict was 'accidental death'. In 1890 John White advertised the inn as the Victoria Inn but in 1891 it became the Victoria Jubilee. Sadly in March 2018 the pub closed and is awaiting new tenants.

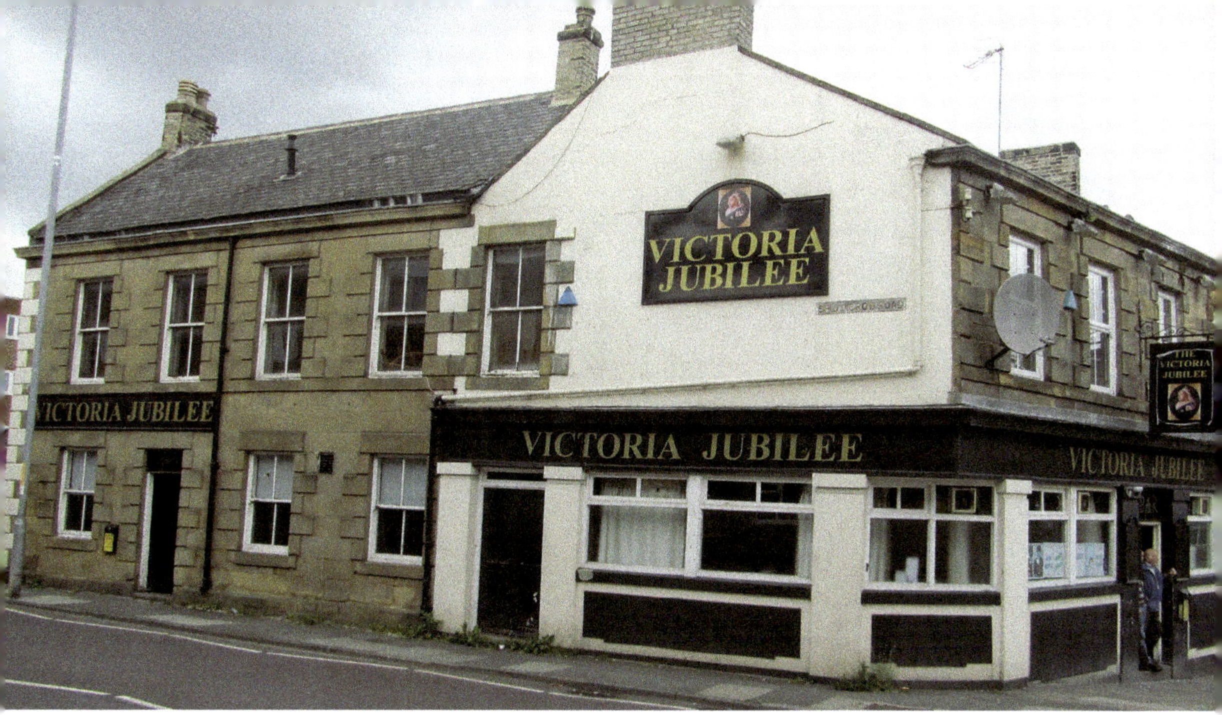

The Victoria Jubilee, originally the Barley Mow Inn, Split Crow Road and Victoria Square.

Hare and Hounds

This beautiful photograph of the Hare and Hounds, Windy Nook, was possibly taken in the early 1900s. Ann Swallow first advertised the inn as the Horse and Hounds in 1828. It probably started in the front room of Ann's cottage with ale brewed in the kitchen – as a lot of people did at the beginning of the 1800s. In 1839 Ann changed

The Hare and Hounds, Windy Nook.

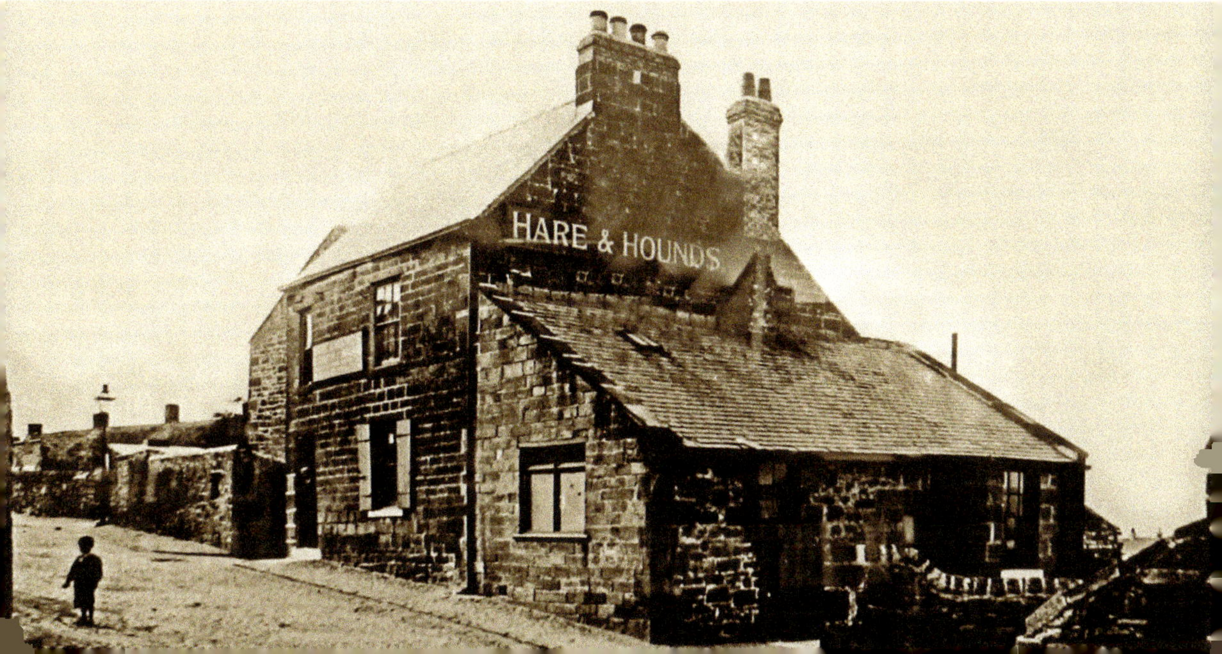

the name to the Hare and Hounds. Foster Stephenson became the licensee in 1855, and John Hall was the last landlord to advertise in 1894. In June 1915 Thomas Walker, the licensee, was charged with not having closed to soldiers on 6 June, in accordance with the order made for Northumberland and Durham under the Defence of the Realm Act by Colonel Dashwood. He was fined £5 and costs.

In November 1827 the *Newcastle Courant* advertised an auction to be held at the Hope and Anchor, Windy Nook, on Thursday 29 November at ten o'clock. At the time it was in the hands of a Mr Lowes. In 1839 Margaret Lowes become the licensee, staying until 1854 when William Battersby took over the licence. At the Brewster Sessions in August 1870 David Spedding applied for a licence but did not get it. John Brown was the next innkeeper to advertise the Hope and Anchor in 1871, but it was not advertised again. At the Brewster Sessions in August 1873 John Vickers unsuccessfully applied for a spirit licence and no other applications have been found.

The Bay Horse

The Bay Horse, Windy Nook, was first advertised in 1839 by John Anderson, who was a miner according to the 1841 census. In August 1838 a meeting of the Radical Reformers was held there, when the following resolutions were agreed to:

> 1st. That the meeting was convinced, by bitter experience, that the House of Commons, as at present constitution, does not represent the opinion of the people, and pledges itself to obtaining a real reform of the house by every means within its power.

> 2nd. In order to protect ourselves from future acts of tyranny from the Legislation, we pledge ourselves to establish a Working Men's Association, and by that means

Bay Horse Inn, Coldwell Lane, Windy Nook.

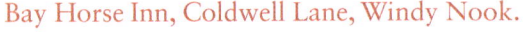

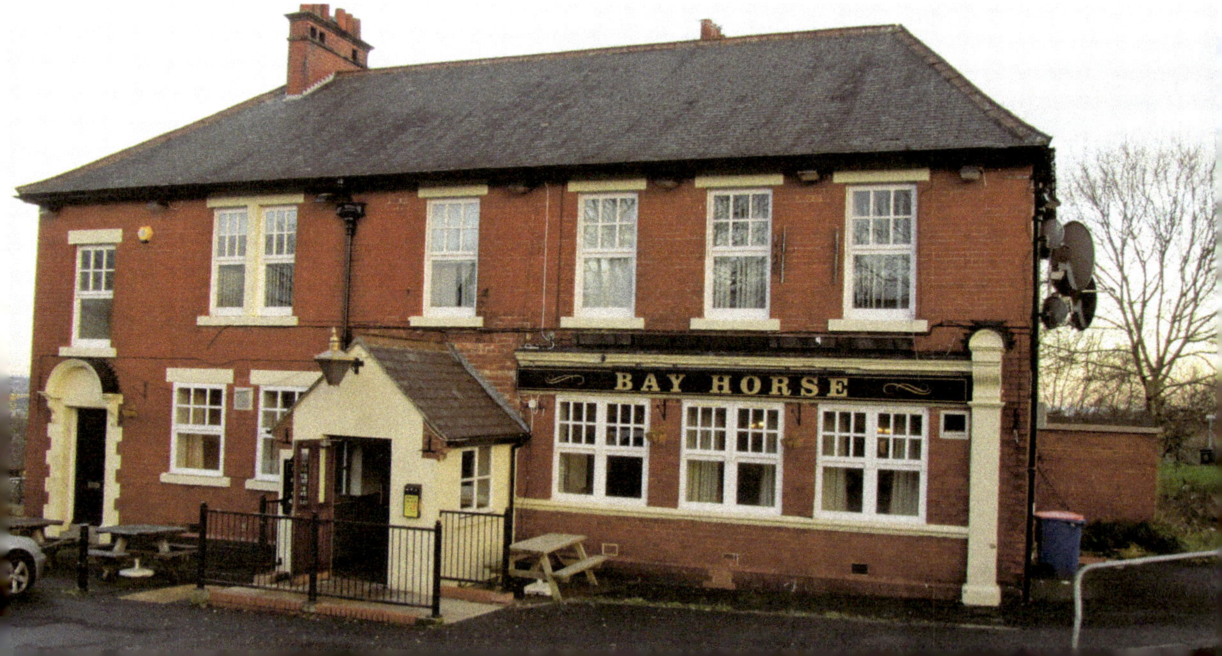

assist our fellow workmen in England to obtain universal suffrage, vote by ballot, no property qualification, and payment of members of Parliament.

Robert Gray was the licensee when on Monday 26 October 1864 an inquest was held by J. M. Favell Esquire, a coroner, into the death of Joseph Bell, aged fifty-five, who was foreman at Mr Forster's Grindstone Quay. The deceased had been knocked into the quay when the wind caught a crane; he fell 14 feet into around 2 feet of water, hitting his head on the rocks below. John Thompson, in a keel below, took hold of him with a hook but after taking one or two breaths was found to be dead when he was taken from the water. The verdict was accidental death. Today the Bay Horse is a more traditional public house, opening from 12:00–11:00 Monday to Friday, 11:00–midnight on Saturdays and 10:45–11:00 on Sundays.

Black House Inn

Tesco Express was originally the Black House Inn. On 27 May 1826 the Black House Inn, Windy Nook, was advertised in the *Courant* to let, as a public house, the Windy Nook, on Gateshead Fell, also known as the Coal Waggon. On 17 June 1828 the Coal Waggon was sold at an auction. It was described as having 1 acre of garden ground attached and consisting of four good dwelling rooms, cellar and other conveniences owned at the time by Thomas Moore. By September that year it was again advertised to let but the tenant does not seem to have stayed long as it was again let in September 1831. On Wednesday 4 August 1841 'The Coal Waggon otherwise the Black House' was again up for auction together with two small closes of adjoining ground. Robert Robson was the occupier. The inn was the meeting place of the Heworth Miners' Lodge all through the nineteenth century. Its banner was stored in one of the upstairs rooms and brought out for parades and the Durham Miners' Gala. Unfortunately it ceased to be in 2013 when it was sold.

The Black House Inn (also known as the Coal Waggon Inn), Coldwell Lane.

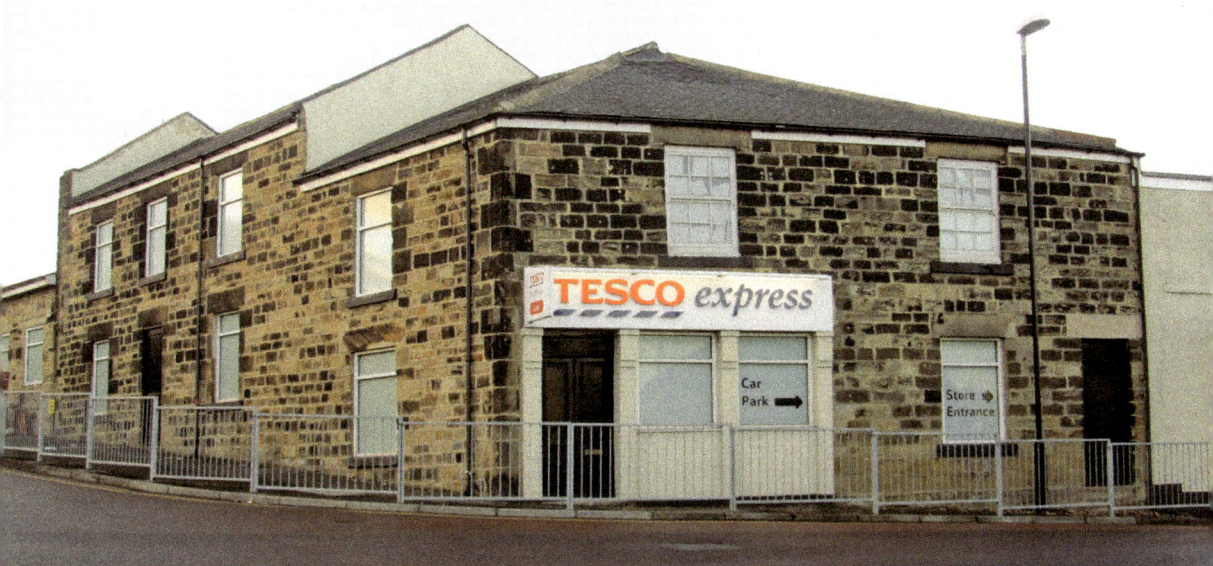

The Bay Horse Inn

The Bay Horse Inn, Coldwell Street, Felling, was first advertised by Mrs Mary Dickinson in 1894 but not much is known about the inn in the early days. It was rebuilt in 1901 for John White of Bennett and White, the Felling innkeepers. Today it had one long room where it would originally have had two – a bar and a snug. The bar is now to the left as you enter a small cosy room that has two giant screens for live sports. Every Sunday afternoon there is a live act at four o'clock. The inn is open 10:00–23:00 Sunday to Thursday and 10:00 to 00:00 Friday and Saturday. With a bus stop not far away there is no need for a car.

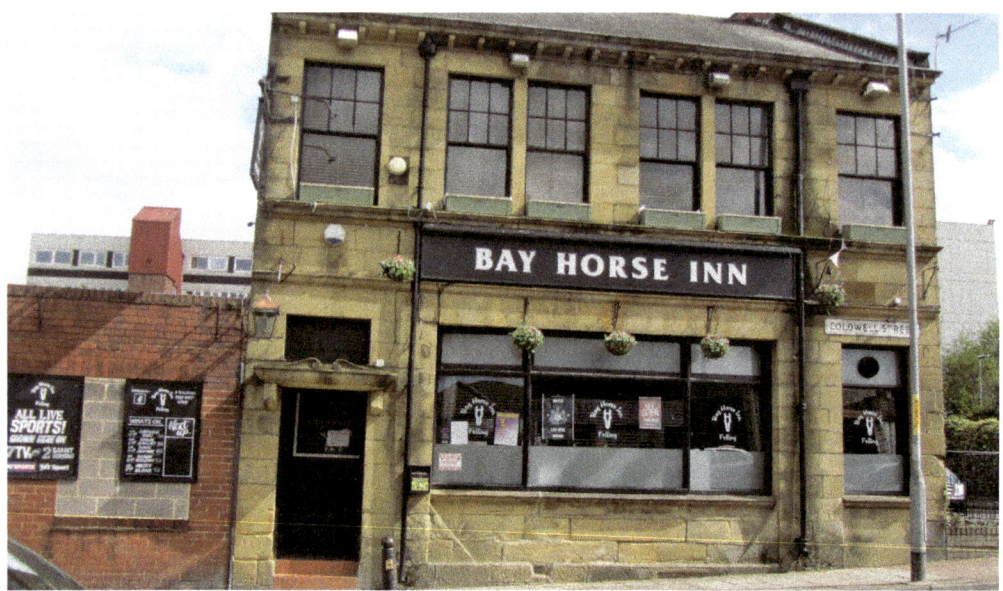

Bay Horse Inn, Coldwell Lane, Felling.

The Portland Arms

The Portland Arms, Split Crow Road, Felling, previously called the Shakespeare Inn, was built before March 1805, when Robert Miller, the licensee, held an auction there. It was first advertised by John Gray in 1828 with a High Felling address. In 1834 Thomas Hutchinson was the licensee but Stephen Laws advertised the inn in Robson's Directory of 1839 for the next twelve years. These two interchanged as licensees – they were possibly co-owners. On 12 December 1851 this old established inn came up for sale by private contract while occupied by John Barras Esquire or under tenants. It was described as having an 'excellent cellar, two stables and suitable conveniences attached'. This gives rise to the speculation that it could have been a coaching inn. In August 1877 Mrs Alice Atkinson, who had taken over the Shakespeare on the death of her husband, William, was up before Gateshead Court for breach of the licensing act for selling a pint of gin that was 32 per cent underproof. Alice was fined £1 plus costs. The Shakespeare Inn was rebuilt by John White in 1898.

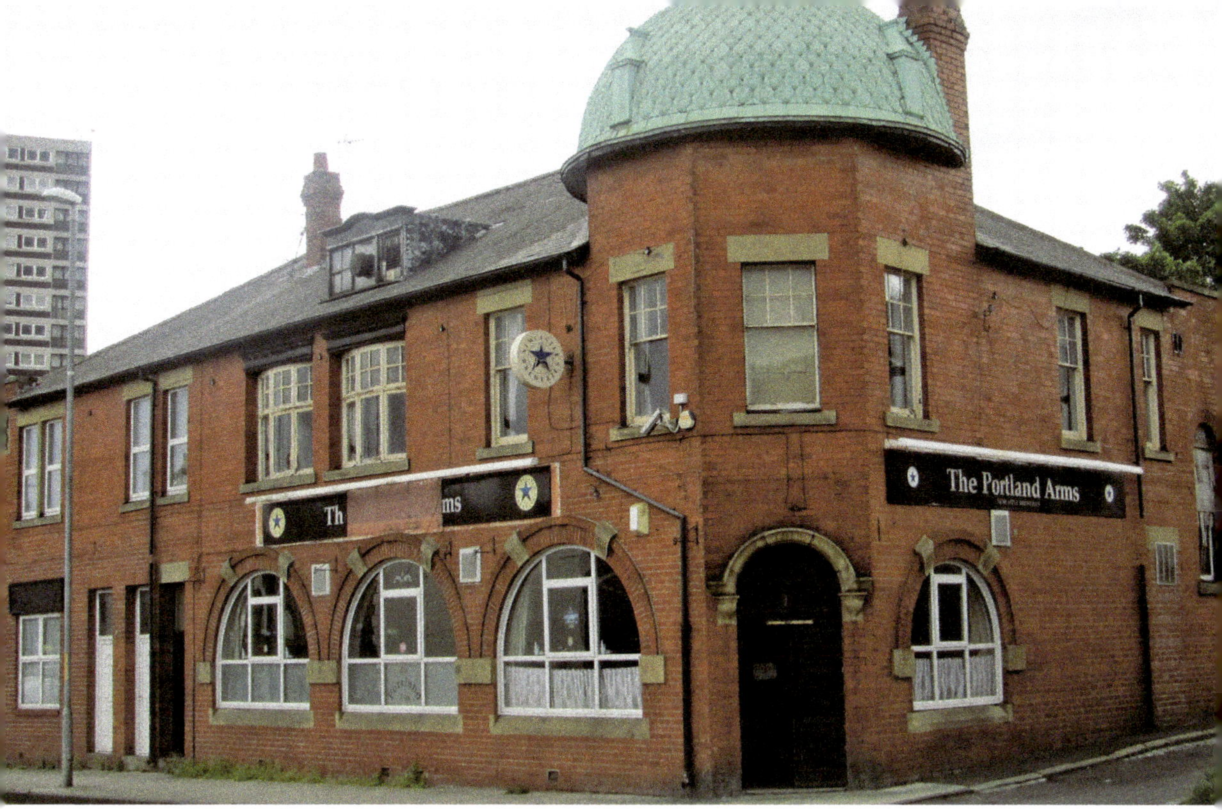

Shakespeare Inn, now The Portland Arms, Split Crow Road, Felling.

Saji's Halal Punjabi Indian Cuisine Restaurant

Saji's Halal Punjabi Indian Cuisine restaurant was originally the Pear Tree Inn, which stood beside the Tollbar at Felling Gate. Built in 1812 (if the plaque above the sign is correct), it was first advertised by Charles Stewart in 1827. In August 1873

The Pear Tree Inn, now an Indian cuisine restaurant.

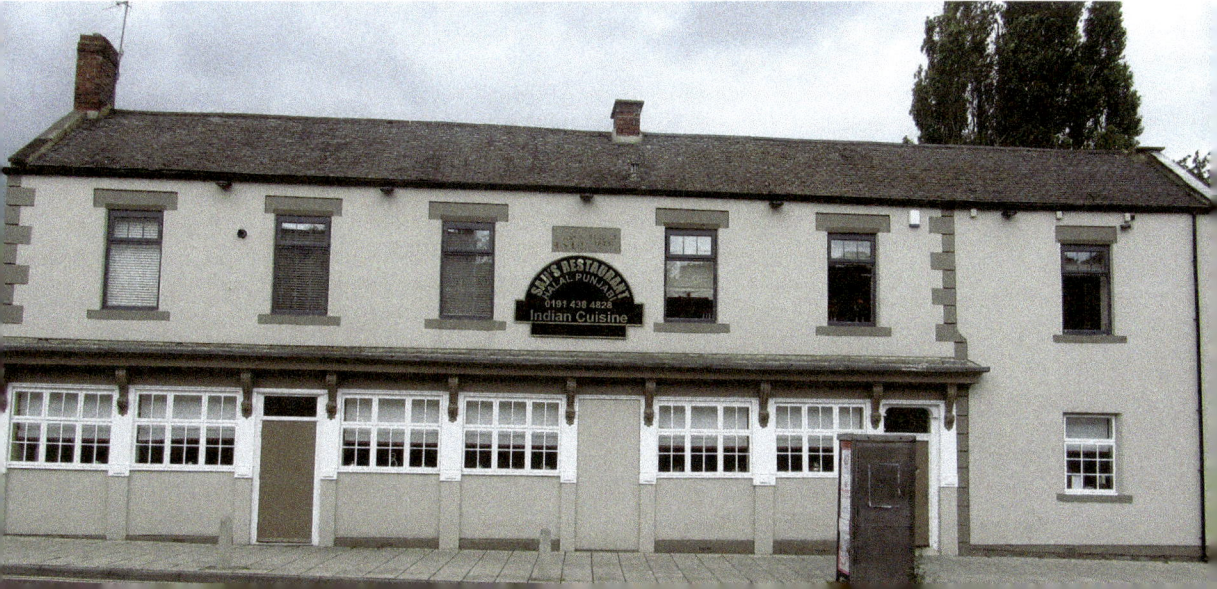

at Gateshead County Brewster Sessions Robert Bell applied for a full licence for the inn. Applications were again made in August 1880 and in September that year a wine licence was granted. At the Brewster Sessions in August 1881 Robert Bell applied for a spirit licence, which was granted. On 21 August 1882 Robert Bell died at the age of forty-one, leaving his wife to run the inn. Elizabeth Bell last advertised the Pear Tree in 1884. By 1897 Alex Deuchar was the owner, Thomas Dawson was the licensee and no other licensees are recorded after this. On 18 November 1939 Gateshead Harriers restarted the club's activities with meetings held at the inn for a training spin.

The Mallard

The Mallard was originally two public houses, the Railway Tavern and Speed the Plough Inn, which were situated in Gosforth Street, Felling. In February 1869 a new lodge opened in connection with the order of the Ancient Free Gardeners in the Railway Tavern when John Collins was landlord. In August 1870 an application was made at the Brewster Sessions, East Chester Ward, for a beer licence, which was granted on 6 September. On 5 January 1874 John Grundy, John Wilson and Thomas Jenkins were charged at Gateshead County Police Court with refusing to quit Mr Temple's tavern

The Mallard, Gosforth Terrace, Felling.

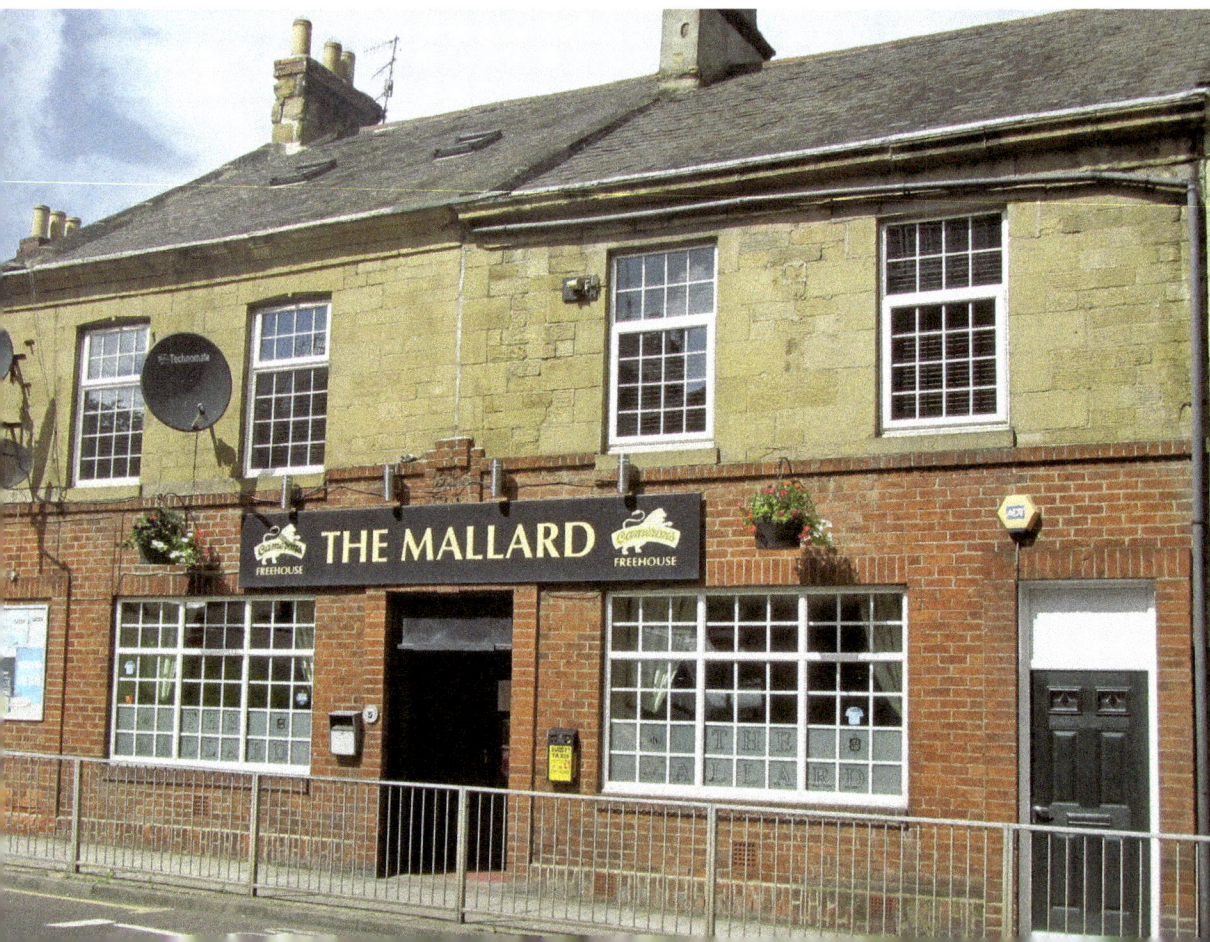

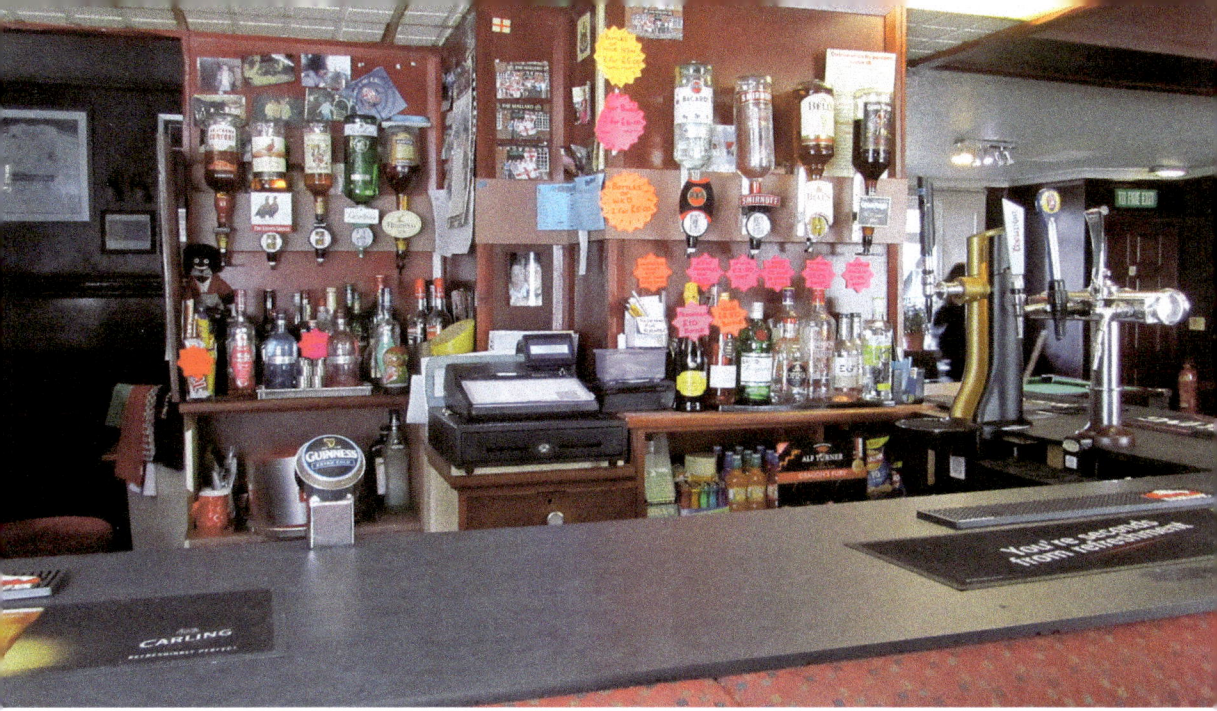

Central Bar in the Mallard facing the door.

on 27 December 1873. They were also charged with assaulting the landlord. Each was fined 11s on each account. In May 1879 John Harrison, landlord, was charged with offences under the Licensing Act for permitting drunkenness on his premises on 17 May. He was fined 40s and costs. No licensees were advertised after this date.

Edward Bennett was the first licensee to advertise the Speed the Plough Inn in 1871, although it could be older as licensees did not always advertise. Nothing has been found regarding the public house and it was not advertised again until Mrs Catherine White was the licensee in 1890.

Bought by Stanley Crawford around thirty years ago, it was knocked into one room with a central bar. An original photograph of the Railway Tavern is top right. To the left is an area for darts and to the right is a snooker area. It is a cosy welcoming pub.

Lord Collingwood Hotel

This impressive building was originally the Lord Collingwood Hotel, Collingwood Street, Felling, which was advertised by Thomas Gourley in 1828 with a Low Felling address. In 1834 Mary Gibson took over the lease of the inn. By 1845 Isaac Brown was the licence holder and like many public houses auctions were being held there. Isaac did not stay long as Matthew Davison was the licensee in 1848. In 1859 Thomas Pigg, a tailor, took on the lease of the inn along with the brewery. Unfortunately Thomas passed away in 1862. The inn, with its goodwill and the brewery, was up for auction on 19 November 1862, which was held at the direction of the administrators of Thomas Pigg's estate. George Henderson became the leaseholder as it was he who advertised the inn in 1865. In 1871 Hannah Henderson, George's wife, was the licensee, and in

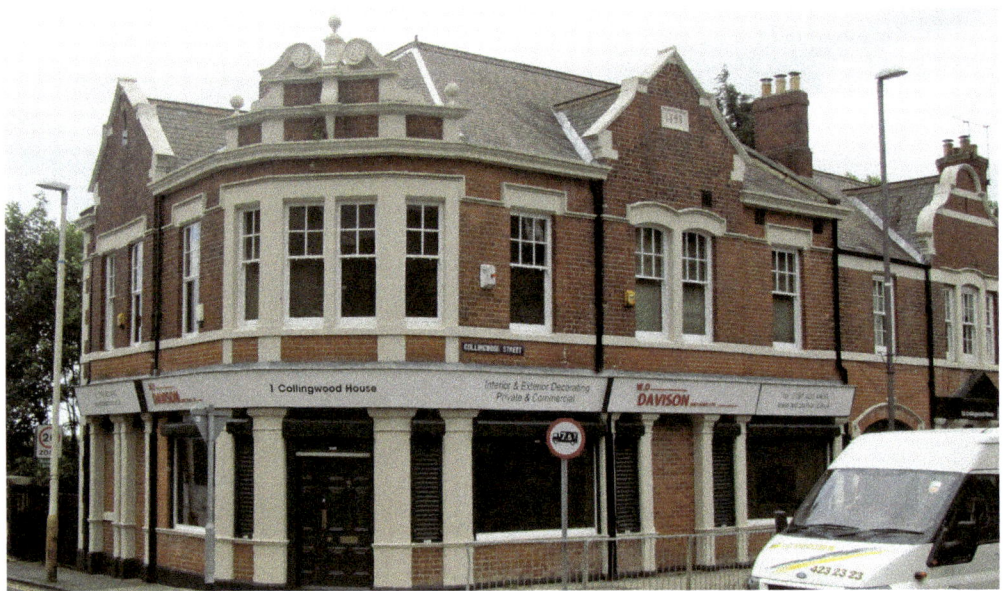

Formerly the Lord Collingwood Hotel, Collingwood Street, Felling.

1873 Edward, their son, had taken over. In 1879 Henry Selkeld Coxon, a contractor and coal merchant, became the licensee, but did not stay long. In 1882 Andrew Holmes became the owner, although in 1884 it was in the hands of A. Chisholm & Co. The Lord Collingwood Hotel was rebuilt in 1895 when Albert H. Higginbottom became the owner.

Mulberry Inn

On Tuesday 14 April 1846 John Cook held Felling Annual Ball at the Mulberry Inn; tickets were *6s* and *6d* including refreshments. In 1848 John Cook advertised as the Mulberry Tree Inn, Felling Hall. The inn, a conversion of Felling Hall, the residence of John Grace Esquire, was the old seat of the Brandling family, who built the Brandling railways in the North East. Unfortunately the hall was shaken by underground workings from Felling Colliery. In 1859 William Hunter advertised the inn as the Mulberry Bush Inn, Felling station. During his time as landlord many auctions were held there. When John Henderson became the licensee in 1865 he reverted back to the Mulberry Tree, Low Felling. On 10 July 1872 the Felling Hall estate was auctioned off in fourteen lots by Mr Samuel Donkin at the Beeswing Inn by order of the court in Chancery. The estate was a substantial one consisting of 56 acres of freehold arable land and gardens, with farm offices and numerous cottages and other buildings, and 7½ acres of leasehold land under the dean and chapter of Durham. Unfortunately there was little competition and only five lots were sold at that time. By 1879 it had been rebuilt in Mulberry Street. The Mulberry Tree closed in 2014 and was converted into houses.

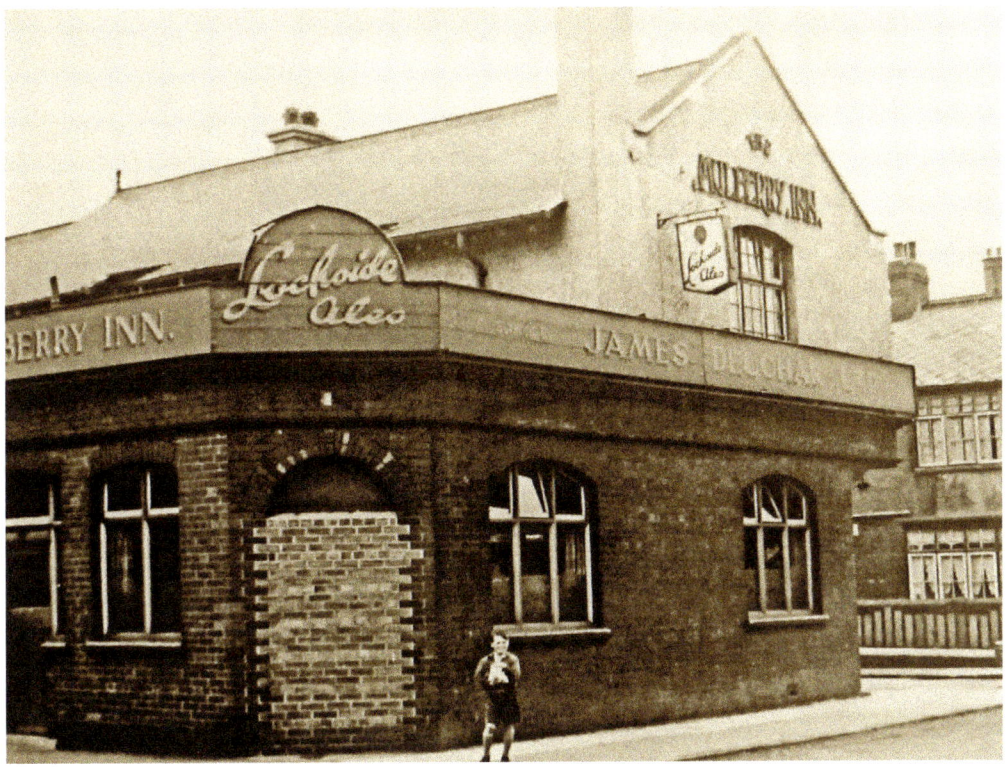
Mulberry Inn, Mulberry Street, Felling.

The Old Fox

The Old Fox was originally the Station Hotel, Carlisle Street, Felling. The Station Hotel was never advertised in any directory, although Alexander Dickson was stated in the *Courant* as promoting a novice handicap horse race in May 1880, the heats having taken place in April. In April 1924 John William Joseph Conlon, licensee, and William Winter were charged with committing a felony. In May John Conlon was fined £5 and costs for harbouring a reputed thief. William Winter, a machinist, was found at the hotel with a set of housebreaking implements. In April 1939 the hotel was top of Felling darts league with G. Byers as the individual champion. Today The Old Fox has a lounge area besides a pool area. The bar has a real fire – a lovely treat on those cold nights – and with real ale being available you're in for a cosy time. To the rear there is a pub garden with a smoking area and it is dog friendly. It is also a family-friendly pub with traditional pub games like darts, dominoes and poker being played two nights a week. Live music can be heard four nights a week with buskers' night being on a Monday. Sports television and Wi-Fi is available. LocAle accredited (locally brewed ales) Jarrow or Maxim real ales are usually available. The pub is close to Felling metro station with buses a short walk away.

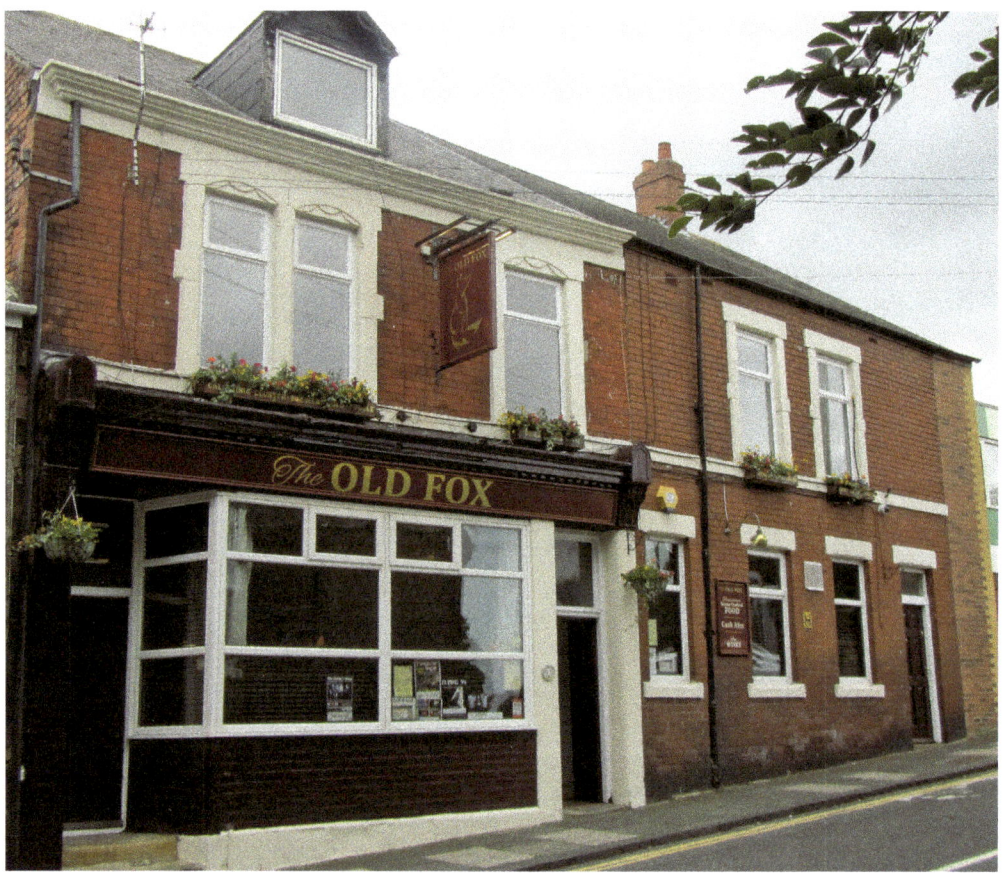

The Old Fox (originally the Station Hotel), Carlisle Street, Felling.

The Wheat Sheaf

The Wheat Sheaf, Carlisle Street and Williams Street, Felling, was not advertised in the 1800s but was an older public house rebuilt in 1907. Originally the Wheatsheaf was next to the pinfold (cattle enclosure) in Nether Heworth. Cattle drovers on their way south or to market would stop to quench their thirst while the cattle or sheep rested in the enclosures. In the early nineteenth century vestry meetings were often held in the parlour, instead of the presbytery of the church nearby. When the North Eastern Railway decided to excavate a tunnel to make a cutting crossed by a new bridge, the old Wheat Sheaf was pulled down and rebuilt on its present site. Today the Wheat Sheaf is a cosy public house with a real fire. It is owned by Big Lamp Brewery, which not only sells real ale and cider but also has LocAle accreditation. A family-friendly pub, it has live music, traditional pub games, sports TV, Wi-Fi and a smoking area. Behind the bar is an original CAMRA clock, and retains some of its original features including outdoor Victorian urinals. Every other Monday night there is a quiz, Tuesday nights there is traditional folk music by local musicians and Wednesday nights are dominoes nights. With the metro and buses not being far away you can leave the car at home and have a good night out.

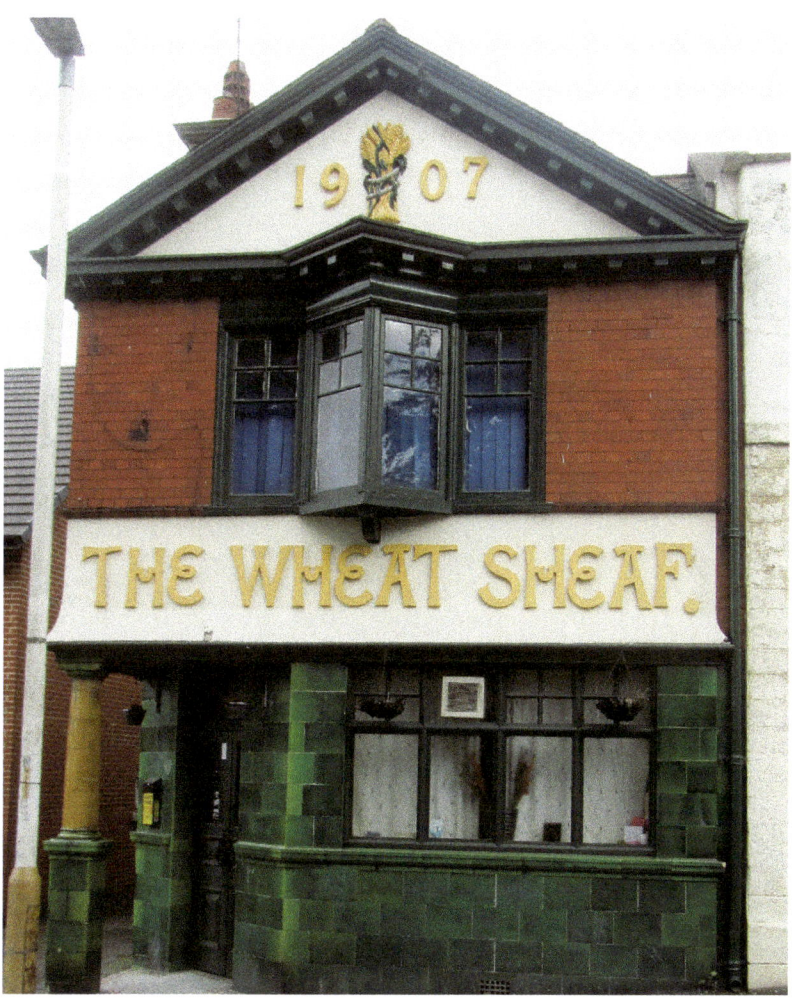

The Wheat Sheaf, Carlisle Street, Felling.

The Malting House

The Malting House, William Street, Felling, stands near the site of an ancient brewery which was next to Dempster Ville Reservoir. This provided a good supply of water, which would have been needed to make its ales and porter. In 1870 Michael Ward applied for a full licence for the Malton House, Low Felling, at which time it contained eight rooms, a long bar, two stables and every convenience. In September 1877 William Forster, the licensee, was granted a licence to sell wine. In January 1925 James Crinnion, the licensee, was fined £5 with £4 4s costs at Gateshead Court for permitting drunkenness. A charge of selling drink to a drunken person was withdrawn on the payment of costs. The case was the sequel to the death of a Mr Cullen, who had fallen downstairs, receiving fatal injuries. In July 1993 the Malting House beat Blaydon Railway Staff 2-0 at darts to win the Cooney Champion of Champions Memorial Trophy, one of the region's longest-running competitions.

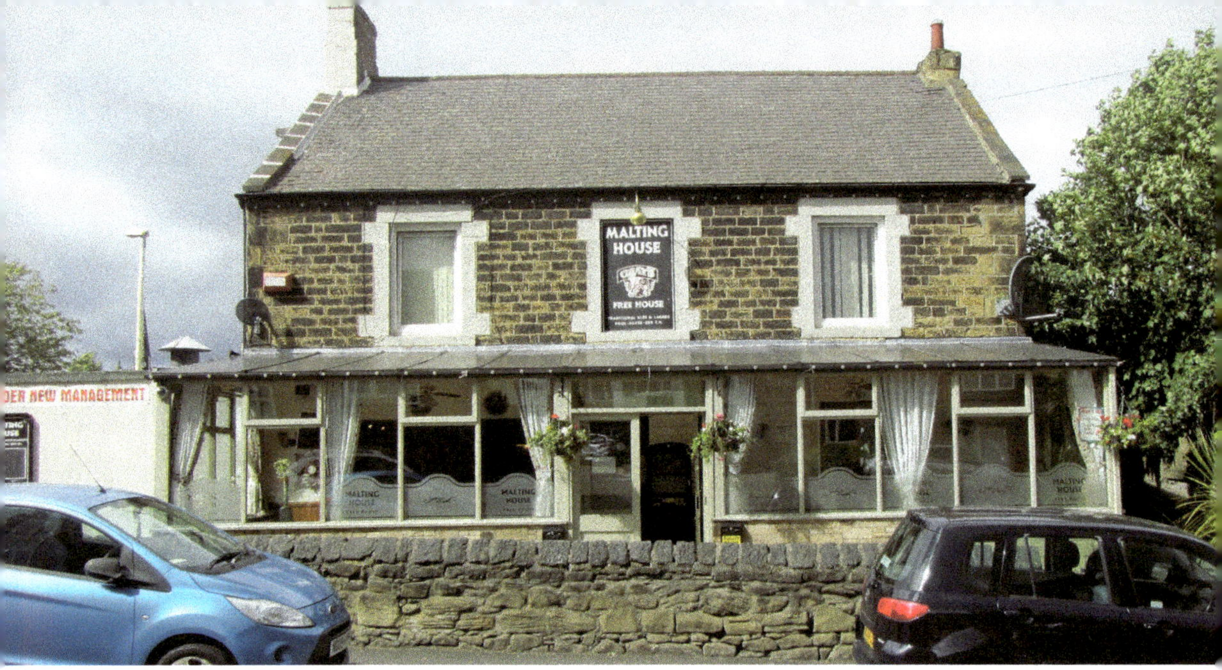

The Malting House, William Street, Felling.

Felling Shore
This old photograph of Felling Shore shows a tightly packed community where many public houses were tucked snuggly alongside houses, factories and shipyards. In 1828 only four inns were advertised: the Unicorn, Thomas Emmerson; the Wherry,

The tightly packed dwellings on Felling Shore.

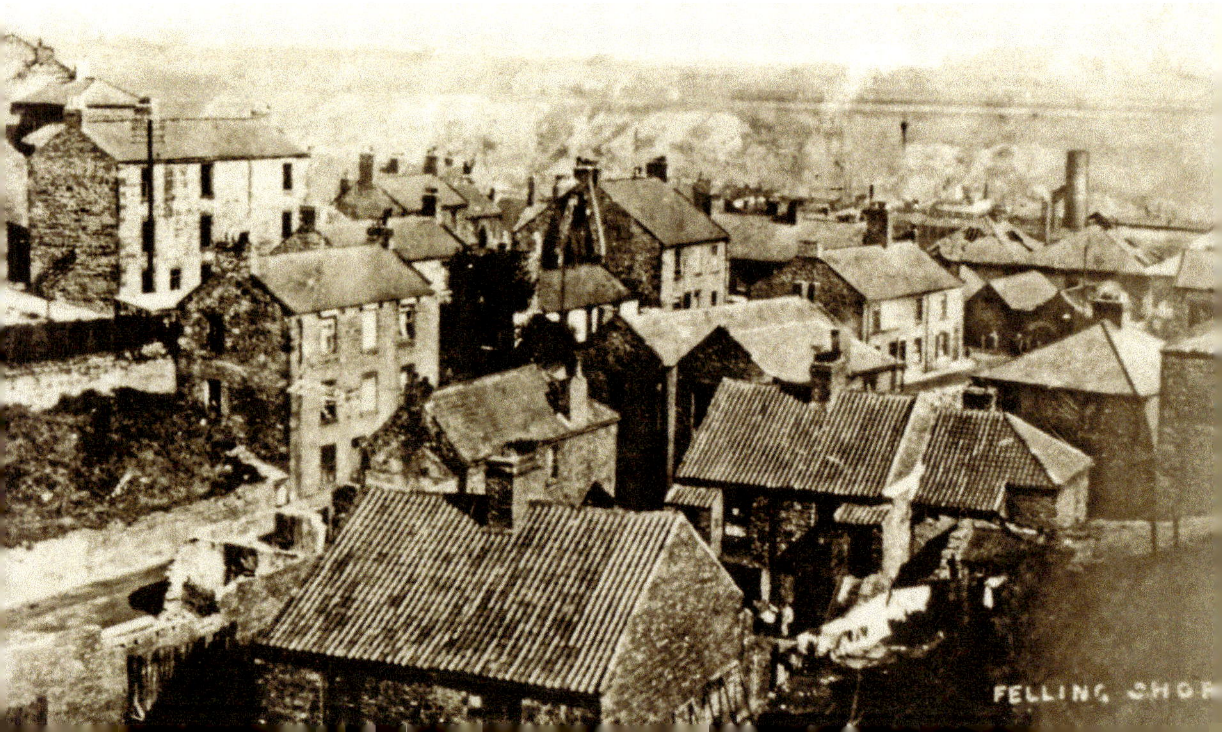

William Forster, a pilot; the Bee Hive, George Noble; and the Ship, Roland Richardson. In 1834 the Anchor was advertised by Edmond Hodgson, and in 1839 the address was given as Tyne Street, with Thomas Meadows adding the Oak Tree. The Grindstone came in 1848, but like most of the inns was possibly much older. In 1850 William Ward ran the Green Tree Inn. As time went on many more inns were added: the Brandling Arms, the Yarmouth Arms and another Ship. In 1895 both ships were in Tyne Street: one at No. 35, in the hands of Mary Dawson Hogarth; and the other in the hands of John Cunningham. Robert Lightfoot had the Anchor Inn also in Tyne Street along with the Grindstone that William Wilshire had for many years. In 1903 when Mrs Sanderson had the Brandling Arms Inn, the address was in Nest Road.

The Pelaw Inn

The Pelaw Inn, Shields Road, Pelaw, was originally the Station Hotel. The Station Hotel was first advertised in 1907 by John Allan, the manager, although it is possibly much older as it has stables out the back. On Thursday 23 August 1900, Vasey and Reed held an auction at the hotel to sell houses in both Coxon Street and in Brack Terrace opposite the Wardley Arms. With bidding starting at £140 per house in Coxon Street and Brack Terrace starting at £200, the lots were withdrawn at that figure. In February 1902 an inquest was held into the death of James Lawson, who appeared to have been struck by a train on the tracks around three quarters of a mile from Pelaw station. There was nothing to indicate why he had been on the track as an unused ticket found in his pocket was for the train from South Shields to Newcastle. On Tuesday 28 May 1907 the land between White Mare Pool and Laverick Hall was auctioned there by

The Pelaw Inn (formerly the Station Hotel), Shields Road, Pelaw.

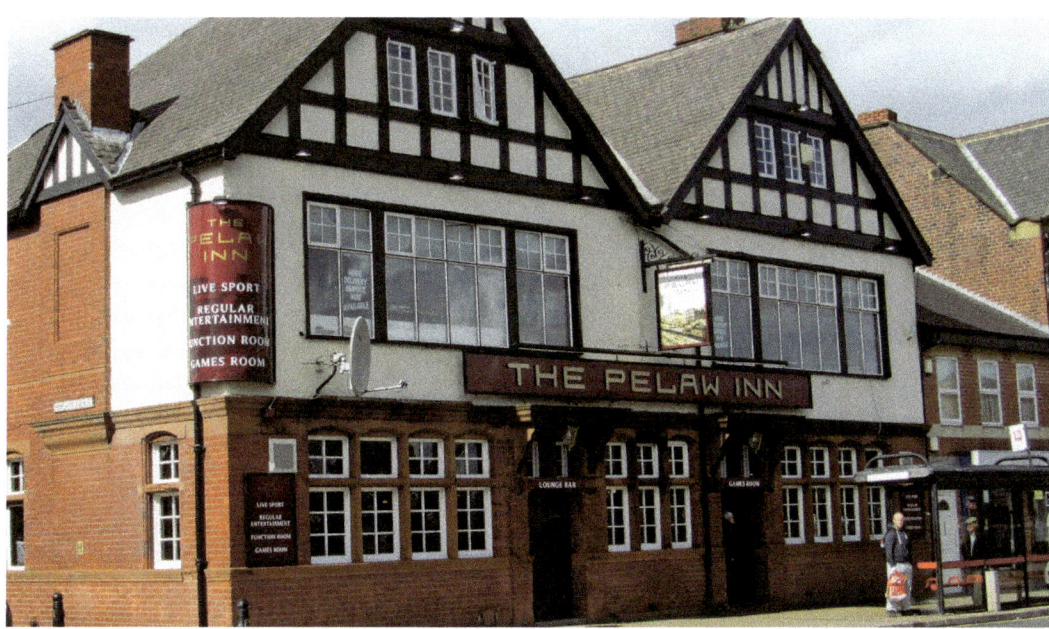

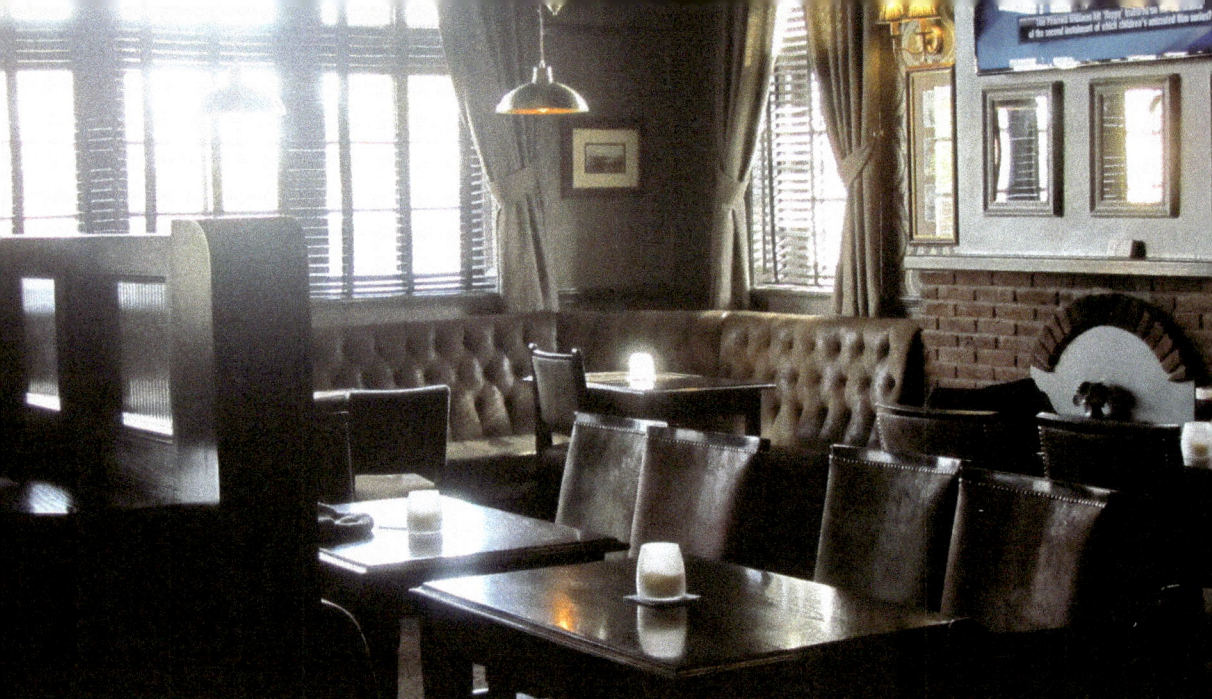

Inside the Pelaw Inn.

Messrs R. and W. Mack. On 21 December 1960 members of the District Council of Conservative Trade Unionists held their annual smoking concert here after a fortnight of lectures.

Graham and Maria Richardson took over the inn three years ago. They added an extension to the back of the lounge where musicians can play.

The Albion Inn

The Albion Inn, Bill Quay, was first advertised as the Bird Inn by William Madison in 1865, who changed the name to the Albion Inn in 1871. James Stewart took over the Albion in 1879, staying until 1883 when Benjamin Jude became the licensee. In May 1893 an inquest was held by Coroner Graham on James Armstrong, who had been found dead in bed on the Monday morning. Medical evidence showed his death was due to prussic acid the deceased had taken. The empty bottle had been found beside his bed, with the following note dated 19 May 1893:

> This world offers now no attraction for me
> Since bereaved of my hope and joy;
> I am weary and tired of earthly cares,
> So bury me with my boy.

A coloured photograph was found, with the following written on the back:

> At my death and burial I desire there will be no hat, bands or scarves used – everything plain and orderly, and that the priest or minister be not allowed to say

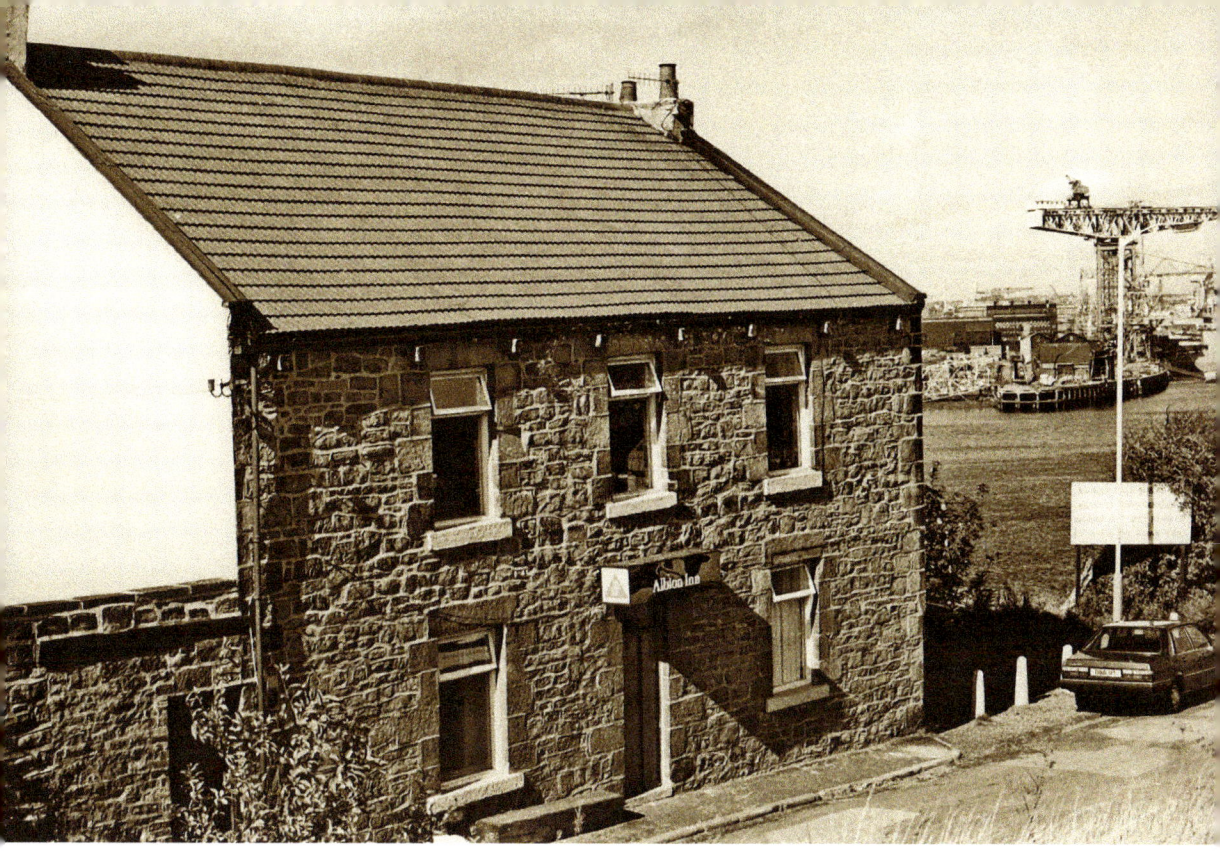

Albion Inn, Reay Street, Bill Quay.

prayers over my corpse, as I do not believe in them. From the time I was able to judge for myself I have been of Republican notion, embraced in no faith, but an a Free-thinker, and will die in the same opinion, knowing that in a few years hence Church and State separated, priest craft abolished. People see the absurdity of the teaching, and laugh at this generation as being led by the idea of others and not exercising their own judgment.

After further evidence the jury returned a verdict in accordance with the medical testimony. The Albion Inn, later run by Ian McConnell, closed in 2012 and is now a private dwelling.

The Cricketers' Arms

The Cricketers' Arms, Joel Terrace, Bill Quay, was originally called the Board Inn when first advertised by Mrs Jane Wynn in 1850. When advertised in 1865 Jane had changed the name to the Letter Board Inn. In 1871 Jane was just listed as an innkeeper, but in 1873 Jane had changed the name to the Quay Inn. At the Brewster Sessions in August 1886 Jane Patterson applied for a spirit licence for the Cricketers' Arms but was refused as Superintendent Harrison said that there was a fully licensed house two doors away. Ethel M. Gladman was the longest-serving landlord, having been in the business for forty-six years, serving many generations of the same families. Ethel knew

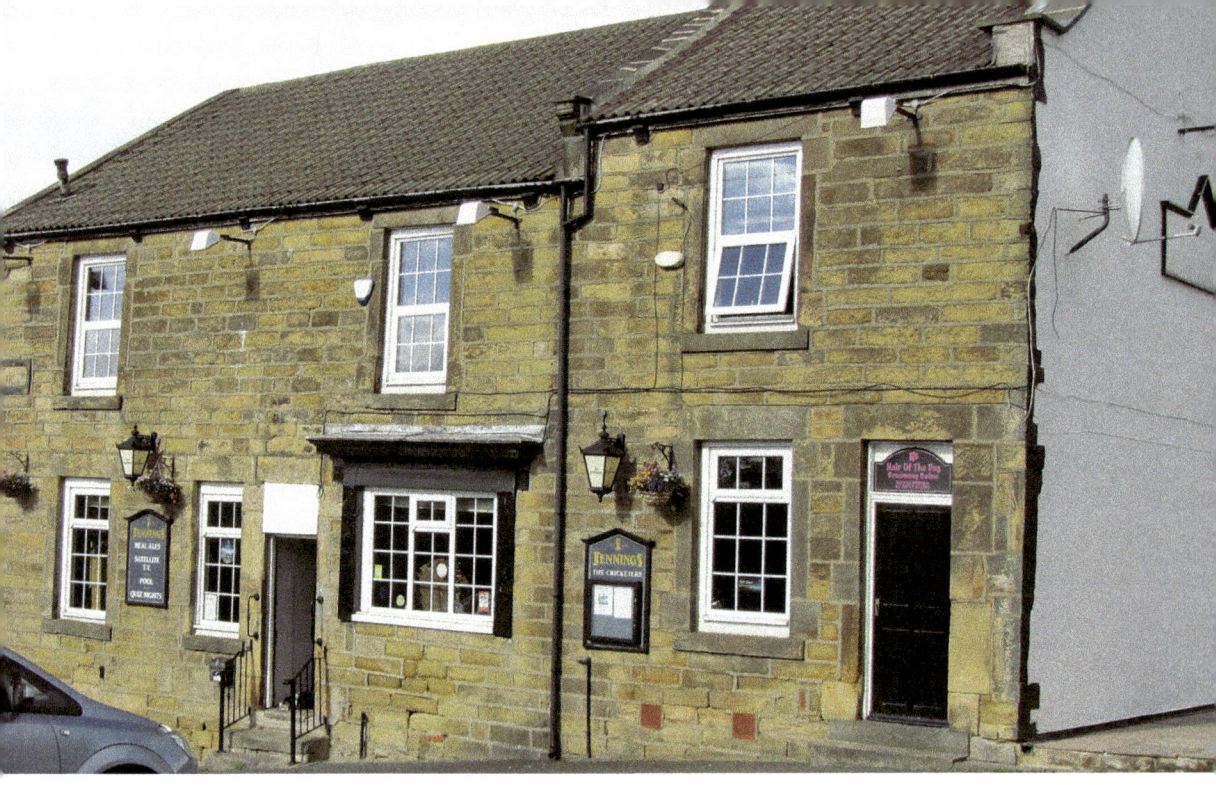

The Cricketers' Arms, Joel Terrace, Cromwell Road, Bill Quay.

her clients so well that she would have their drinks ready for them by the time they reached the bar. Today real ale is available in this unusual split-level pub where you can read the paper with your tipple. There is plenty of parking, a garden for warm days and dogs are welcome – you can call in after a walk along the riverside.

The Wardley

The Wardley, Brack Terrace, Bill Quay, although not advertised in a trade directory until 1895, was first noted in the Brewster Sessions for Gateshead in 1868. William Gilchrist was applying for a licence and the case was adjourned. In August 1870 William was again applying for a new public house licence for the Wardley Inn. Mr T. Hoyle, appearing for the case, stated 'that the Inn was situated near Pelaw Main Railway Station, and would be a boon to the passengers'. The case was deferred for two weeks for the magistrates to make their decisions, and the licence was granted. In August 1873 William Gilchrist, owner, applied for a full licence for the Wardley Inn, which was refused. He reapplied each year bur was still being refused in 1885 with no reason given. Rebuilt in 1897, this inn was popular with the mining community. With the decline of local industry and demolition of the former streets, the pub stands alone but it is no less popular. Real ale is available and it is Cask Marque accredited with one regular beer and one change of beer. With disabled access this family-friendly pub had an L-shaped bar with a snug at the rear. There is a weekly quiz, traditional pub games and sports TV for those all-important matches. There is also a pub garden and parking.

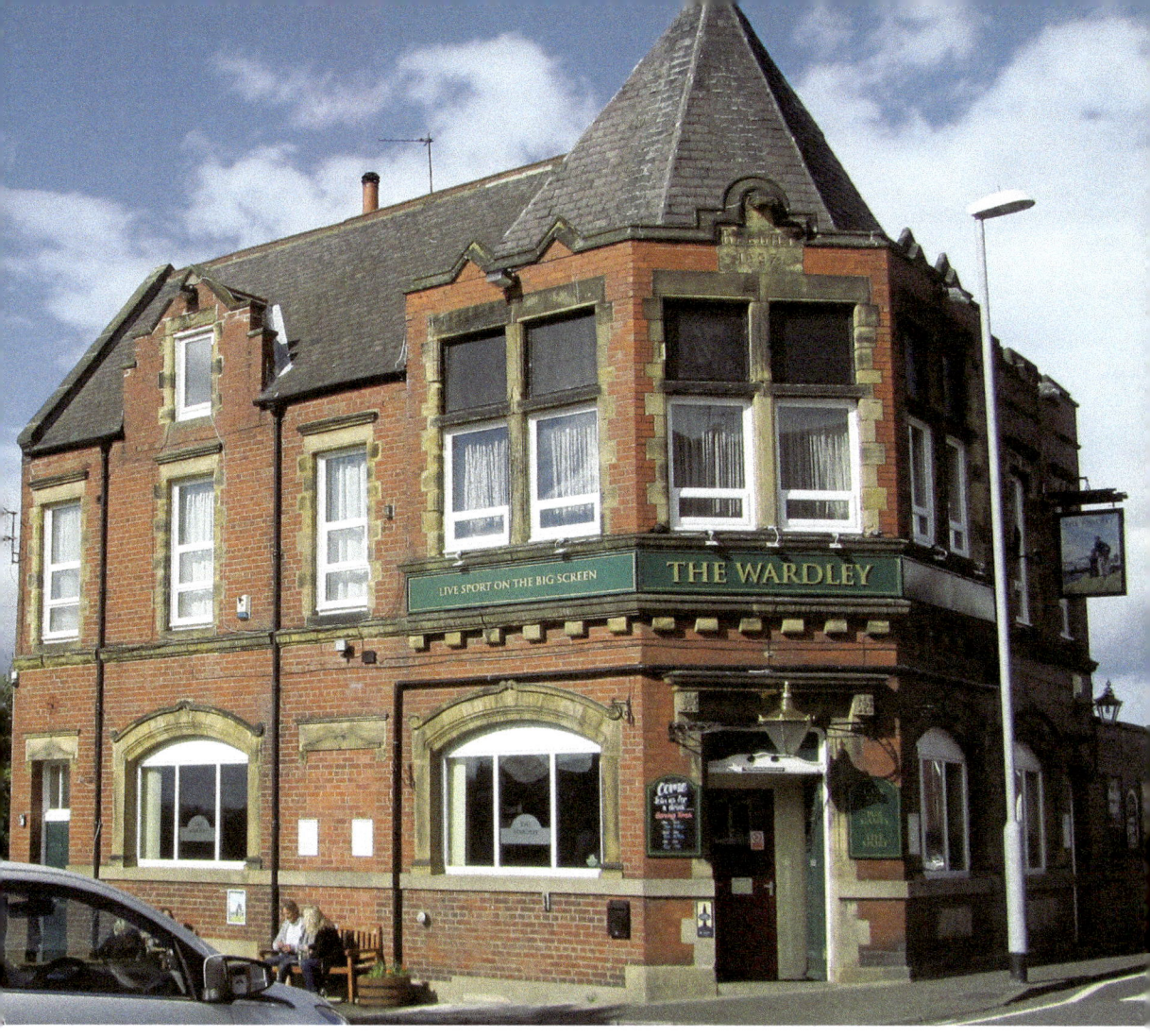

The Wardley, Brack Terrace, Bill Quay.

The Ramada Restaurant

The Ramada Restaurant at the Junction of Victoria Road West, Hebburn, was known for most of its life as the Argyle Hotel. The Argyle Hotel was originally the Hebburn Hall Hotel. In 1856 Hebburn Hall Inn stood not far from the Fire Brick Factory, which was near to Hebburn Quay. In 1839 John Moore first advertised the inn, holding the licence until 1859 when William Barnfather became the licensee. For quite a number of years the Hebburn Hall Inn was not advertised. In the Post Office Directory of 1879 Robert Alexander advertised the Hebburn Hall Hotel as being on Shields Road, Hebburn New Town, not Hebburn Quay as the previous directories had stated. Possibly the old Hebburn Hall Inn had been pulled down and rebuilt in the 'New Town'. On 20 June 1895 an assault on a constable in Hebburn occured: 'The officer was ejecting the men, William McLaren and his brother, from the Argyle Hotel, Hebburn New Town, when he got them into the street they made an attack on him.' The men were later apprehended by two other officers.

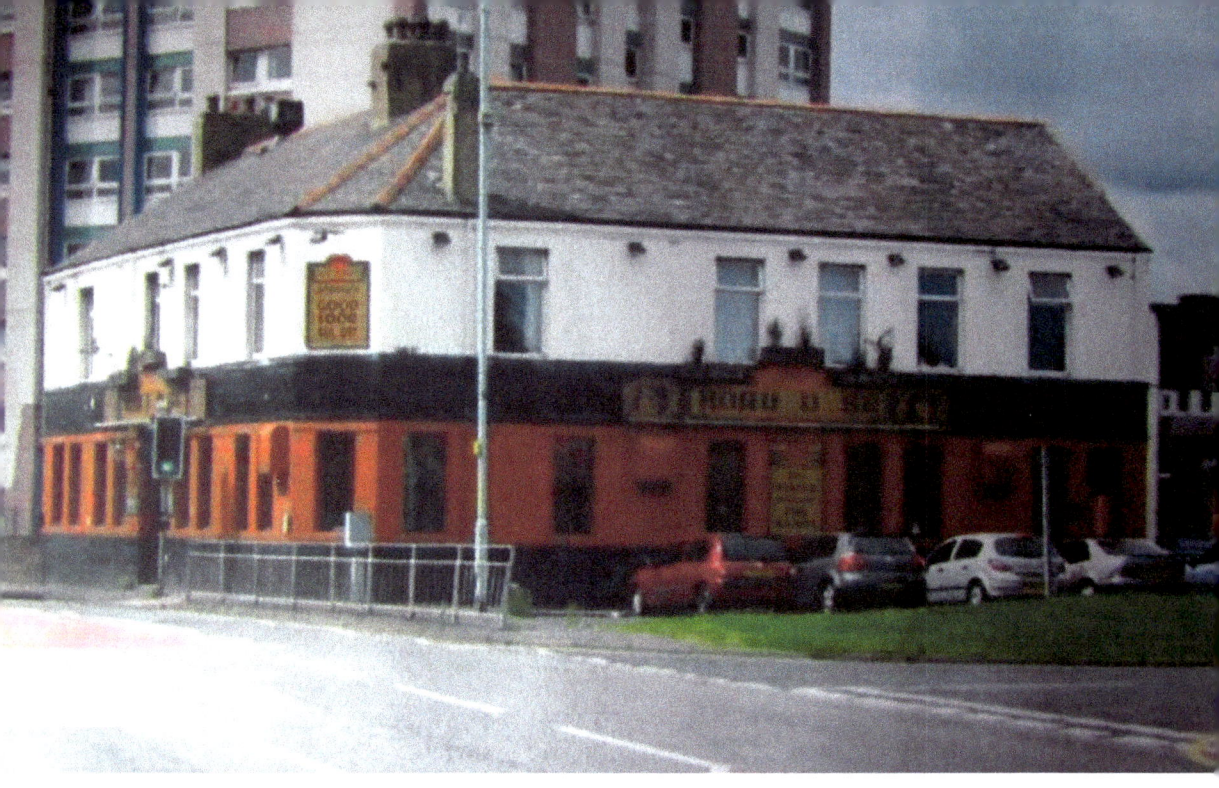

The Ramada Restaurant (formerly the Argyle Hotel), Victoria Road, Hebburn.

Leroy's

Leroy's nightclub on Station Road, Hebburn, was better known as Roy's, which was named after previous owner and councillor John Styles Roy. John Roy first advertised the Station Hotel in 1879, and in the following years many functions are recorded as being held there. From 1896 Hebburn Urban District Council along with their employees held their annual dinners there, with around sixty guests. In February 1900 the Station Hotel was described as having 'A good Dinner and Comfortable Smoke Room. Dinners, Luncheons, and all classes of catering provided for. Wines and Spirits of the best quality. Wm. Younger's Ales. Billiards. John S. Roy, Proprietor'. On Saturday 11 September 1903 twenty Hebburn men started a circular walk from the hotel to Washington and back, a distance of some 14 miles. Accompanying the men were a number of cyclists and other conveyances, with a large crowd seeing them off. An even larger crowd gathered for their return home, to see Mr J. W. Cox win at a time of two hours twenty-six minutes, while G. Johnson came second in two hours twenty-eight minutes and in third place was William Holtham in two hours thirty-two minutes. Mr James Milne, aged fifty-three years, was the first of the veterans home. On Friday 24 February 1906 the hotel hosted a billiard match organised by John Roy in aid of the Clog Fund. This fund helped shoe the many needy children of the town's poorer families. After it became Leroy's nightclub it was beset by many problems and in January 1992 receivers were called in because of unpaid debts. It suffered an arson attack and all its windows were shattered. The Glen Centre now stands on the site.

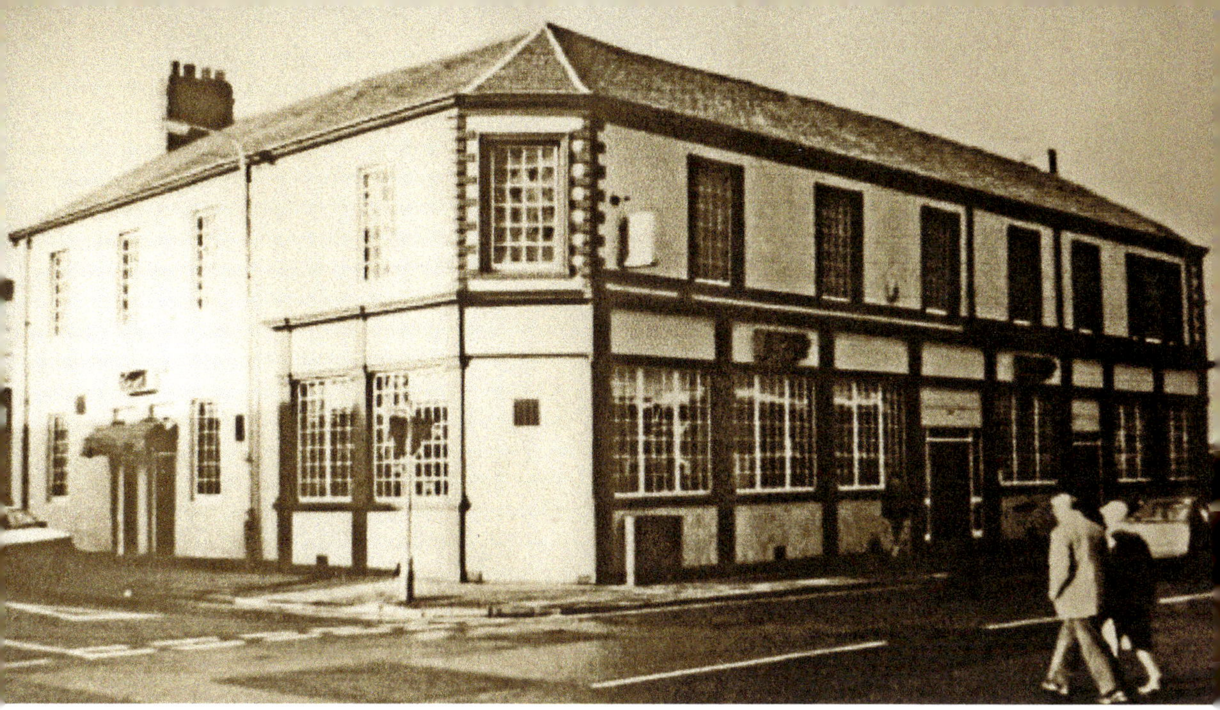

Station Hotel, Station Road, Hebburn.

Mambo II

Mambo II on Station Road, Hebburn, was originally the County Hotel, which was first advertised by Mrs Elizabeth Hall in 1893. Previously a Mr J. Hutchinson, in February 1887, had sent a contribution of 10s to the miners in dispute at Hebburn Colliery on

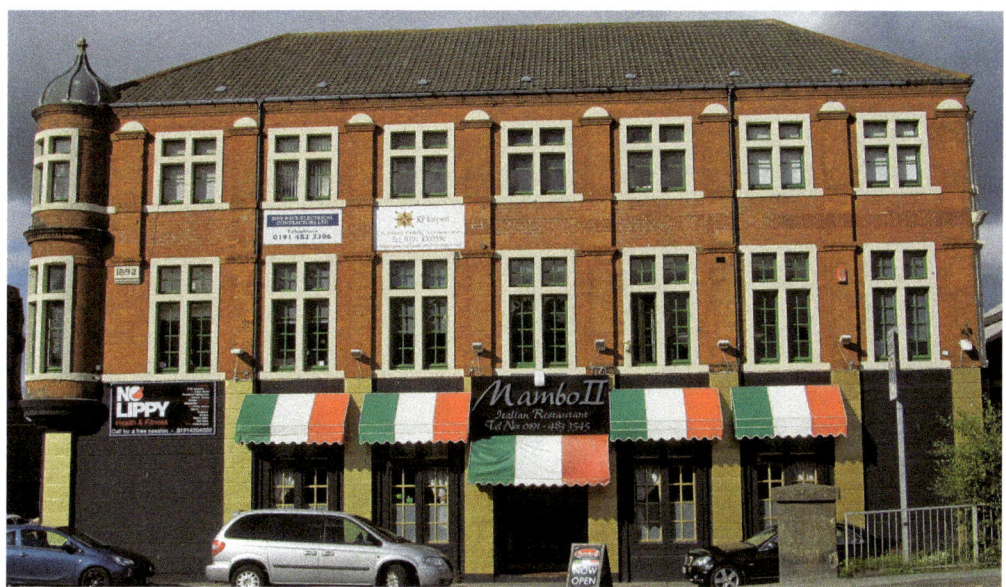

Mambo II, formerly the County Hotel, Station Road, Hebburn.

behalf of the hotel. In January 1893 Jarrow and Hebburn Burns' Club held their fourth annual dinner in the Assembly Room in the hotel. Six courses were served to the many guests. In January 1899 the Simson and McPherson Permanent Benefit Lodge was opened with around 150 members assembling for its opening. McPherson Simpson Ltd were the hotel owners at the time. In the early 1990s a series of arson attacks on the County Hotel left its already deadbeat image even more tarnished. In January 1992, after someone smashed windows and ignited petrol in the bar, a number of pensioners had to be evacuated, two of which had to be treated for smoke inhalation.

Wardles Wine Bar

Wardles Wine Bar, Albert Street, Hebburn, was originally the Albert Hotel, the name which can still be seen in the decorative façade of this Edwardian building. The hotel was first advertised in 1890 by John M. Burn with a William Street address, although Mr J. M. Bruce had the hotel before him. On 6 January 1887 Mr Bruce had provided a dinner for one hundred of Hebburn's poorest children. The local clergymen and Inspector Harrison had handed out tickets to the neediest children. St Andrew's Lodge of the NUOF Gardeners also held their meetings in the hotel in December 1887 – the address was Hebburn Quay then. In October 1893 the Albert Leek Club held its first

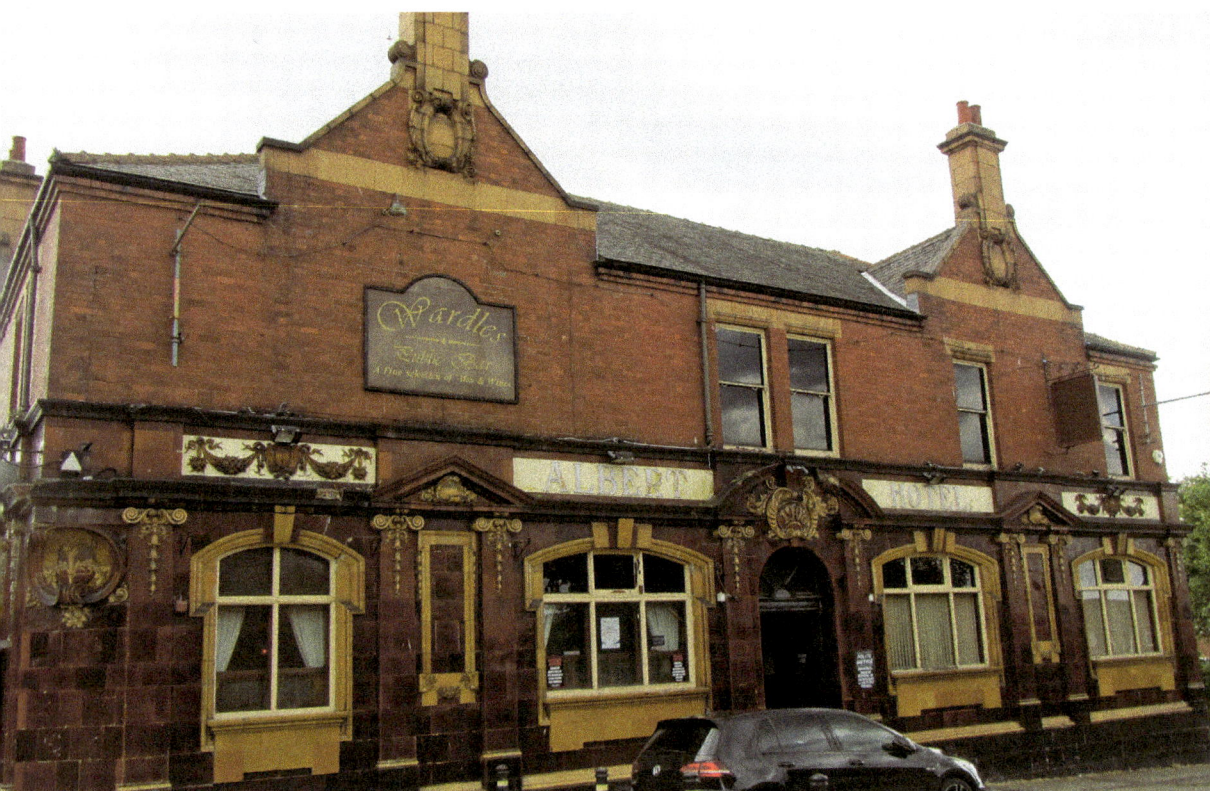

The Albert Hotel (now Wardles Wine Bar), Albert Street, Hebburn.

annual leek show. Mr J. Allison and Mr J. Hunter officiated as judges; thirty-five prizes were given for leeks, four for vegetables, four for celery, three for red cabbage, two for Savoy cabbage, two for Scotch cabbage and three for parsnips. The hotel was the headquarters of the Hebburn Argyle Football Club. On Wednesday 17 May 1899 the players from the previous season showed their appreciation to Mr Mitchell for his service to the club over the last season. Mr Mitchell was presented with a Meerschaum Pipe, a tobacco pouch and a novelly designed matchbox inscribed 'Presented to Mr J. B. Mitchell from the players of H.A.F.C. 1899'. Unfortunately a fire in the hotel caused a sensation in 1907 when the hotel was razed to the ground. On 23 July 1909 the new hotel was opened and was described as the most modern Edwardian licensed premises in the town, having been fitted with electric lights as well as gas. The electricity for the hotel was being supplied by the Ellison House Hotel, Carr Street, where the company had its own generating plant.

The Clock
The Clock public house is on the corner of Victoria Road and Black Road, Hebburn, just on the boundary between Jarrow and Hebburn. The granting of a licence in 1932 was a great surprise at the time as the trade was suffering from the effects of the depression and profits were small, Hebburn Colliery having closed in 1931. The building of the hotel in 1933 was confirmed to be the first licensed house to be built on the south side of the railway.

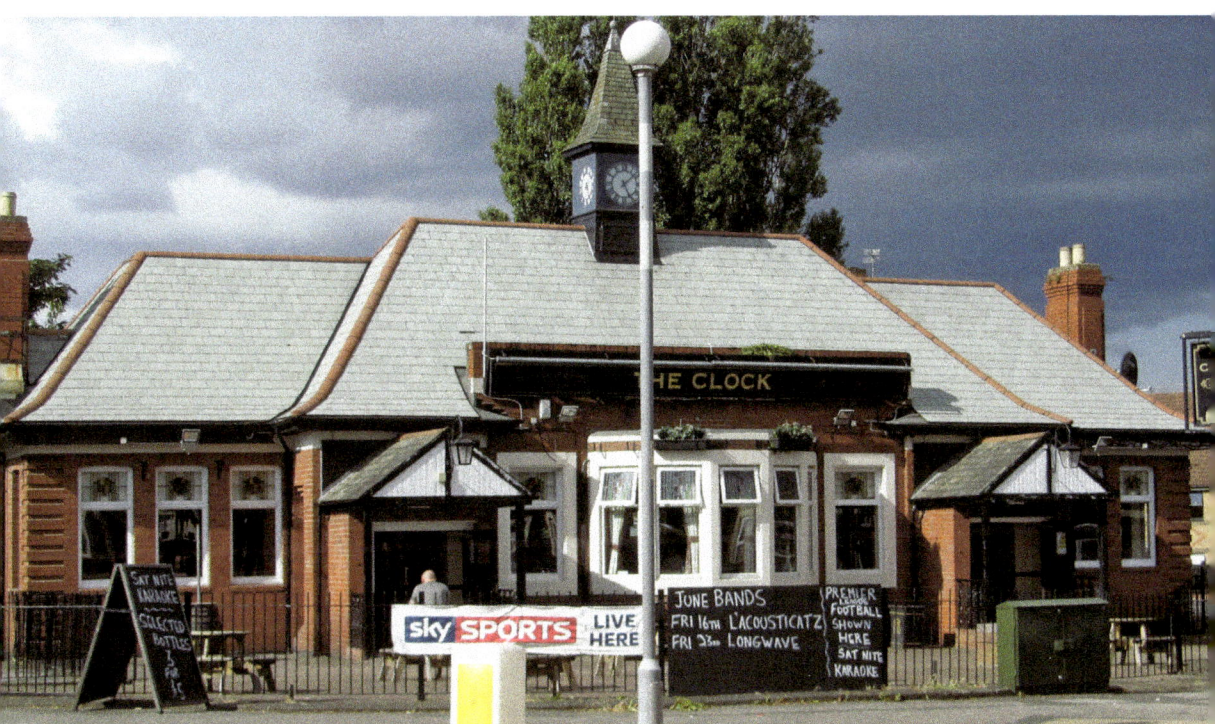

The Clock, Black Road and Victoria Road, Hebburn.

In October 1943 Mr D. Arams, manager, had taken a collection among his customers for 'Bob' Young, a seventy-five-year-old merchant sailor that had been repatriated from a German prison camp. The collection of £16 was presented to 'Bob' on 31 October and 'Bob then entertained the company with racey tails of the lighter side of camp life.' The Clock was a popular meeting place on a Sunday in the 1950s for people going on coach trip to places such as Plessey Woods, Seaton Delaval, Seaton Burn and Shotley Bridge.

The Caledonian

The Caledonian, Lyon Street, Hebburn, was not advertised until 1884 when Thomas Charlton was the licensee. In August 1880 Thomas Charlton applied for the fifth time for a licence at the Brewster Sessions to sell liquors on or off his premises. He was granted a licence to sell beer off the premises, and permission to sell beer on the premises was later granted. By 1889 John Styles Roy had become the owner and on 31 October a complimentary supper and presentation was given for Brother John McDonald of the Boilermakers and Iron Ship Builders, No. 2 Branch, attended by eighty gentlemen. On 15 November 1905 the annual meeting of the Workingmen's Sick and Benefits Club was held in the Caledonian. At the close of the meeting all 141 members received 19s 3d. The expenses for the sick and funeral benefits had amounted to £17 3s 11d and although there had been a great deal of sickness, the society was still able to pay out the stated sum to its members. In September 1984 the Caledonian was hit by a fire that severely damaged the bar, causing heat and smoke damage to the rest of the pub and flat upstairs. A double raid within days of the fire robbed landlord Alex McConnell of thousands of pounds' worth of property. On 1 October, despite the fire, the lounge was opened for business as usual by Alex and his wife Christina.

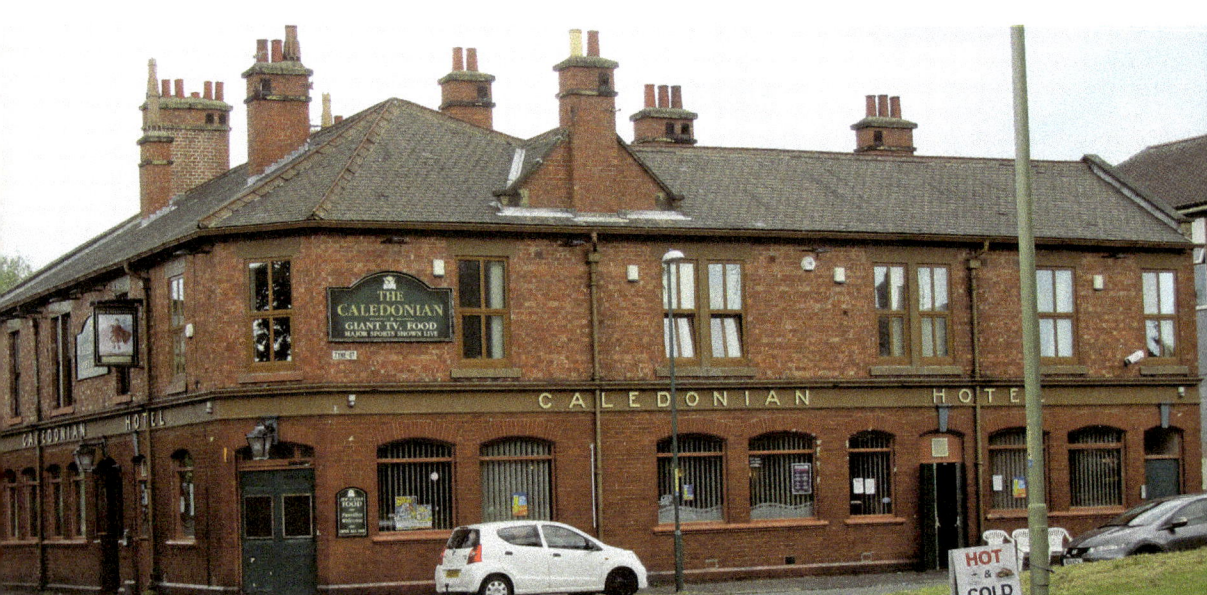

The Caledonian, Lyon Street, Hebburn.

The Banks O' the Tyne

The Banks O' the Tyne, Hebburn, originally the Ellison Arms Inn, just a stone's throw from Hebburn Colliery 'A' Pit and Staiths, was first advertised in 1850 by Charles Stewart. At the time it was the centre of the mining community, which by 1856 had its own post office, chapel and school. This community was hemmed in by the waggon way to three sides, Hebburn Staiths and the river on the fourth. In October 1912 the first potted leek show was held with twenty-four stands of leeks alone and red cabbage and parsnips also being displayed. In August 1988 the pub's £250,000 revamp transformed it with special facilities. Lindsay Wade thought the work, which included a 100-seat restaurant and a conservatory, was a major investment. The games room and bar were knocked into one with a carvery becoming one of its special features. The décor incorporated 'Olde Worlde' styles. When staff turned up on 4 July 1994 they found the pub had been stripped bare. Carpets, paintings, tables, ovens and all other valuable items had been removed during the night and the owners, Scottish and Newcastle Brewery, were trying to contact Mr Wade, the tenant. On 12 July 1994 Lindsay Wade was declared bankrupt, leaving as many as forty couples' wedding plans in tatters. An arson attack a few days later left the pub in ruins. At the end of December the Banks O' the Tyne was demolished.

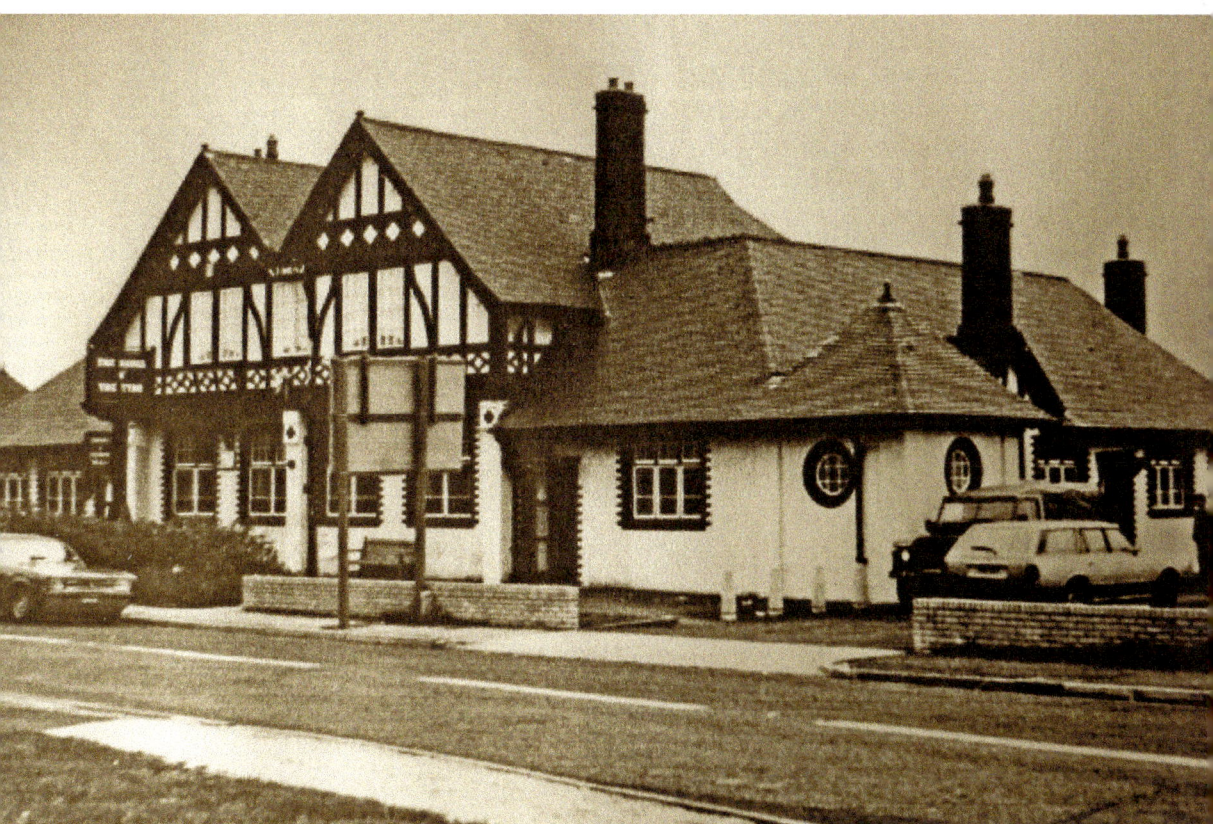

Banks O' the Tyne (originally the Ellison Arms), Hebburn Colliery.

The White Lead

The White Lead, Blackett Street, on the Jarrow and Hebburn border, which was originally called the Royal Hotel, was advertised by Thomas Charlton in 1871. In 1865 an inquest was held into the death of Thomas Charlton, who kept the hotel for eleven years before John Hutchinson became the licensee in 1882. On 8 May 1889 an inquest was opened by John Graham, a coroner, into the death of Daniel Button, forty-nine, and James Kennedy, thirty-four, who had been killed in an explosion at Hebburn Colliery on Tuesday 7 May. In total three people were killed that day. On Saturday 15 July 1893 after the first-round match in the Cricket Challenge Cup between Tynemouth and Newcastle Volunteer Artillery Sergeant's Mess the teams had dinner together at the Royal Hotel. The Royal, built opposite the White Lead Works, eventually got the nickname the 'White Lead'. Later it became Dougie's Tavern, but after a complete refurbishment it became the White Lead once more. The White Lead became a 'Sonnet 43' gastro restaurant and bar. The dining area has an open kitchen at the end of the room.

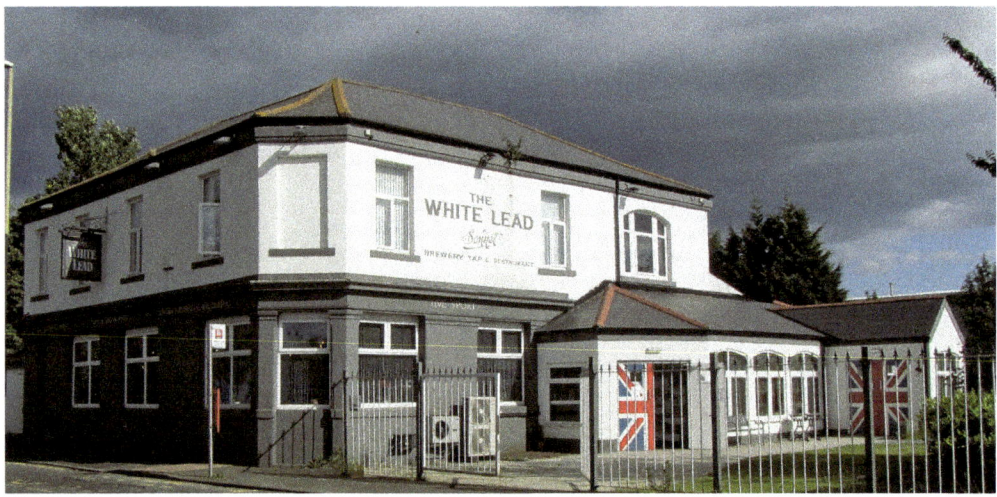

Above: The White Lead (originally the Royal Hotel), Blackett Street, Hebburn.

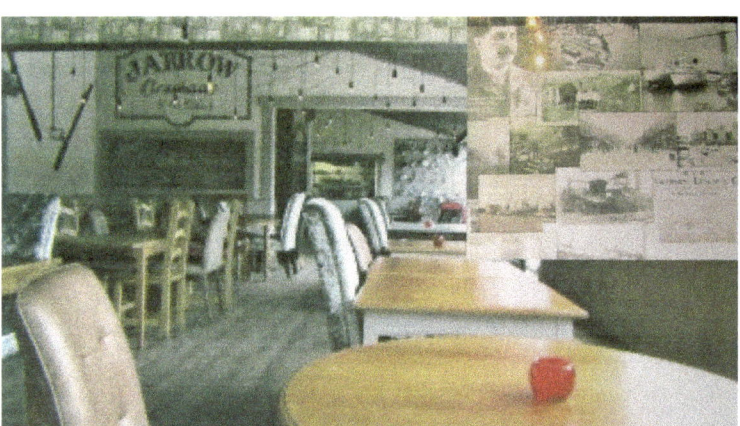

Left: The dining area and mural that is in the bar area.

Western Hotel

It is hard to imagine this as the Western Hotel, Western Road, Jarrow. The Western Hotel first came to light on 28 March 1874 when an advert for houses to let stated that the particulars were to be collected from Mr D. McVay at the Western Hotel. Ward's Directory 1875/6 has David McVay as the licensee but David had already died. On 29 August 1874 David McVay died suddenly aged forty-two from a liver complaint he had had for some time, leaving a wife and one son. The Western Hotel was not advertised again until 1883 when Alexander Donaldson was the licensee. Alexander Donaldson had been the licensee since 1878 when tragedy struck the family: their only daughter had died on 16 January 1878. In June 1881 the Caledonian Society held their meeting in the club room of the Western where it was agreed to hold their annual sports on the recreation ground. There was also an agreement of £50 in prizes to be given. At the Brewster Sessions in September 1886 Mary Donaldson, beerhouse keeper, applied for a full licence for the hotel. Mr C. W. Newlands was presenting a petition from residents of the district and members of friendly societies that met at the house. Although the hotel had an ale licence unsuccessful applications had been made for a full licence since 1874, according to the petition. Mary Donaldson was still the licence holder in March 1904 when she was in court and fined £5 for serving a drink to a policeman while he was on duty. In June 1910 B. F. Simpson applied for planning permission to create a new front to the Western Hotel.

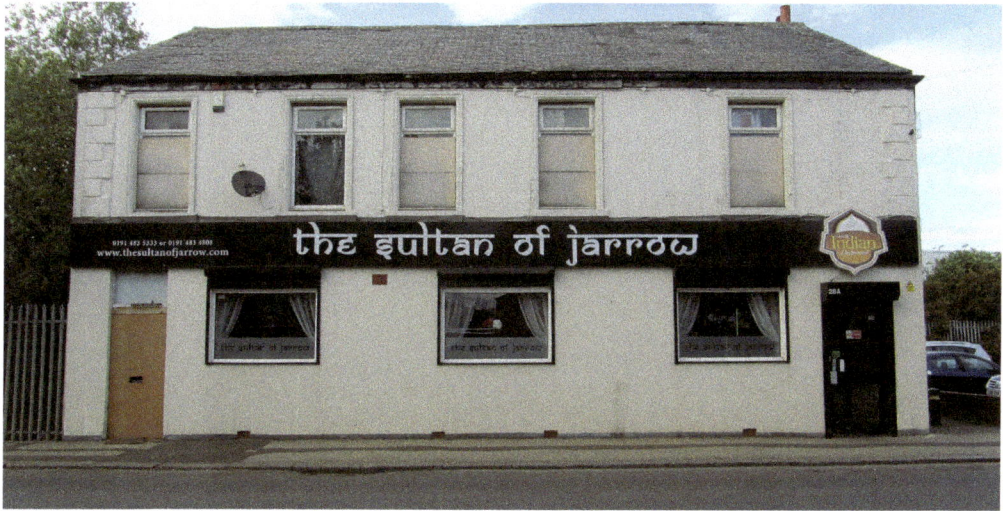

The Sultan of Jarrow restaurant (formally the Western Hotel), Western Road, Jarrow.

Rolling Mill Hotel

James Atkin was the first publican to advertise the Rolling Mill Hotel, whose address at that time was given as Straker Street, Jarrow, in 1871. The Rolling Mill Hotel took its name from the rolling mills used in the processing of the steel in Palmers shipyards that were near the public house. In 1885 John Graham advertised the Rolling Mill Tavern

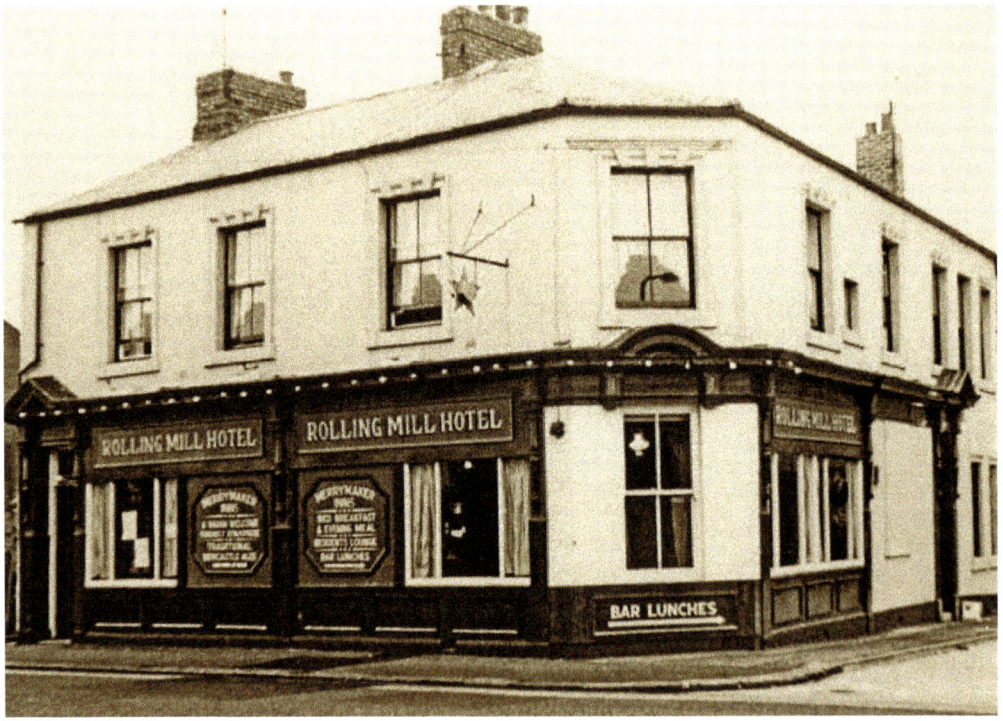

The Rolling Mill Hotel, Western Road, Jarrow.

as being at Nos 40 and 42 Western Road, which is the hotel above. It is unlikely to be the same one advertised by James Atkin. As street names changed and neither street is named on the 1856 map it is hard to tell. Newcastle breweries had alterations carried out in March 1938 when toilets were added. Bill Walker was one of the last licensees, being at the hotel for four years. The Rolling Mill closed around 2006.

Queen's Hotel

This lovely photograph of the Queen's Hotel is thought to be from the 1960s. The Queen's Hotel, Western Road, opposite the Rolling Mill, was built in the late 1860s. In January 1870 the Jarrow branch of the Amalgamated Society of the Engineers, Machinists, Millwrights, Smiths and Pattern Makers held their annual supper at the Queen's Hotel with thirty-four members sitting down to an excellent repast, when Thomas Watson was the licensee. In October 1872 James Henry, a mason's labourer, was given one month's hard labour for stealing two bottles of sherry from the hotel. In August 1884 Alexander Smithfield applied for a transfer of his licence from the Wellington Hotel in the High Street to the Queen's Hotel, which was was granted. On 14 January 1887 Alexander Smithfield placed an advert in the *Jarrow Express* for the 'Queen's Luncheon Bar, to have Superior Foreign and British Wines and Spirits, to be supplied in prime condition'. On Thursday 9 October 1890, members of the Mid-Tyne Committee of the Society of Engineers met to agree to the ending of piece-work at the

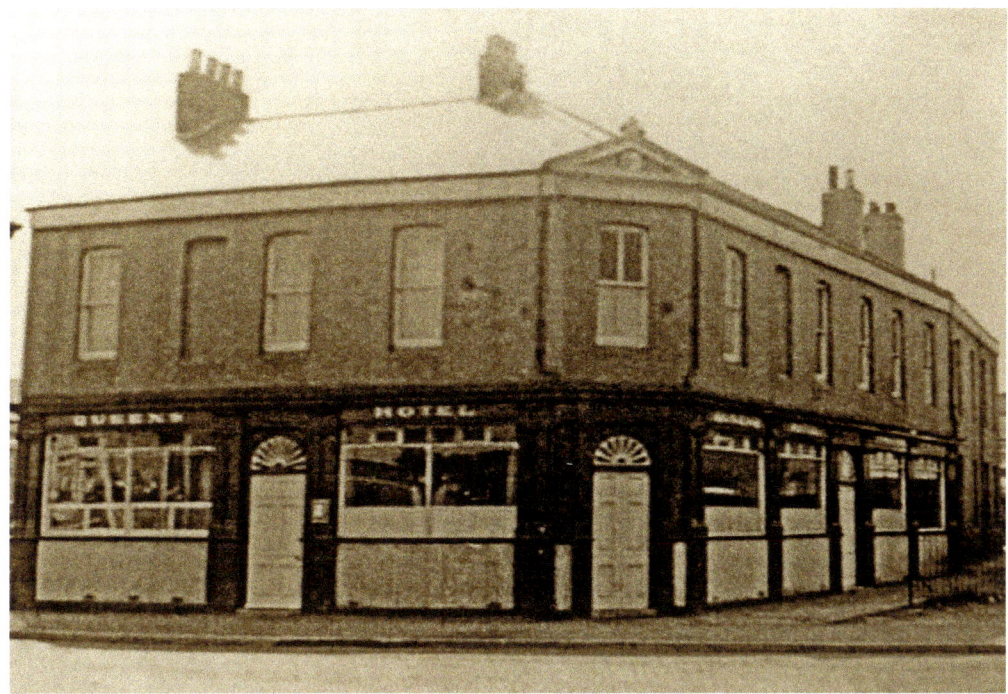

Queen's Hotel, Western Road, Jarrow.

Wallsend and Willington Quay Slipway Co.'s shipyards. The directors of the company, on their part, agreed, allowing fifteen or more extra men to be employed. In April 1895 Alexander Smithfield, owner of the Queen's Hotel, had his plans for a new club room passed. Monday 8 July 1903 John Metcalf, the licensee, opened a billiard room to the public. Mr J. Sweeney, South Shields, and Mr J. Roy, Hebburn, played a match of 500 up. Sometime in the late 1900s the Queen's Hotel was renamed the Jarrow Lad. With the closure of the shipyards and other local industry the Queen's Hotel sadly closed and was demolished.

The North Eastern Hotel

The North Eastern Hotel, on the corner of Clayton Street and Wear Street opposite the railway station, was first advertised on 8 April 1876 in the *Jarrow Express* by John Forster informing the public that the North Eastern Hotel would be opened on 11 April for the purpose of 'Accommodating Commercial Travellers and other Business Gentlemen, and thereby suppliers a want long felt in the district'. He described the bedroom accommodation as simple and the commercial and dining rooms sufficient to accommodate large parties. A carefully selected stock of British and foreign wines, spirits, ales and porter were available, and no effort was spared in making it a first-class family and commercial hotel. In 1888, after extensive alterations and improvements, it was described as having a 'handsome dining hall, coffee, billiard and smoke rooms'. The hotel was also described and considered as one of the best in the north of England.

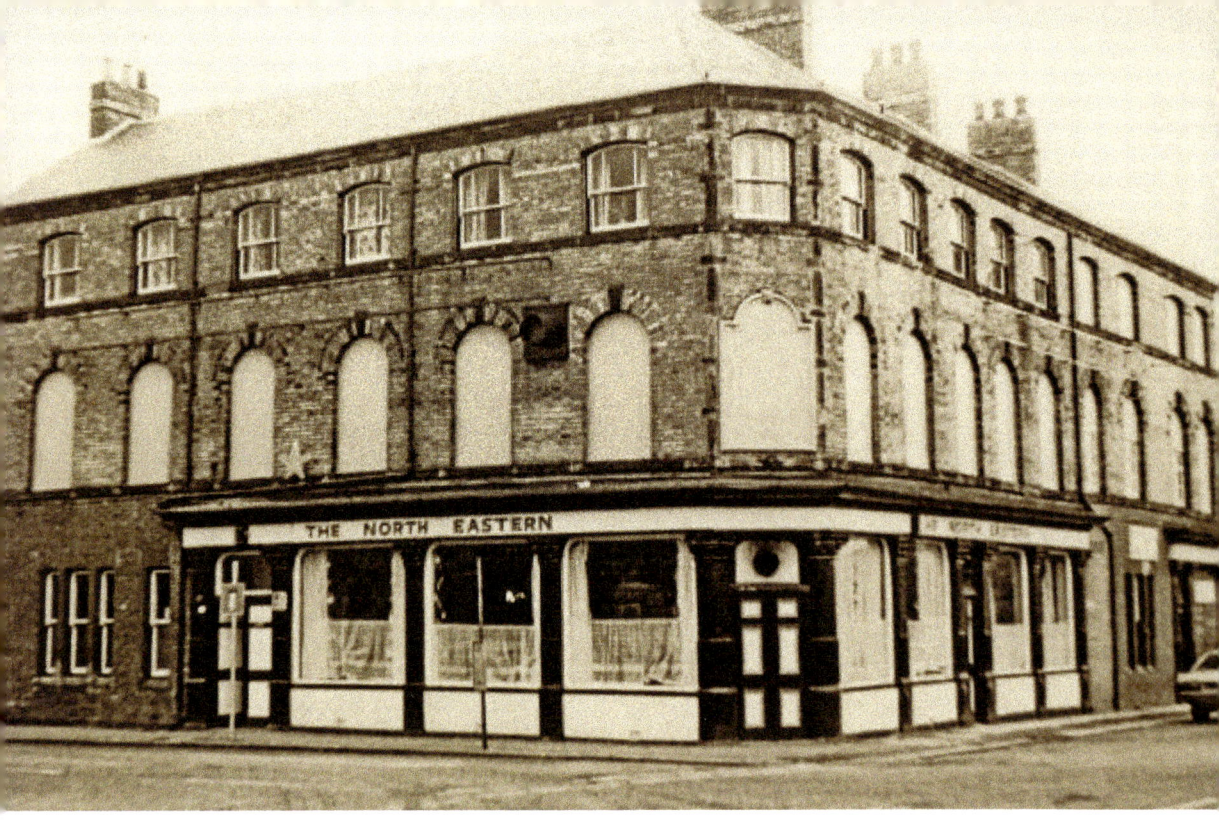

North Eastern Hotel, Clayton Street and Wear Street, Jarrow.

The main entrance fronted onto Clayton Street. By 1897 Simpson and McPherson Ltd had become the proprietors of the North Eastern Hotel. On Friday 4 August 1899 Archibald Lidgate, who had been manager for two and a half years, was presented with a silver-mounted walking stick and a gold ring as a mark of the esteem in which he had been held. He had recently transferred to the Ben Lomond. Just after the war in 1949 Robert Deuchar carried out alterations on the buffett to meet the requirements of the growing clientele. Sadly the North Eastern was demolished, and the bus station now stands on part of the site.

The Ben Lomond Hotel

The Ben Lomond Hotel, Ellison Street, Jarrow, was first advertised by George Albion Barrasford in 1890. In 1881 George Albion Barrasford, a wine and spirit merchant living at 'Ben Lomond House', No. 65 Ellison Street, applied for a licence for these premises, which he now owned. For many years he had been unsuccessful in acquiring a licence for a new hotel he was proposing to build. Objections came from the temperance movement and the Methodist community in the town. In 1886 George Barrasford, now a counsellor, applied for a transfer of his licence from the Ship Inn, Tyne Street, to the Ben Lomond; after much discussion the licence was granted with conditions. In 1887 plans were drawn up for the new hotel by Mr James Walter Hanson, an architect from Jarrow. The main frontage to Grainger Road would be 61 feet and 56 feet along Ellison Street. The front elevation was to be faced with stone, with ornamental facings of pillars, four large windows – one in the centre, one over the vestibule – and three circular windows at the top of the building. A wholesale department to the left of the stone portion would be with brick front and two large windows for lighting. The basement was to contain an extensive cellarage. The entrance, a fine doorway, would lead into a vestibule 9 feet by 9 feet, then into the hall that would be 16 feet by 13 feet 6 inches. Off the hall there was to be a spacious bar and refreshment room; on the right of the vestibule a dining room 28 feet by 19 feet with a grill room of the same size; and to the left a commercial room 19 feet 6 inches by 15 feet, and a sitting room or office 15 feet by 11 feet. Lifts went to the first floor where there was a stockroom, a billiard room (30 feet by 19 feet) five bedrooms, lavatories and bathrooms, etc. The kitchen on the second floor was to be 28 feet by 19 feet with a scullery, larder, bedrooms, bathrooms, etc. It was indeed to be a first-class commercial hotel. In 1888 work was well underway in pulling down Ben Lomond House for the building of the Ben Lomond Hotel. Robert Deuchar had alterations carried out in the 1950s, but by the late 1960s the Ben Lomond looked unchanged on the outside. The years had taken its toll on the inside and it needed much doing to it. Scottish and Newcastle Breweries, the owners, leased the Ben Lomond to Derek Armstrong, a local entrepreneur, who took on the refurbishment and renamed it the Viking, possibly after the new precinct across the road. Unfortunately less than forty years later it once again needed some love and care as there was a threat the building would be razed to the ground. Wetherspoons Brewery took on the refurbishment and restored it to some of its former glory and original name. Today it is a Greene King Brewery house.

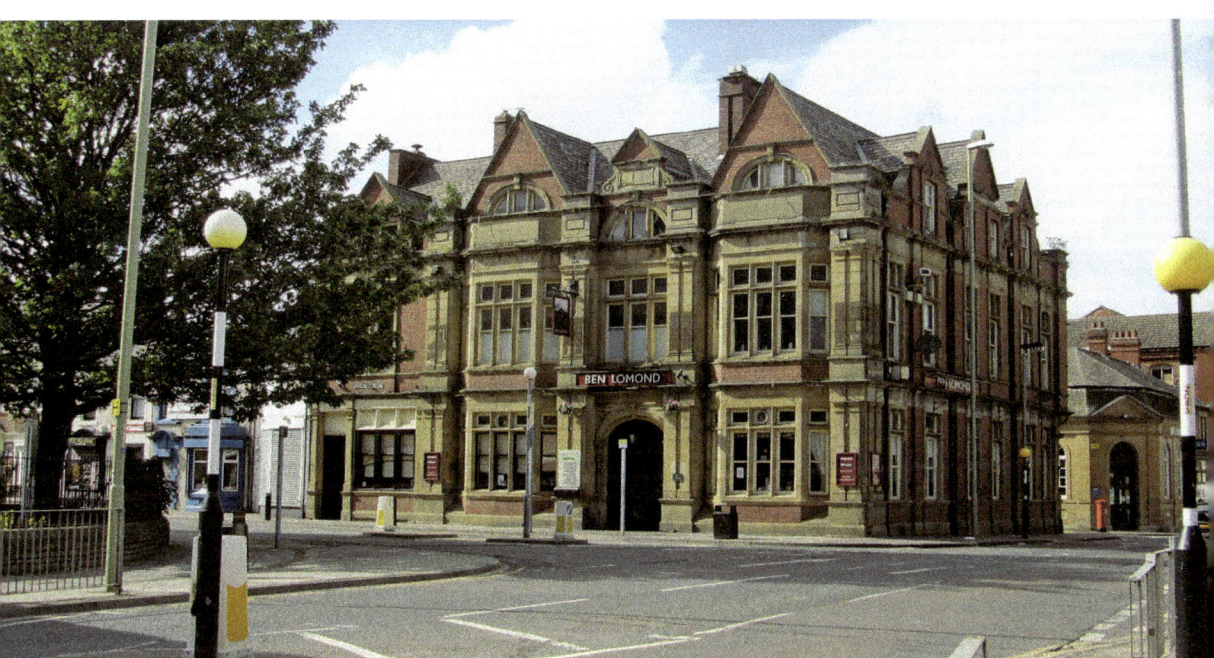

Ben Lomond Hotel, Ellison Street, Jarrow.

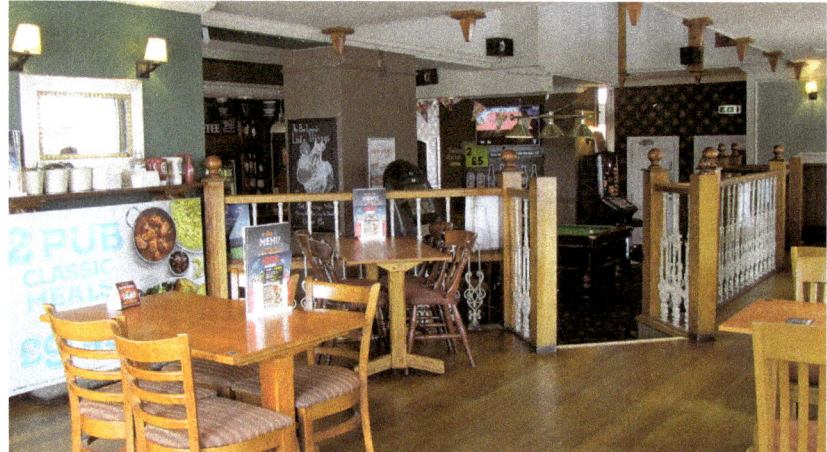

The dais to the right of the front entrance.

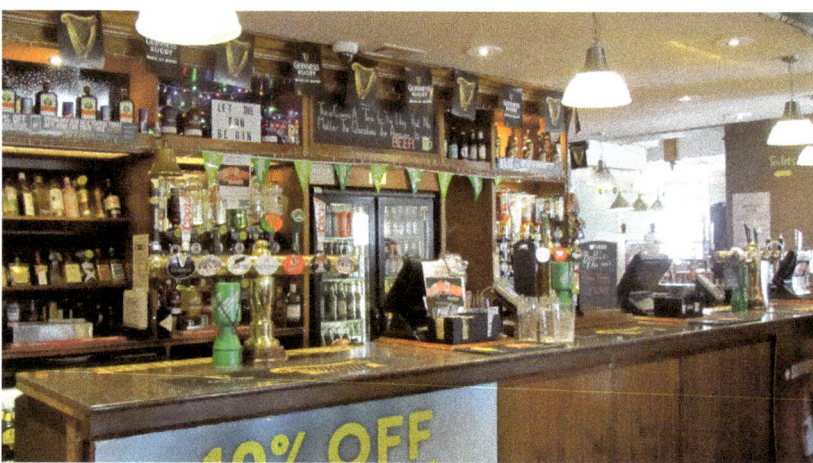

The bar to the left of the entrance.

The Station Hotel

The Station Hotel, Ellison Street, Jarrow, was first advertised by James Talbot in 1871. In February 1872 an inquest was held there by J. M. Favel on Edward Schaughlesy, who had been killed at Hebburn Colliery on Tuesday 20 February from injuries received on the Monday when being run over by a waggon. Many such inquests were recorded over the years – it was quite common for an inquest to be held in a public house local to the deceased because there were no coroner's courts. On Saturday 30 April 1892 Luke Seymour, the forty-five-year-old landlord, died after a brief illness, leaving a wife and four children. Jarrow Cricket and Athletics Club held their annual general meeting in the hotel on Tuesday 21 April 1891 with a good attendance present. Owing to the failure of the sports held at the end of the season, they showed a deficit but the cricket secretary's report detailed a fairly successful event. The principal batting honours went to Thomas Mearns of the first team with an average of nineteen runs per match. In November 1908 Mr Moffett, landlord, had a curiosity he kept in a glass bowl in the

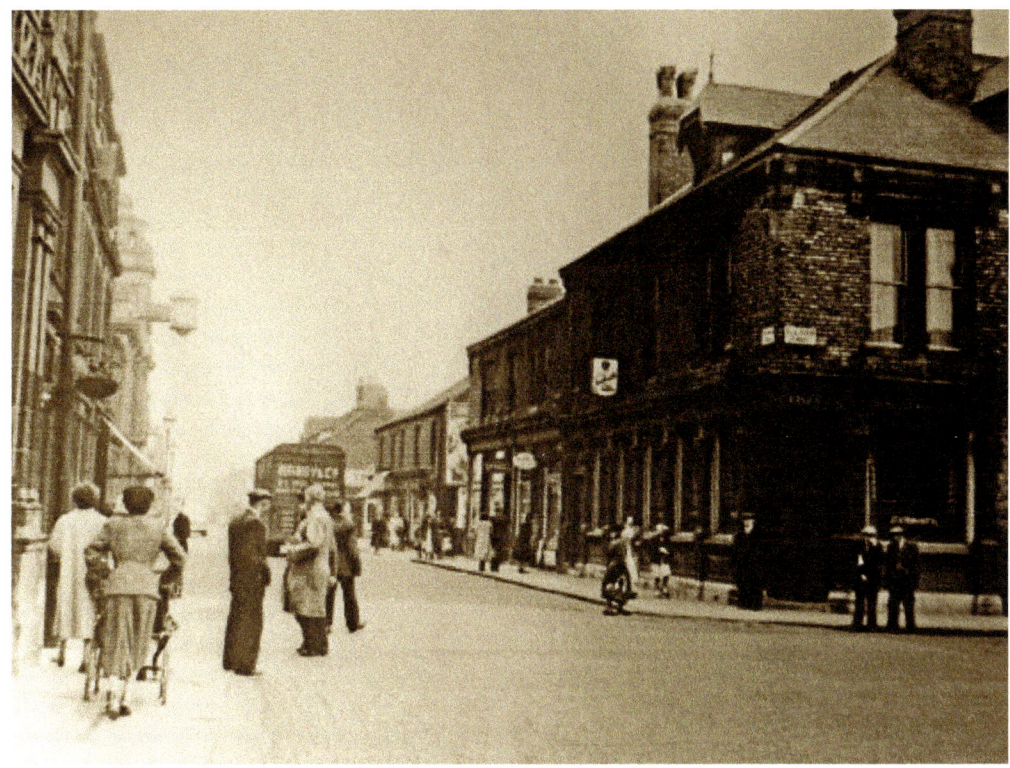

Station Hotel, Ellison Street, Jarrow.

shape of a hen's egg. At first sight it looked like a bowl and stem of a clay pipe, but turning it out it was nothing more than an empty shell with what might have been described as a small pipe or outlet curled up at one end. Apparently it was the last egg laid by a hen that had previously laid an egg that was 2½ ounces. The Station Hotel was demolished to make way for the new Viking shopping centre.

The Ellison Arms Hotel

The Ellison Arms Hotel, No. 1 Western Road, Jarrow, was first advertised by Zephaniah Harrison in 1884 as the Ellison Arms Inn. In 1890 James Dudgeon became the licensee but did not advertise the Ellison Arms after this. In March 1894 a large egg was on view in the bar, which had been laid by a hen bred by Robert Ironsides, James Street, the length of which was 3⅕ inches, the diameter 2 1/32 inches and the weight 4 ⅜ ounces. In January 1902 members of the National Union of Gas Workers and General Labourers employed at the Hedworth Barium Works held a smoking concert for the purpose of making a presentation to Mr H. Lynas, district secretary. In October 1904 James Dudgeon stood for the Central Ward in the Jarrow Municipal Elections at the request of a large number of voters. In his campaign poster he stated that he was in favour of erecting public baths and believed in efficiency and economy with local funds.

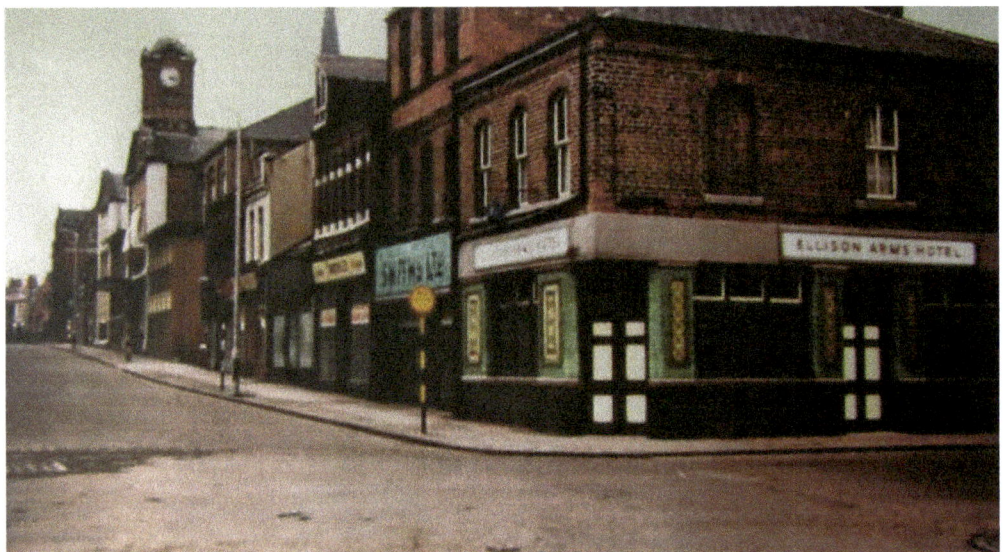

The Ellison Arms Hotel, No. 1 Western Road, Jarrow.

The Royal Oak

The Royal Oak, which is still standing on the corner of Grange Road and Staple Road, is better known as Kitty Monro's or the 'Long bar'. In 1875 J. and J. Meikle first advertised the Royal Oak Hotel. At the time Jarrow was starting to grow with quite a few Irish immigrants settling into the area seeking work in the nearby shipyards. Thomas Barrasford

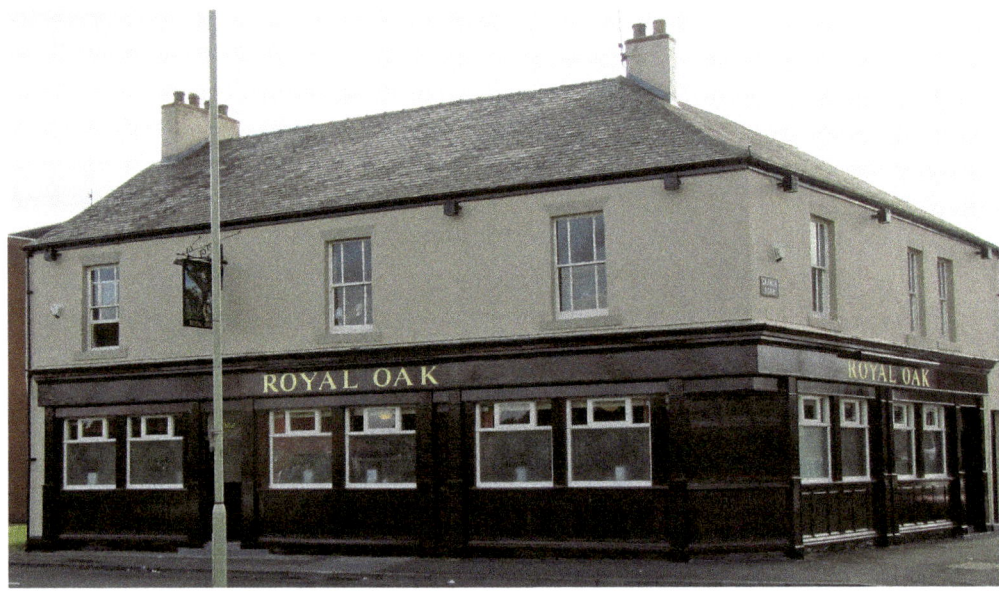

The Royal Oak, Grange Road and Staple Road, Jarrow.

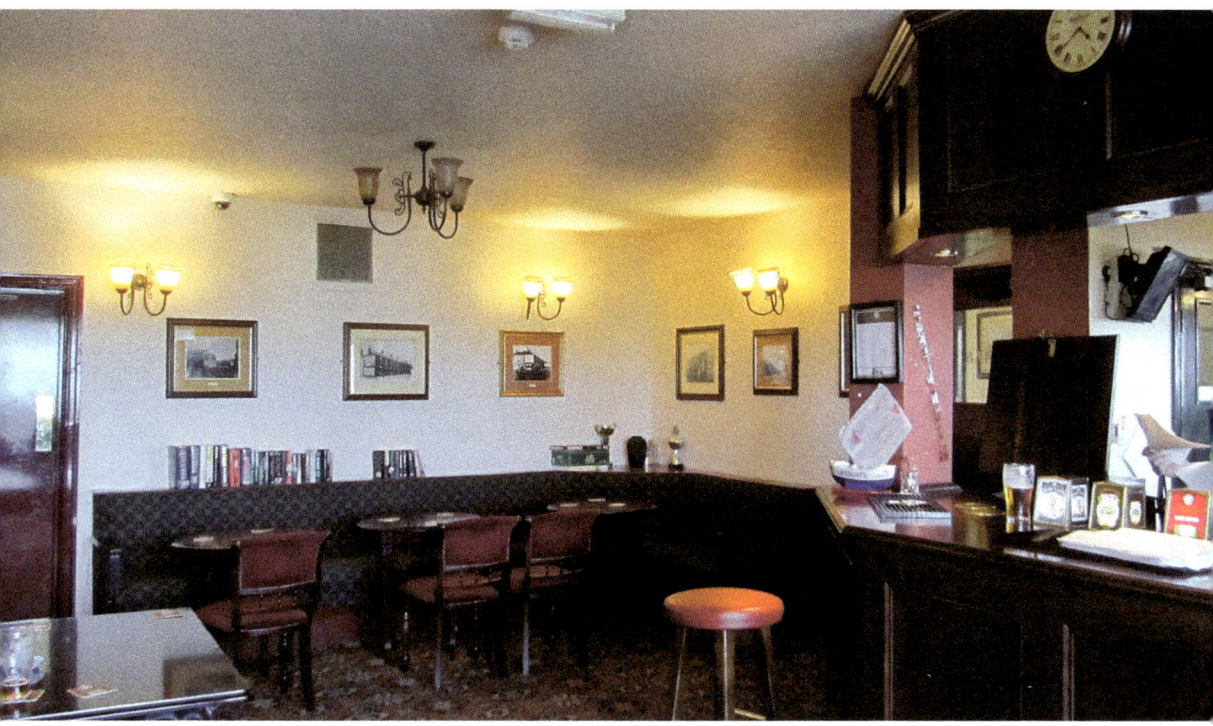

The lounge with old photographs on the walls.

took over the Royal Oak in 1893. Thomas had taken over the wooden circus, Ormond Street, turning it into the Palace of Varieties, advertising in *The Era*, a London paper, for musicians who must 'be steady and accustomed to the variety business'. This was to fill vacancies in the theatre. In 1897 Walter Arrol became the new licensee.

Today the Royal Oak is a pleasant friendly pub. The lounge is a small cosy room with old photographs on the walls, and the oak-panelled bar serves both it and the long room.

The Bell Rock Hotel

The Bell Rock Hotel, Nixon Street, Jarrow, showing the winners of the Ingham Infirmary Challenge Cup of 1923–24, was first advertised by John Jackson in 1873 as the Bell Rock House. In June 1893 licensee Robert Bowey was in the *Newcastle Courant* as the gentleman taking subscription on behalf of the Royal Humane Society, who proposed giving a medal to Thomas Urwin, who lived at No. 52 Walter Street and over the previous twenty years had shown great heroism and courage by saving many people from drowning. On Thursday 10 October 1901, Robert Bowey hosted a smoking concert (which were popular live performances, usually music, for men-only audiences) in connection with the Bell Rock Break Club, which was attended by forty people. A cold collation was served followed by a harmonious evening. On August bank holiday Monday 1903 the Bell Rock Break Club had their twelfth annual trip visiting the 'ancient cathedral city of Durham'. Twenty-four members of the club left

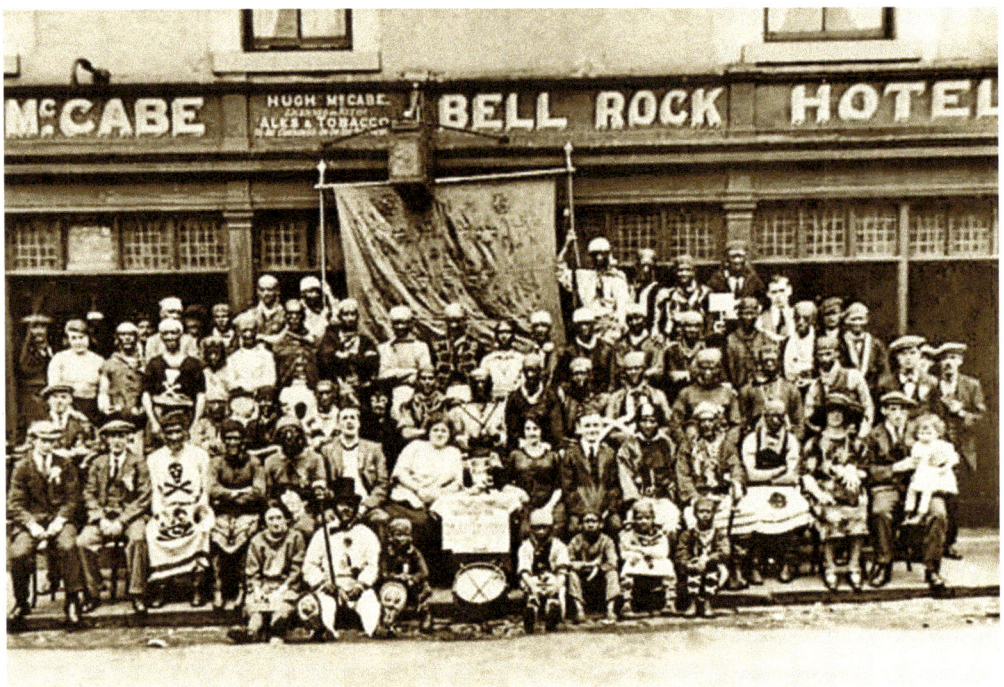

Bell Rock Hotel, Nixon Street, Jarrow. Hugh McCabe was landlord at the time.

the hotel and drove to the Lord Nelson, Monkton, picking up the landlord, Mr Dunn, their president. Friday 27 December 1908 Robert Bowey hosted a social gathering for the members of the Black and White Club. An excellent roast turkey supper was provided by the host, assisted by John Mellor, who supplied the exceptionally fine bird. In April 1939 Newcastle Breweries Ltd surrendered its licence.

McConnell's Gin and Alehouse

McConnell's Gin and Alehouse, Walter Street, Jarrow, was originally called the Albion Inn, whose first landlord was Edward Winspear, who in 1859 gave the address as Jarrow Dock. It was once popularly known as Frankie Dennim's, before being changed to the Crusaders. Later it became the Jarrow Crusaders, renamed as a tribute to the 1936 crusade when Jarrow men marched to London. It was later taken over by Mr McConnell and renamed the Gin and Alehouse. Out the back of the pub there is a small 'detention' room adorned with old photographs of St Bede's School, Jarrow, which Mr McConnell once attended – there is even a door marked 'Head Master' with a cane upon the desk. Little has changed inside the pub over the years. Once a Barras & Co. public house selling both India pale and mild ales, it went on to sell Irish stout. Now it is selling Jarrow Brewery hand-crafted ales.

McConnell's still has that 'Olde Worlde' look with its wood-panelled walls adorned with historic photographs of Jarrow.

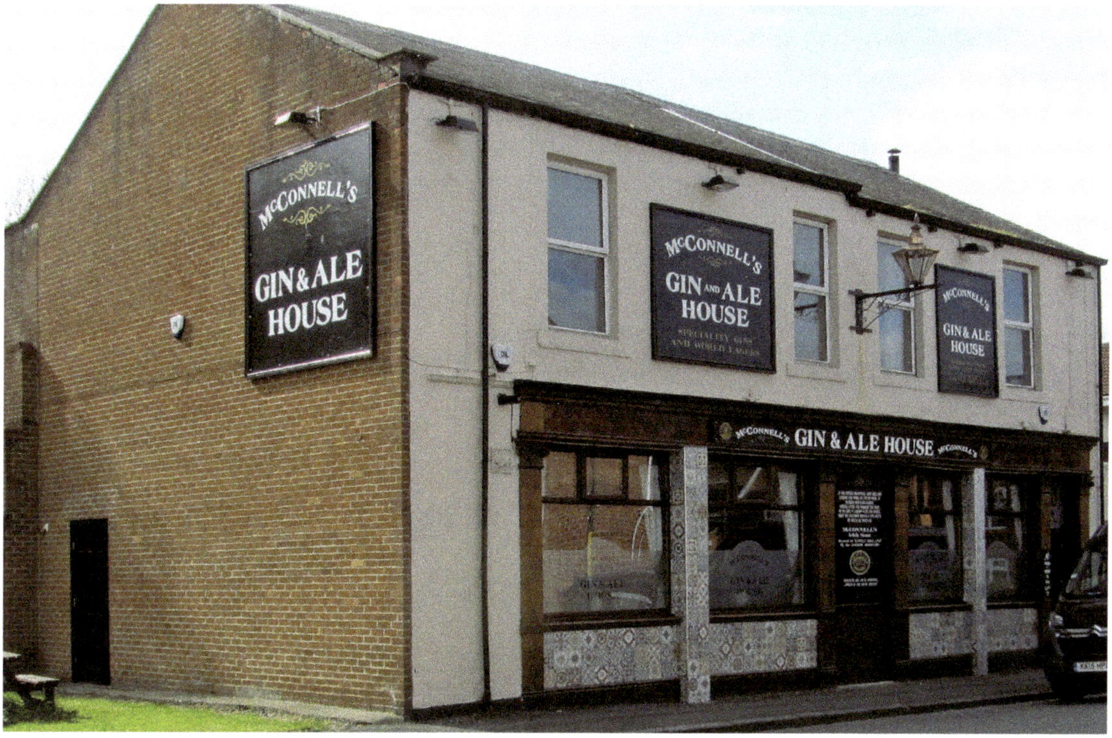

Above: The Gin and Ale House (originally the Albion Hotel), Walter Street, Jarrow.

Below: The oak-panelled walls inside McConnell's with the original fireplace.

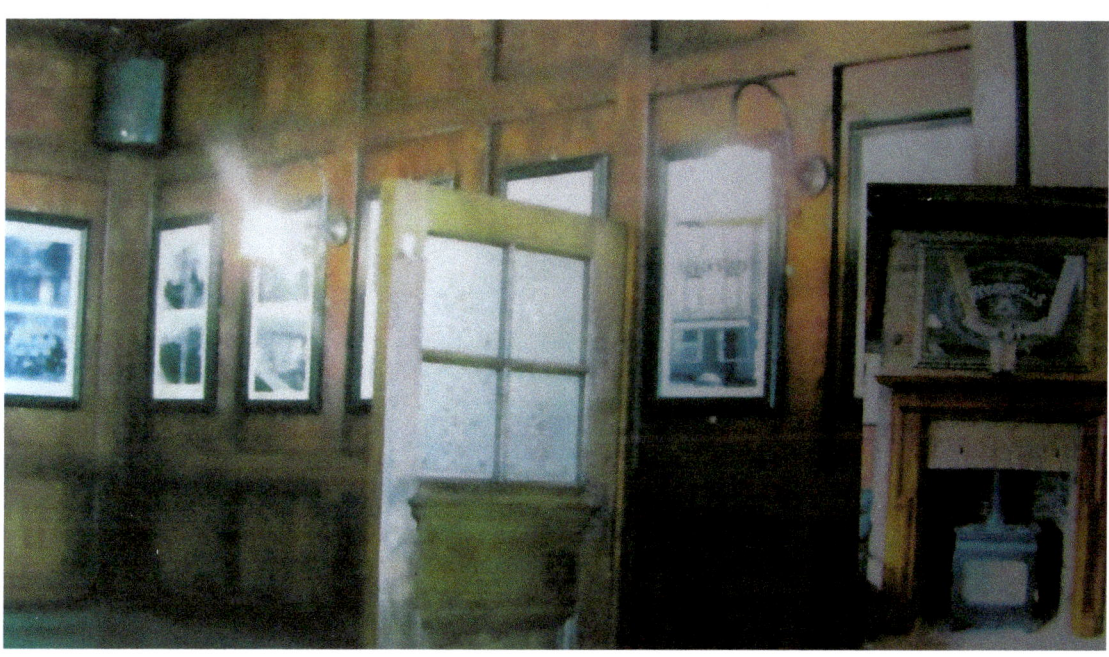

The Alnwick Castle Hotel

The Alnwick Castle Hotel on the corner of Walter Street and Grange Road, Jarrow, was first advertised by Thomas Thompson in 1871 but could be much older with friendly societies having held their annual dinners there. On 5 March 1870 the Court Venerable Bede of the Order of the Foresters held their annual supper there with between forty and fifty members sitting down for an excellent supper. In March 1874 R. Wylan & Co. were advertising fine 'Scotch and Irish Whiskey from 2 shillings, the very best 3 shillings and 4 pence a bottle, Martel's and Hennessey's Celebrated Brandies, from 4 shillings and 6 pence to 5 shillings; Fine old Rum and the finest Burton and Scotch Ales'. On 14 July 1875 Miss Wylam, owner of the Alnwick Castle, had plans approved for alterations to the hotel. In May 1892 plans submitted by Benjamin F. Simpson for alterations to be carried out on the hotel were passed when John Duncan was the manager.

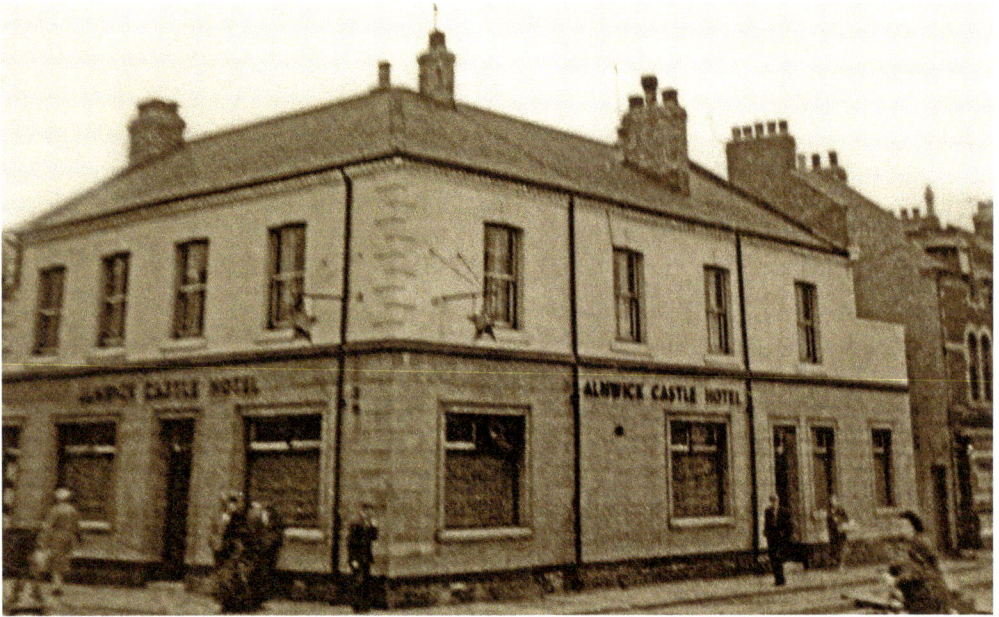

The Alnwick Castle, Walter Street and Grange Road, Jarrow.

The Cottage

The Cottage public house on the corner of Walter Street and North Street was originally the Forge & Hammer and was purpose built by Sarah Derry, who originated from Wolverhampton. Sarah Derry, with her six children, moved north after her husband left for America and was not heard of again. Selling her shares in a brewery, an iron and steel company and a brickworks, she capitalised on workers flooding into Jarrow. Not only did her wealth enable her to build the Forge & Hammer public house but

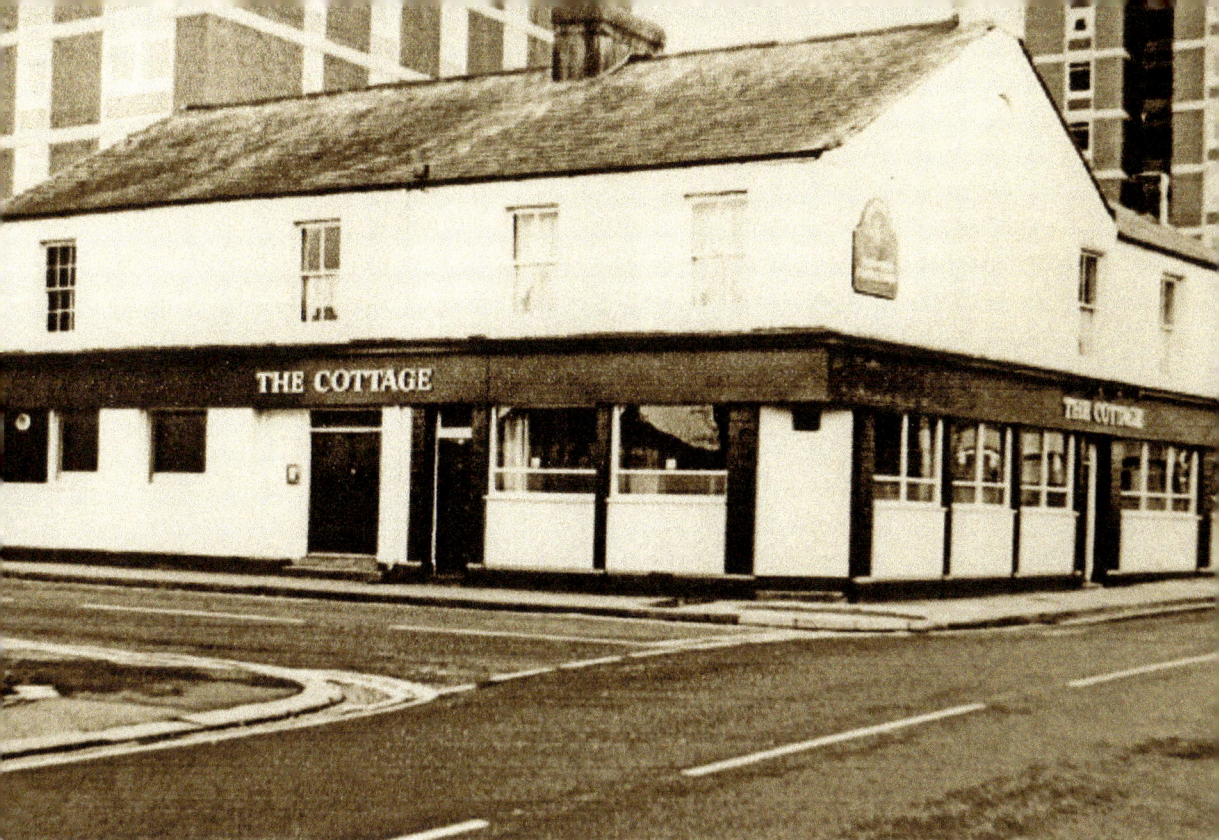

The Cottage (originally the Forge & Hammer), Walter Street and North Street, Jarrow.

also Caroline and Edith streets in the town. On Wednesday 7 July 1886 friends of the little sisters Ada and Annie Wright, Serio-comic vocalists, duettists and dancers, gathered there to present the charming sisters with a splendid silver necklet and locket each, which were engraved in recognition of their ability. On 13 April 1892 John Rutherford, the new owner, had plans passed for alterations to be carried out and lavatories put in. Although surrounded by the apartment blocks built in 1963, trade from them was not sustained and at the beginning of 2000 it was pulled down to make way for car parking for residents.

The Royal Hotel

The Royal Hotel in the Market Place was first advertised by Thomas Holmes in 1871, although he built it in 1865. As well as being the licensee of the Royal Hotel, Thomas Holmes was also proprietor of the music hall in the Market Square, and he also owned the twelve shops and dwelling houses. Thomas stayed at the hotel until he retired in 1889. In 1900 North Eastern Breweries Co. Ltd had become the owners and Richard Murry was the licensee. In October 1925 William Carr, the bar manager, of No. 101 Commercial Road, fell down the steps into the cellar, injuring his leg. Unfortunately cellulitis set in and William Carr died on 16 October at the Royal Victoria Infirmary. The Royal Hotel and the music hall were demolished to make way for new housing.

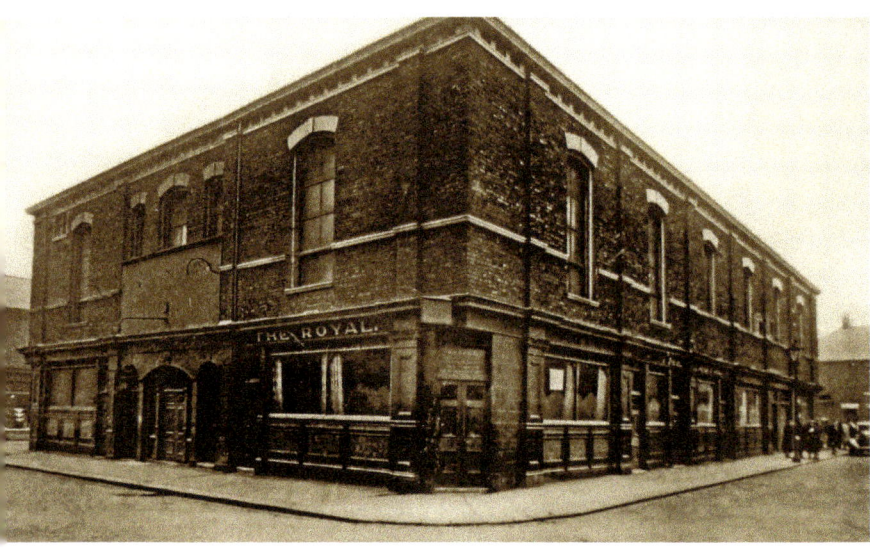

The Royal Hotel, Market Place, Jarrow.

The Borough Arms

The Borough Arms, North Street, Jarrow, which was originally called the Turf Hotel, was first advertised in 1871 by Andrew Liddle. In 1879 Joseph Wilson had become the licensee. In June 1883 George Leighton, the owner, had plans passed to have the Turf Hotel altered; John Rutherford was licensee at the time, staying until 1900.

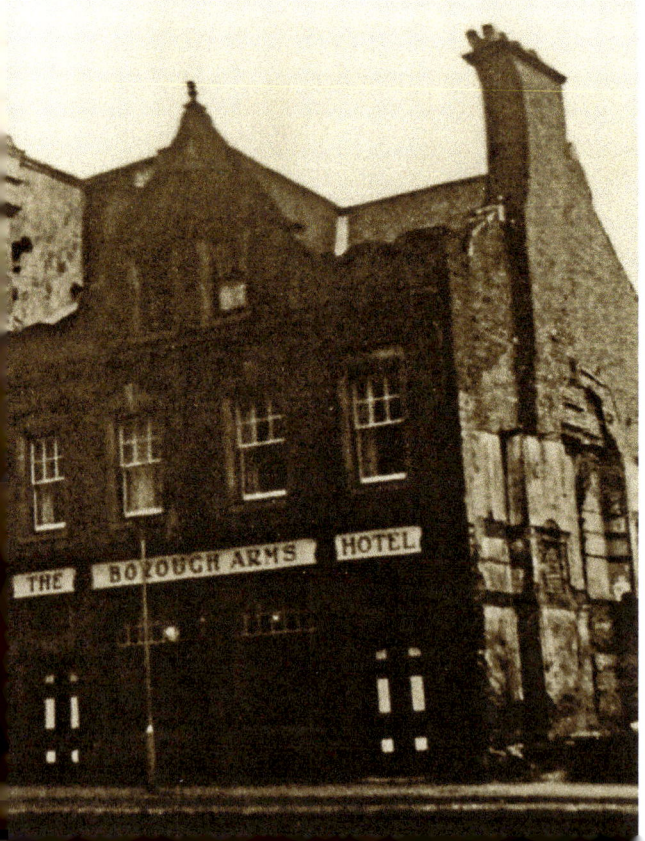

The Borough Arms (formerly the Turf Hotel), North Street, Jarrow.

John Rutherford stood in the Jarrow Council Elections for the Grange and West wards in March of 1895, giving the Turf Hotel as well as No. 3 Claremont Terrace, South Shields, as his contact addresses. By 1904 the Turf Hotel had been taken over by Newcastle Breweries Ltd, who changed its name to the Borough Arms, no landlord having been listed since. On entering from the door on the left there was a small bar to the right and straight ahead was a back room with the toilets still outside.

The County Hotel

The County Hotel, No. 78 Ormonde Street, Jarrow. When Edward Forster & Son first advertised the hotel in 1865, it was the Railway Hotel, but it is older than that. In August 1860 when the erection of the gasworks were proposed, particulars were to be applied for from Mr J. Forster at the Railway Hotel. On 19 August 1861 Ralph Brown, an auctioneer, had been instructed by Anthony Watson, Jarrow Red House Farm, to sell by auction all away going crops of corn, wheat and oats. Edward Forster Snr died in 1872, and his son Edward took over the hotel on his death. He was also a spirit merchant at the same address in 1873. In 1881 Edward Forster changed the name to the County Hotel when auctioneer Mr Thomas Medd was offering to the public five lots of property that had come up for sale in the town.

An 1897 advert for the County Hotel had a very good ditty.

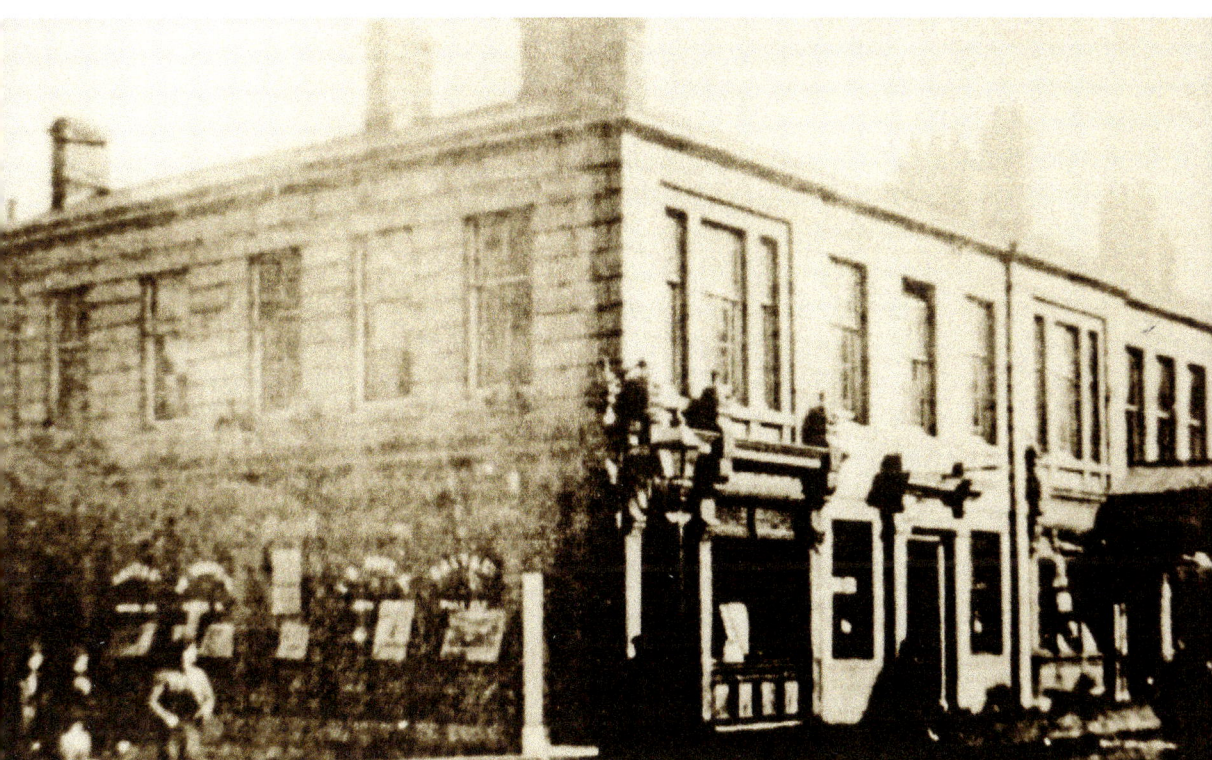

The County Hotel (formerly the Railway Hotel), No. 78 Ormonde Street, Jarrow.

THE PLACE TO DINE

Have you heard tell:	Viands and cooking
The best place to dine	Fit for a Queen;
Is the COUNTY HOTEL	Waiters all looking
JARROW ON TYNE	Tidy and clean,
Why it's almost	After you dine,
A household name	Then a good rest
The name of the host	A glass of good wine
Is JOHN RUTHERFORD.	And cigar of the best
Joints, steaming hot,	Treated like this,
The beast that can be,	We never complain,
With a TABLE D' HOTE	But consider it bliss
From twelve until three.	To call back again.

The Royal Engineers Hotel

The Royal Engineers Hotel, No. 89 Ormonde Street, Jarrow, was first advertised by Benjamin Strothard in 1884. At the Brewster Sessions in September 1886 Henry Skipsey Beck, the 'beerhouse keeper', applied for a full licence for the hotel. Mr C. W. Newland, who was applying on behalf of Henry Beck, presented a petition from a number of

Royal Engineers Hotel, No. 89 Ormonde Street, Jarrow.

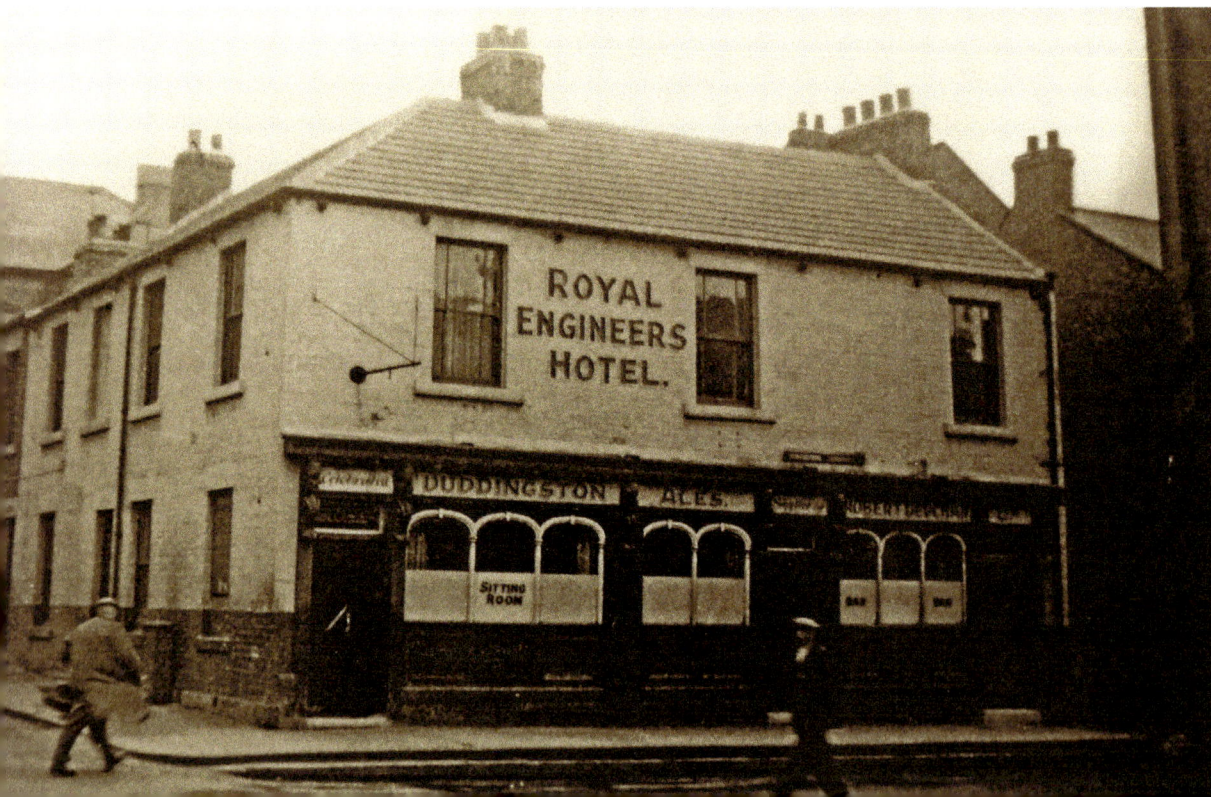

residents and several friendly societies that met at the house. Objecting to the licence, Mr W. H. Richardson said that there was a public house for every 150 men in the borough; Henry Beck thought if a person was qualified to hold a licence it should be a full licence. Jarrow Trade Council had fortnightly meetings in the hotel. This was made up of the Associated Shipwrights, Shop Assistants' Union, Enginemen and Crane Men, Boiler Makers' Society, National Labour Union, Amalgamated Society of Tailors, Amalgamated Society of Carpenters and Joiners, Drillers' Society, United Machine Workers and Amalgamated Coopers. Each trade reported on the previous fortnight's progress, and these meetings were held until the start of the First World War.

Lord Nelson Inn

This photograph of the Lord Nelson Inn, Walter Street, Jarrow, was taken when Sarah Ann Lunn was the licensee. The Lord Nelson Inn was advertised by Sidney Stone in 1883, although it is a much older establishment as it was originally owned by his father. It was not advertised again after this. On 1 June 1889 both a band contest and a bicycle handicap was held at Jarrow Bicycle Ground. Sidney Stone gave £65 prize money (Band Contest £46 8s, Two Miles Professional Bicycle Handicap £10, 110 Yards' Handicap £6 10s, and the 440 yards' Handicap £3). The closing date for entry was 25 May to Joseph Horn, manager of the Lord Nelson. On 30 April 1891 a dinner was given in honour of Joseph Horn, who had been the manager to Mr Stone for twelve years, which suggests the Lord Nelson was open before 1879. The dinner took place at Mrs M. Lockey's Crown & Anchor Inn. Mr Horn was presented with a handsome black-marble clock. Sydney Stone died on 21 March 1912, leaving an estate of £15,700 gross.

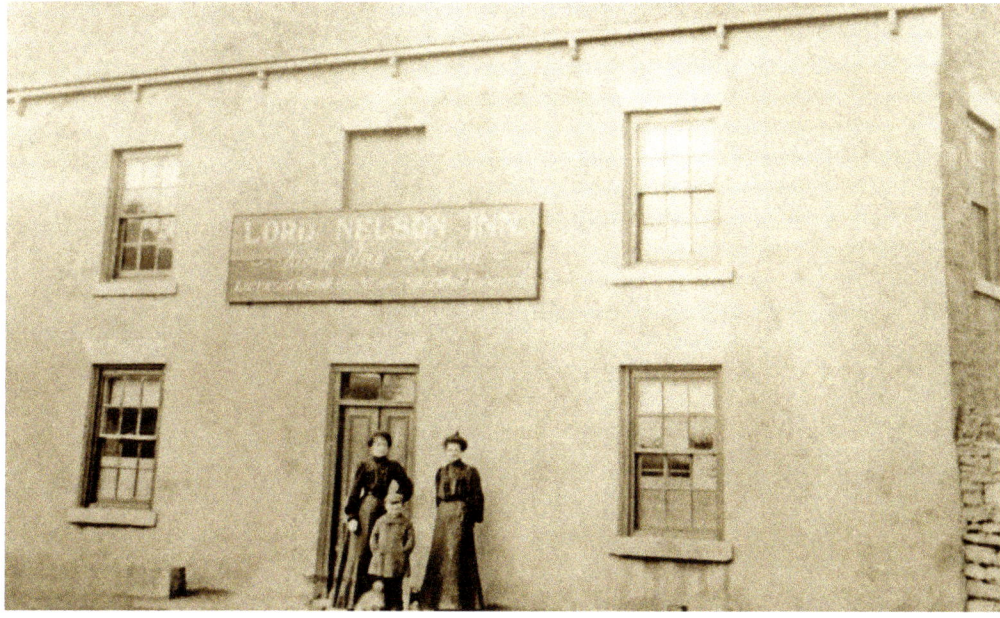

Lord Nelson Inn, Walter Street, Jarrow.

The Golden Lion

The Golden Lion at the Walter Street end of Ellison Place was first advertised by Edmund Calvert in 1871, giving the address as Nos 14–16 Walter Street. By 1875 it had been taken over by H. Marshall, and in 1879 John Marshall was the licensee. In 1885 David Thomas became the licensee and on 18 November 1891 a dinner was held in honour of Daniel Jackson, a foreman plater, for twenty years connected with the Jarrow shipyard on the occasion of his appointment as outdoor manager to the Blyth Shipping and Engineering Co. Ltd, with over sixty gentlemen sitting down for dinner. In October 1896 the first annual supper of the Brake Club was held in the Golden Lion, which it had for its headquarters, with more than fifty members attending.

The Golden Lion bar has a great choice of wines and spirits.

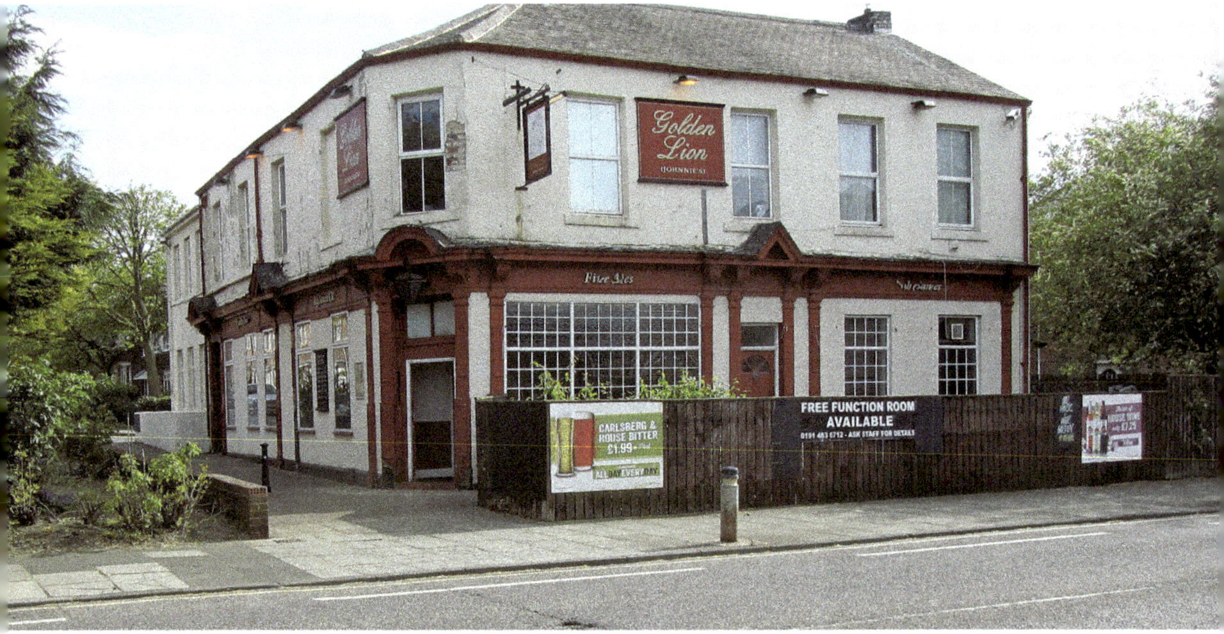

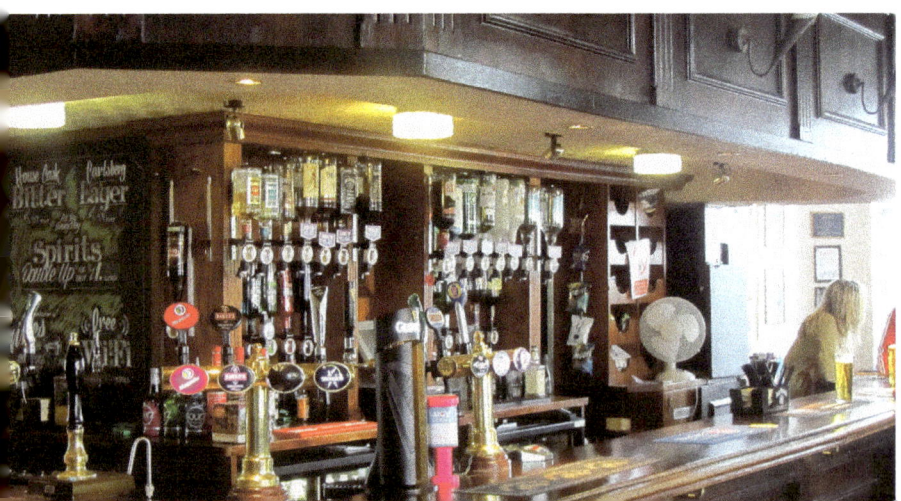

Above: The Golden Lion, Walter Street and Ellison Place, Jarrow.

Left: Bar of the Golden Lion, Walter Street and Ellison Place, Jarrow.

The Queens

The Queens on the corner of Union Street and Ormonde Street back lane was first advertised as the Queens Arms Hotel in 1879 by John Simpson. On Saturday 14 June 1884 the platers employed by Palmer Iron and Shipbuilding Co. Ltd went on strike owing to the reduction of wages being imposed without notice. A meeting was held in the club room of the hotel on Monday 16th. After arriving at a settlement work was resumed on the Tuesday. On 31 May 1908 the hotel

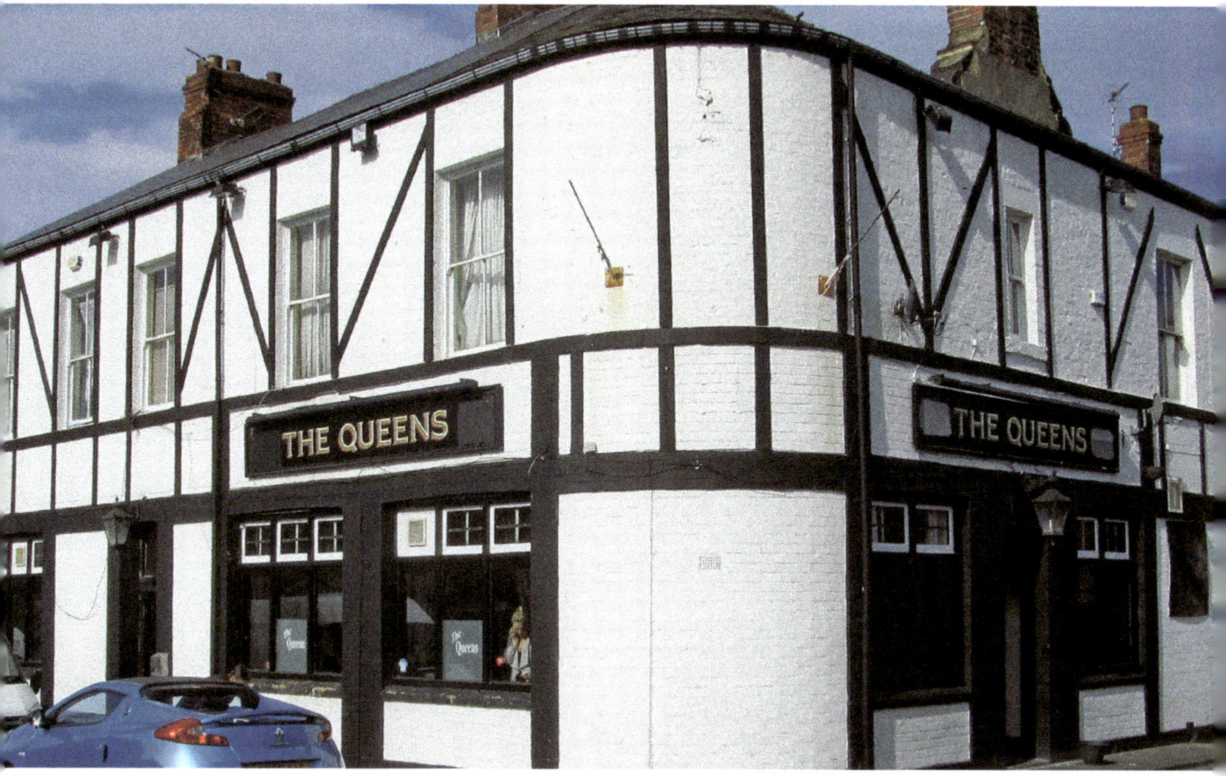

Above: Queen's Arms Hotel, Union Street, Jarrow.

Right: The Small Lounge, Queen's, Union Street, Jarrow.

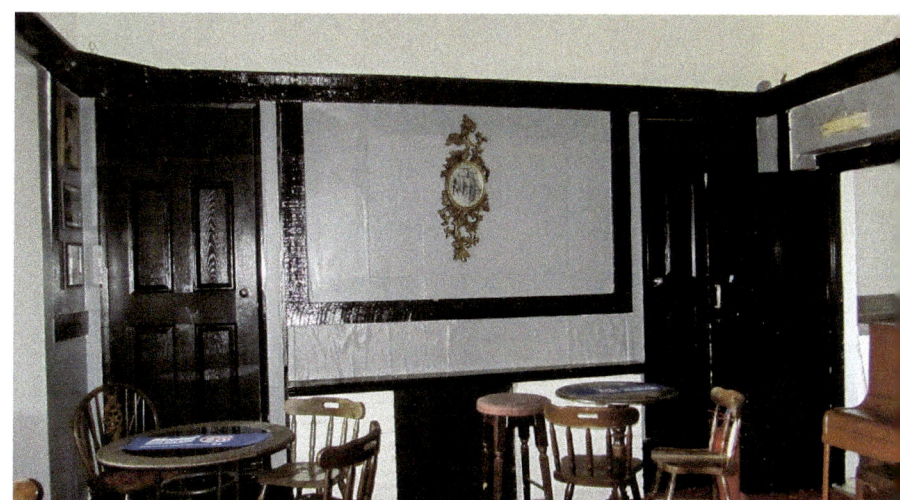

gave away more than 100 pints of lentil to deserving people without tickets and upwards of 260 pints to those with tickets. Made by Mr and Mrs P. McQuire, the licensees, everyone was grateful and also received an allowance of bread.

To the left of the front door is the newly redecorated small lounge.

The Golden Fleece

The Golden Fleece, Ferry Street, Jarrow, was first advertised in 1871 by Thomas Blackburn, and by 1875 Mrs Blackburn had taken over as the licensee. William Burlinson became the new owner in 1879 and in 1881 he was advertising his 'Hearse and Mourning Coach Establishment' from the hotel. William Burlinson was also a builder, undertaker and funeral furnisher. On Friday 23 December 1881 the annual meeting of the Amalgamated Society of Carpenters and Joiners was held. After supper a purse of £18 was presented to Mr John Irwin, who had been off work for some time through sickness, and £50 from the accident fund was given to Mr William Crow, who had lost his eye. The society formed in 1860 was flourishing and had paid out £339,856 in benefits. Robert Errington was the new licensee in 1884.

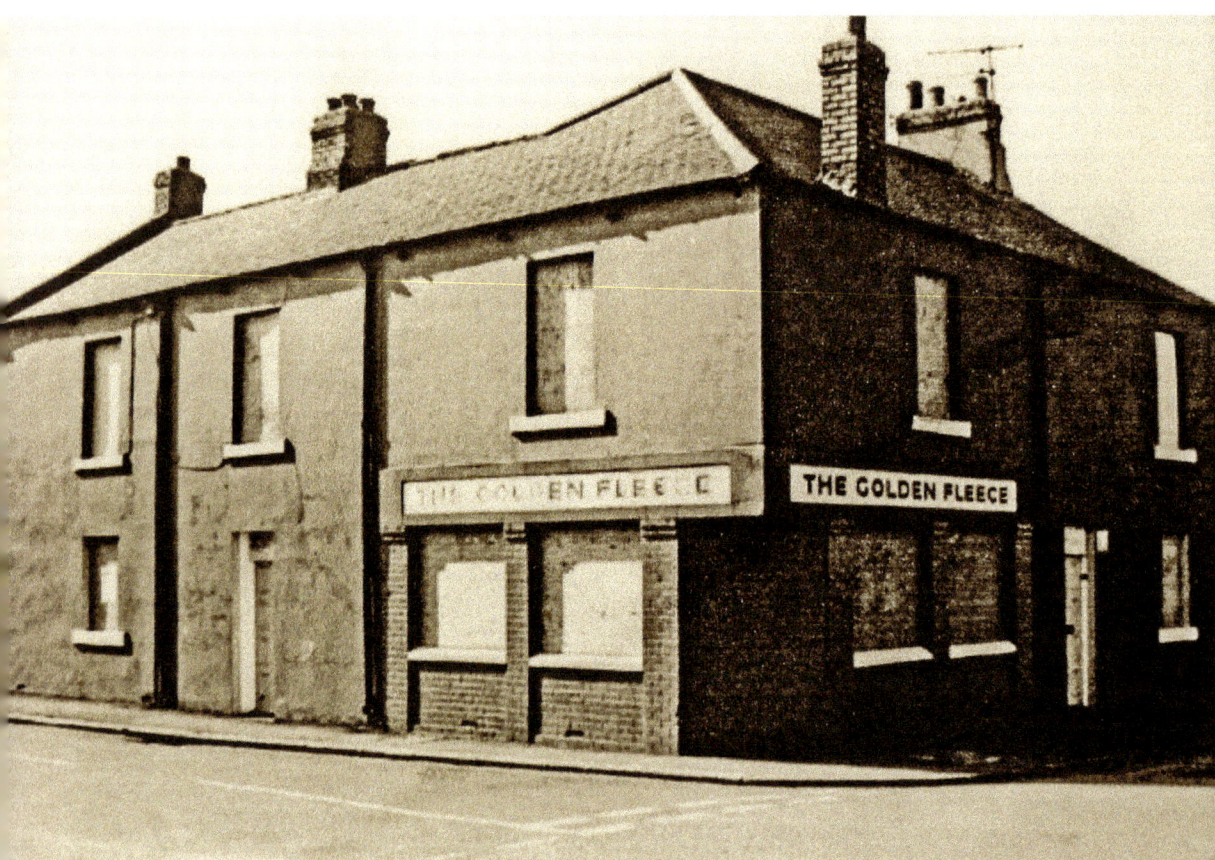

The Golden Fleece, Ferry Street, Jarrow.

The Gas Light

The Gas Light on the corner of Commercial Road and Tyne Street started as the Commercial Hotel, which was advertised for the first time in 1871 by Robert Nixon. Although the Staith House is marked on the 1856 map of Jarrow, the Commercial Hotel is not, giving doubt to its age and the authenticity of the legend that William Jobling's body was taken there after it was taken down from the gibbet at Jarrow Slake in 1832. In an advert in the *Jarrow Express* in July 1876, Henry Eggleton, formerly of the Golden Fleece Inn, Durham, 'wishes to inform his friends and the general public that he had taken over the hotel'. Eggleton's Commercial Hotel became the agents for the Mississippi and Dominican Steam Ship Co. in 1879, advertising passage from Liverpool to both North America and Canada, and also assisting passage for 'Artizans, Mechanics and Agricultural Labourers'. By 1960 the Commercial Hotel had become the Tyne Tunnel Tavern, standing on its own in front of the gasometer. In December 1987 Malcolm and Margaret Nicholson became the new tenants of the Gas Light, but sadly by 2007 it was derelict and awaiting demolition.

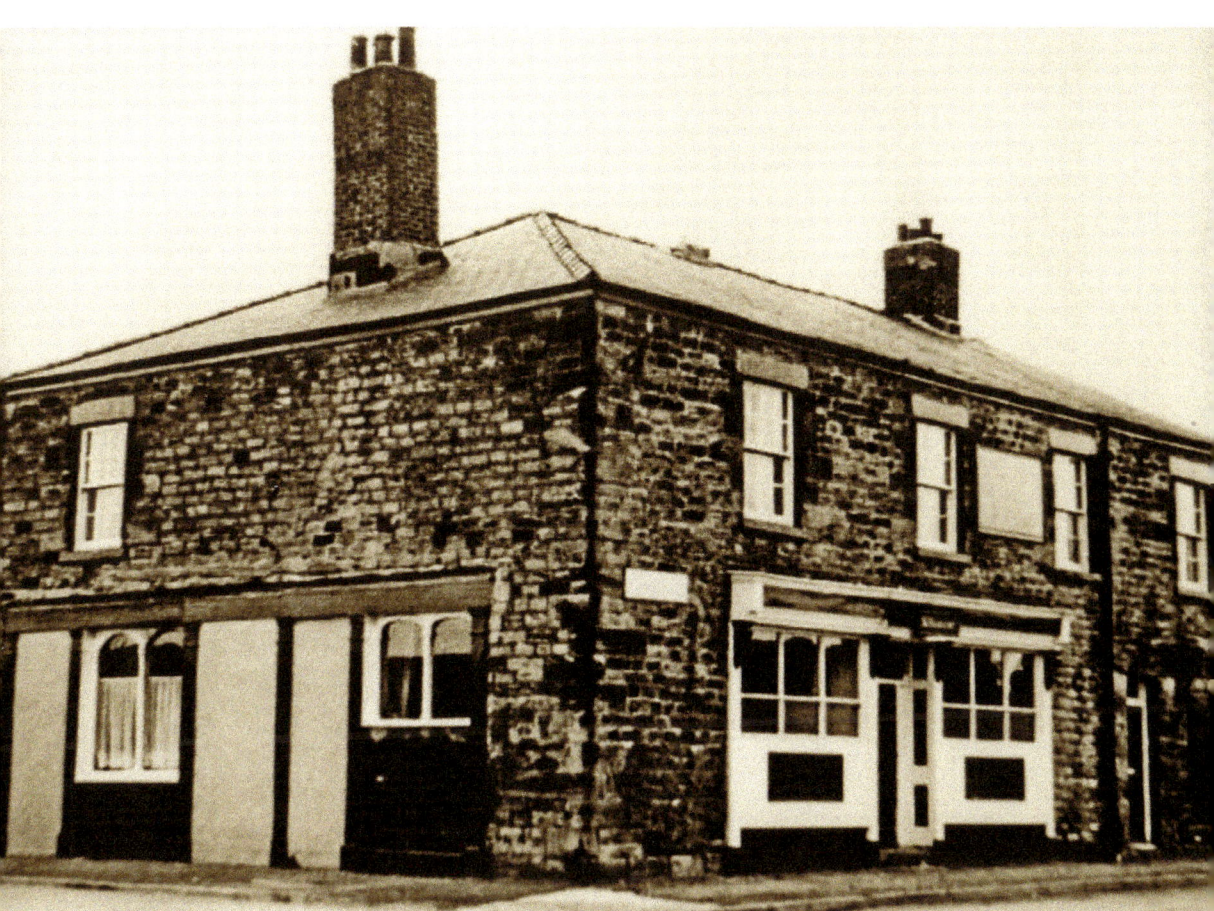

Gas Light (originally the Commercial Hotel), Commercial Road and Tyne Street, Jarrow.

The Staith House

The Staith House on the corner of Pearson Place and Tyne Street was one of Jarrow's oldest public houses. William Wilkinson first advertised the Staith House in 1828 as being at Jarrow Main Quay. It was one of only three advertised at the time, the other two being the Hilton Castle on Long Row (now the High Street) and the Ship at Jarrow Quay. In 1837 Christopher Grant was the licensee when he was selling a coal keel, nearly new with excellent storage. Christopher kept the inn until 1850 when William John Brown became the licensee. On 9 November 1883 Joseph Aynsley placed an advert 'informing his old friends, and inviting the acquaintance of new ones to the Staith House Inn'. In January 1954 tragedy almost struck the family of Mr and Mrs Cunningham, the landlords, when a disused gas tap had been accidentally knocked causing a leak. If the coughing of the three children, Peter (fourteen), Edward (fourteen) and Michael (thirteen) had not been heard by their parents, a great tragedy would have occurred.

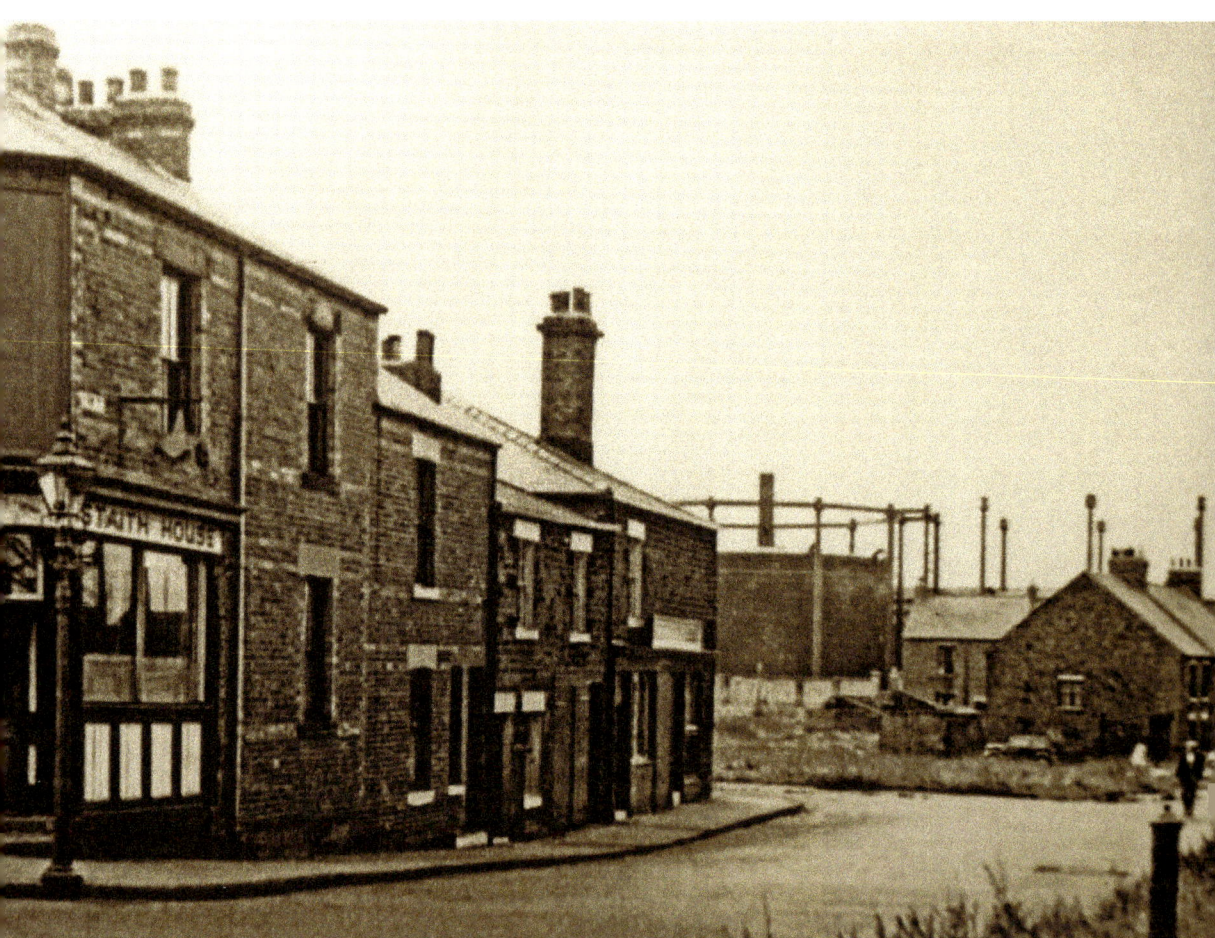

Staith House, Pearson Street and Tyne Street, Jarrow.

Prince of Wales Hotel

This sad photograph shows the Prince of Wales Hotel, on the corner of Commercial Road and Tyne Street, Jarrow, not long before it was demolished. First advertised in 1865 by Joseph Wilson, it was one of only ten public houses advertised at the time. In May 1866 friends of Mr Marr, a builder, held a supper in his honour, presenting him with a timepiece and Mrs Marr with a ring. In 1873 William Burlinson became the licensee and owner. On a planning application for alterations to the hotel in March 1873 he stated he was the builder who would carry out the work. In 1875 William gave the address as Drury Lane. He did not stay long, moving to the Golden Fleece Inn, and the hotel was taken over by John Smith in 1879. On Thursday 6 April 1939 Jarrow magistrates confirmed an application made by Newcastle Breweries Ltd for the removal of the licence from the Prince of Wales, Commercial Road, to a new hotel to be built beside York Avenue.

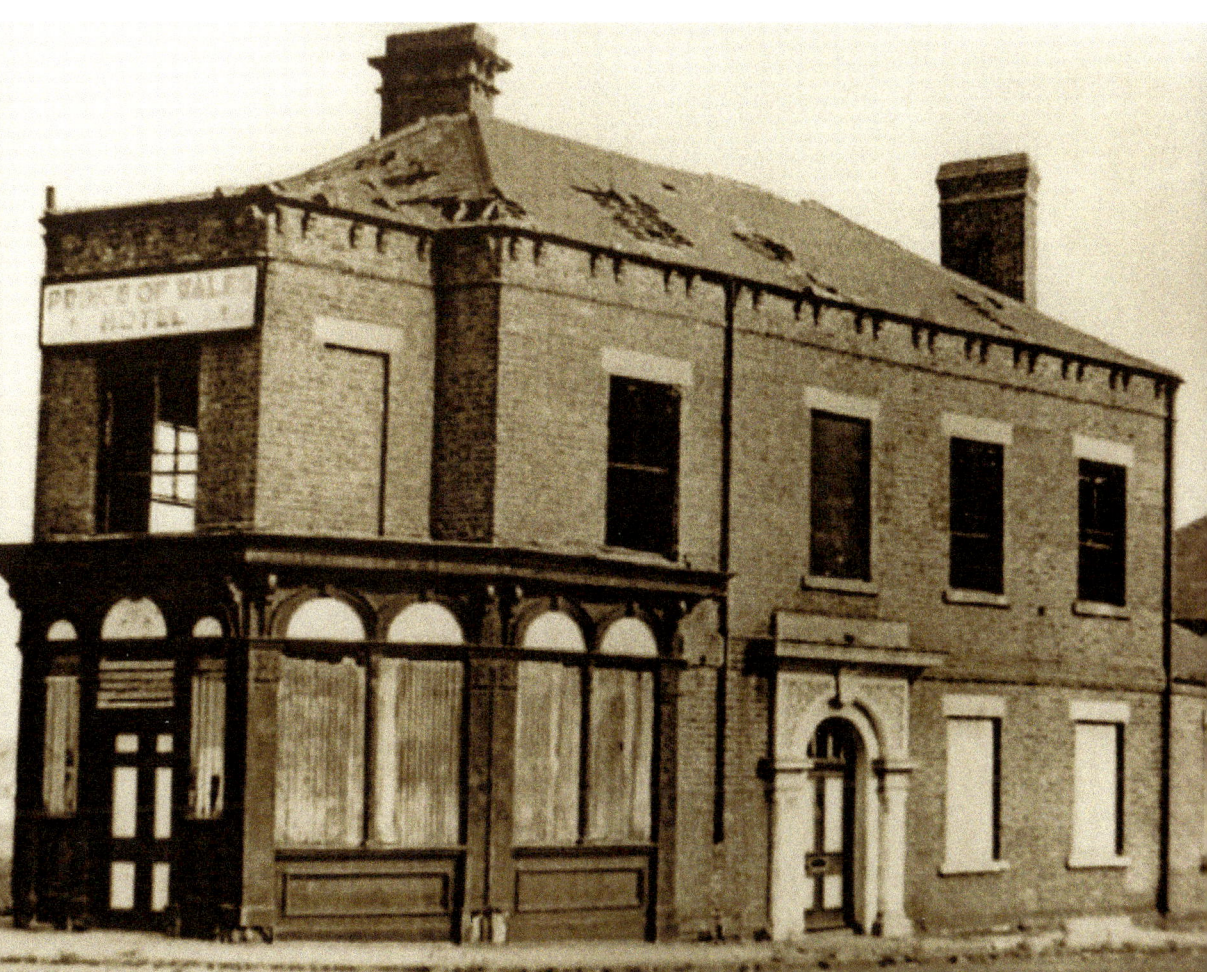

Prince of Wales Hotel, Commercial Road and Tyne Street, Jarrow.

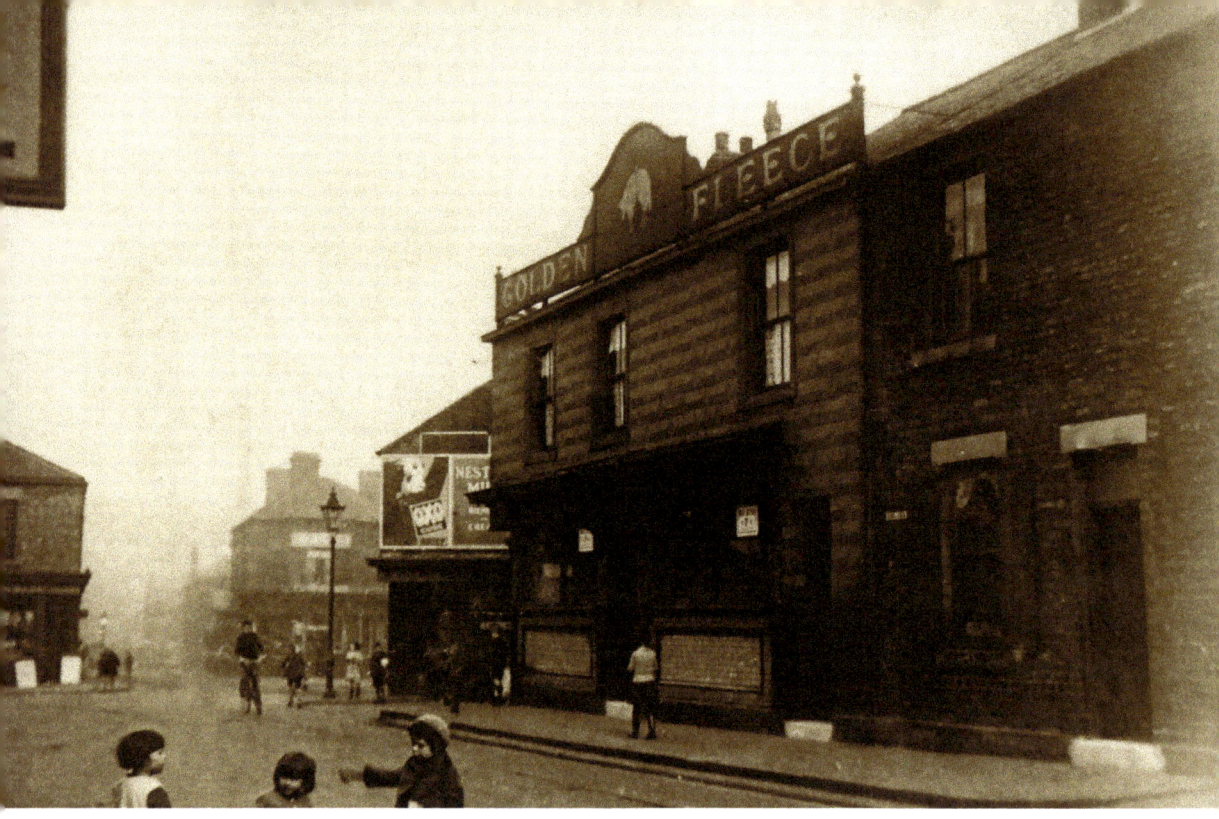

Golden Fleece, Commercial Road and Pit Heap, Jarrow.

Golden Fleece
This photograph shows the Golden Fleece, on the corner of Commercial Road and Pit Heap Jarrow, which was first advertised by Robert Ainsley in 1873. On 27 December 1873 a pigeon shoot was held on the ground next to the Golden Fleece between Henry Arthur of Jarrow and William Graham of Hebburn for £20. William Graham won by six birds to Henry Arthur's four. In July 1903 Roy Stone, the licensee, was promoting a walking craze contest to be held at Boldon flats on Wednesday 15th. The 25-mile contest was confined to the Northumberland and Durham licensed victualling trade. There was a 5-mile contest for the managers and barmaids and a veterans' race with a prize valued at 20 guineas. The Golden Fleece was demolished in the early 1960s to make way for new housing.

The Globe Hotel
The Globe Hotel on the corner of Buddle Street and Princess Street was first advertised by James Jeffrey in 1884, but could have been much older. It was taken over by William Stabler in 1885. William Staverley became the licensee on 26 January 1890, followed by his wife, Mary Ann, a year later. Ballentyne Hall took over the hotel in 1893 and in May 1914 he retired asking that the licence be transferred to Reginald E. McEvily. In March 1919 George Johnson, from Newcastle Breweries Ltd, applied to Jarrow for an order to obtain the living quarters of the Globe. George Wakenshaw, the previous manager, was still living there as he was unable to find a house after returning from

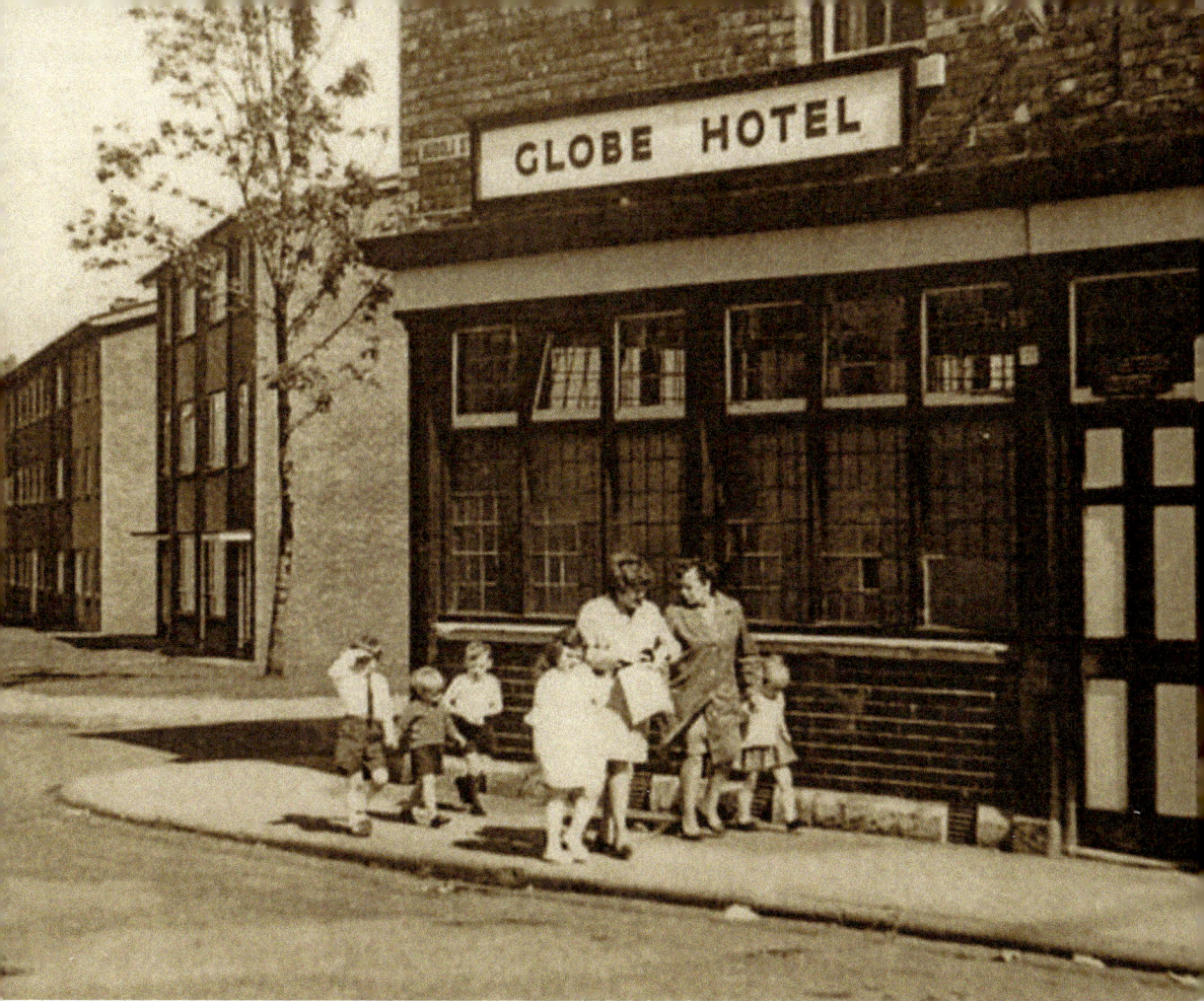

Globe Hotel, Buddle Street and Princes Street, Jarrow.

the army. Because of this, Hugh McCabe, who had been transferred from the Golden Fleece, Ferry Street, was still living at that address. The new manager of the Fleece was still at the Queen's Arms, in Union Street. George Wakenshaw was subsequently given twenty-one days to leave the Globe.

The Royal Oak

The Royal Oak on the corner of Princes Street and Stead Street was first advertised in 1885 by William Stanley, but was advertised after 1890. On Monday 8 August 1893 John Whalen and John Welsh were up before Jarrow Police Court charged with being drunk on licensed premises on the Saturday night. Both defendants admitted the charge and were fined 5s each plus costs. In addition to the above charges nine other offences were on the charge sheet, but after the usual fines these were disposed. In April 1918 Mr and Mrs McDonald, tenants of the inn, were informed their son, Sapper J. McDonald RE, was in the convalescent depot at Rouen with wounds to his right hand. The Royal Oak was demolished to make way for modern housing.

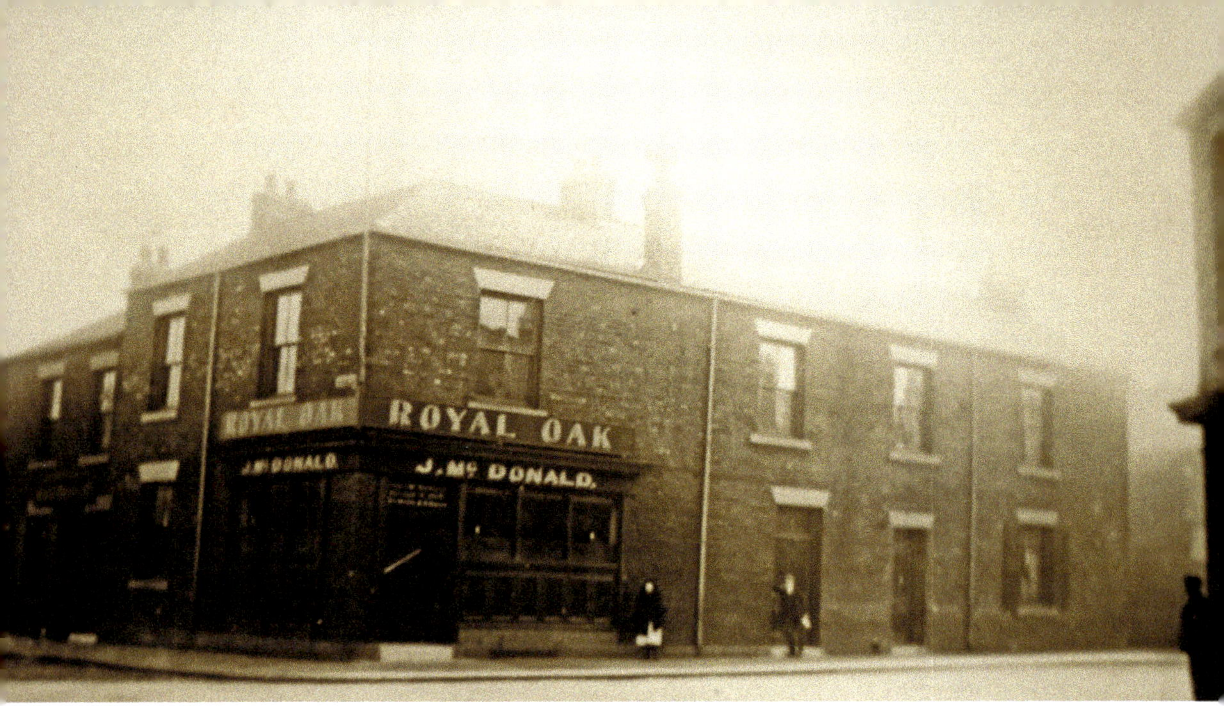

Royal Oak, Princes Street and Stead Street, Jarrow.

The Queens Head

The Queens Head, Monkton Road, Jarrow, was advertised by Peter Watson in 1859 with a Jarrow Dock address. It was not advertised again until 1873 when Hugh McGrorty, a builder, became the licensee. In March 1884 Mr J. Graham, a coroner, held an inquest into the death of Euphemia Campbell, who had died

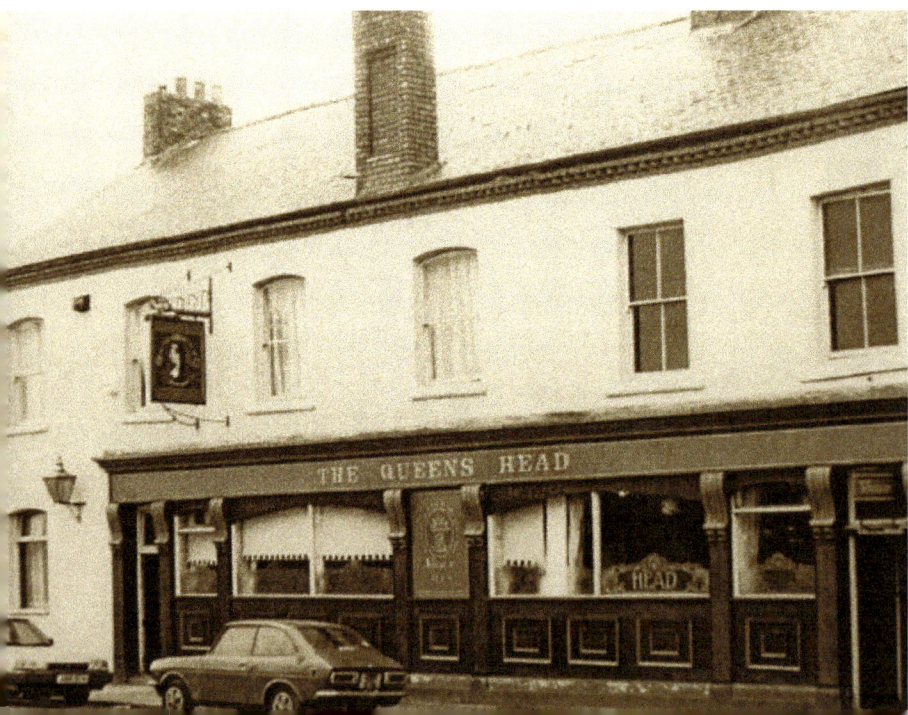

Queen's Head, Monkton Road, Jarrow.

suddenly at her home in Monkton Road early on Monday 24 March. At around five o'clock in the morning the deceased had apparently fallen out of bed, and when her husband had lifted her up, she was dead. The cause of death was given as heart disease. Richard Murray became the licensee in 1890 and it was owned by North Eastern Breweries Co. Ltd in early 1900.

The Crown & Anchor

The Crown & Anchor, Chapel Road, Jarrow, is next to St Bede's Roman Catholic Church, and the plans submitted by Herbert Clay, a builder, for a public house were approved on 12 April 1865. The Crown & Anchor was first advertised by Robert Thompson in 1871. Meetings of the St Bede's Lodge of the Oddfellows' Friendly Society (a friendly society was an organisation whose purpose was to improve people's lives through friendship, care and charitable support) met at the inn during the 1870s and 1880s. In 1890 Redmond Lockey became the licensee but by 1891 his wife had taken over. On Thursday 31 May 1891 a complimentary dinner was given at the Crown & Anchor for Joseph Horn, the late manager of the Lord Nelson Inn, on the occasion of his leaving Jarrow for Sunderland. Now the Crown & Anchor has a central bar area where it was originally split into several rooms like most of the older public houses of its time.

Crown & Anchor, Chapel Road, Jarrow.

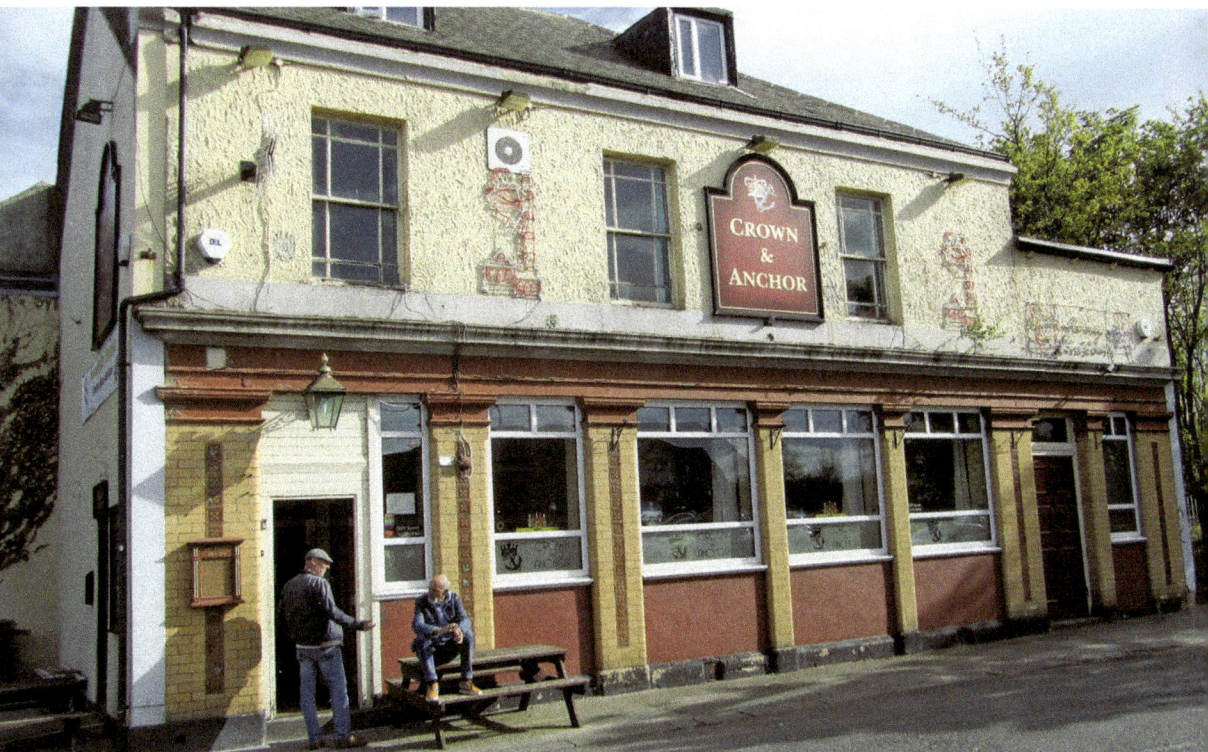

The Alexandra Hotel

The Alexandra Hotel, High Street, Jarrow, was first advertised in 1865 as the Princess Alexander Hotel by Benjamin Stone – in 1866 Benjamin called it the Alexander Inn. In November 1867 Titus Baker was in residence and held a great billiard handicap at the hotel with several of the best northern players taking part. In 1871 Titus Baker was advertising 'Ales, Wines and Spirits of the first-class quality, good stabling, hacks on hire, billiards and near the railway station'. In August 1875 Titus Baker and his wife, along with three other persons, were in an accident when driving along the High Street in a conveyance towards St Paul's Church. The horse took a fright and the carriage knocked against a wall upsetting the occupants. Mr Baker cut his head on some stones. Sadly in April 1881 Titus Baker auctioned all his surplus furniture as he was leaving Jarrow. George Blackmore took over the Alexander Hotel in 1883. In November 1884 an inquest was held in the hotel on the death of a three-year-old girl, Mary Jane Kedger, who had sadly died of convulsion brought about by the shock of being burnt. The Alexander Hotel, as named in Kelly's Directory but known as the Alexandra in Ward's Directory, changed to O'Malley's but is now known as the Alexandra Hotel.

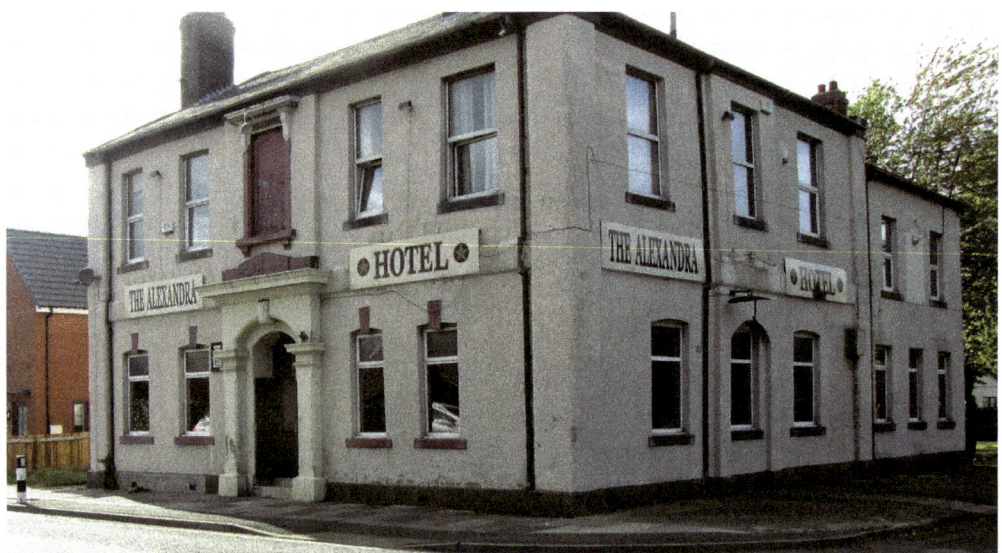

Alexandra Hotel, High Street, Jarrow.

The Duke of Wellington

The Duke of Wellington, No. 79 High Street, Jarrow, was originally called the Wellington Hotel when it was first advertised by Alexander Moffett in 1871. John Hutchinson took over the Wellington in 1875, staying until 1883 when Alexander Smithfield became the licensee, but he stayed only two years. By 1911 John Hockey had become the licensee

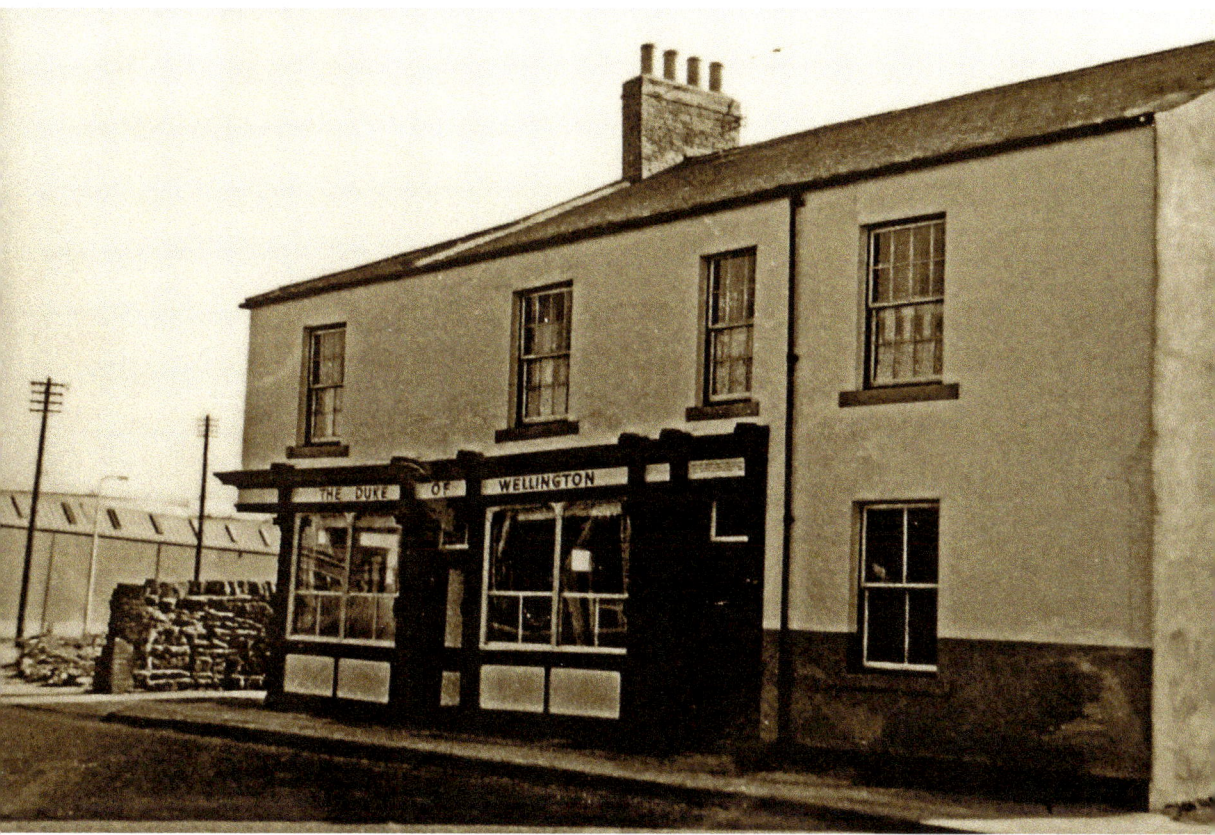

Duke of Wellington, No. 79 High Street, Jarrow.

and he started promoting the leek shows. In December 1915 a supper and smoking concert was held in connection with the No. 1 branch of the Boilermakers' Society to present Brother R. Murray, the branch secretary for sixteen years, with a silver tea and coffee service. In September 1941 James Pilkington, who had been the manager for around twelve years, died at the age of fifty-six. Renamed the Bede Ale House, it was pulled down to make way for new housing.

The East Ferry Inn

The East Ferry Inn, Jarrow Quay, was first advertised in 1859 by John Williamson, although it appears on the 1856 map of Jarrow. The brethren of the Venerable Bede Lodge, Order of Oddfellows, gave a dinner and presentation to Brother R. T. Watson PGM, a chemist, in March 1865. As a token of their respect for his exertion in promoting the welfare of the lodge, Brother Watson was presented with a framed emblem of the order. In September 1869 James Miles Favel Esq., a coroner, held an inquest into the death of William Simon Russell, seventeen. Around six o'clock on a Wednesday morning Robert Errington said he was in a boat alongside the quay

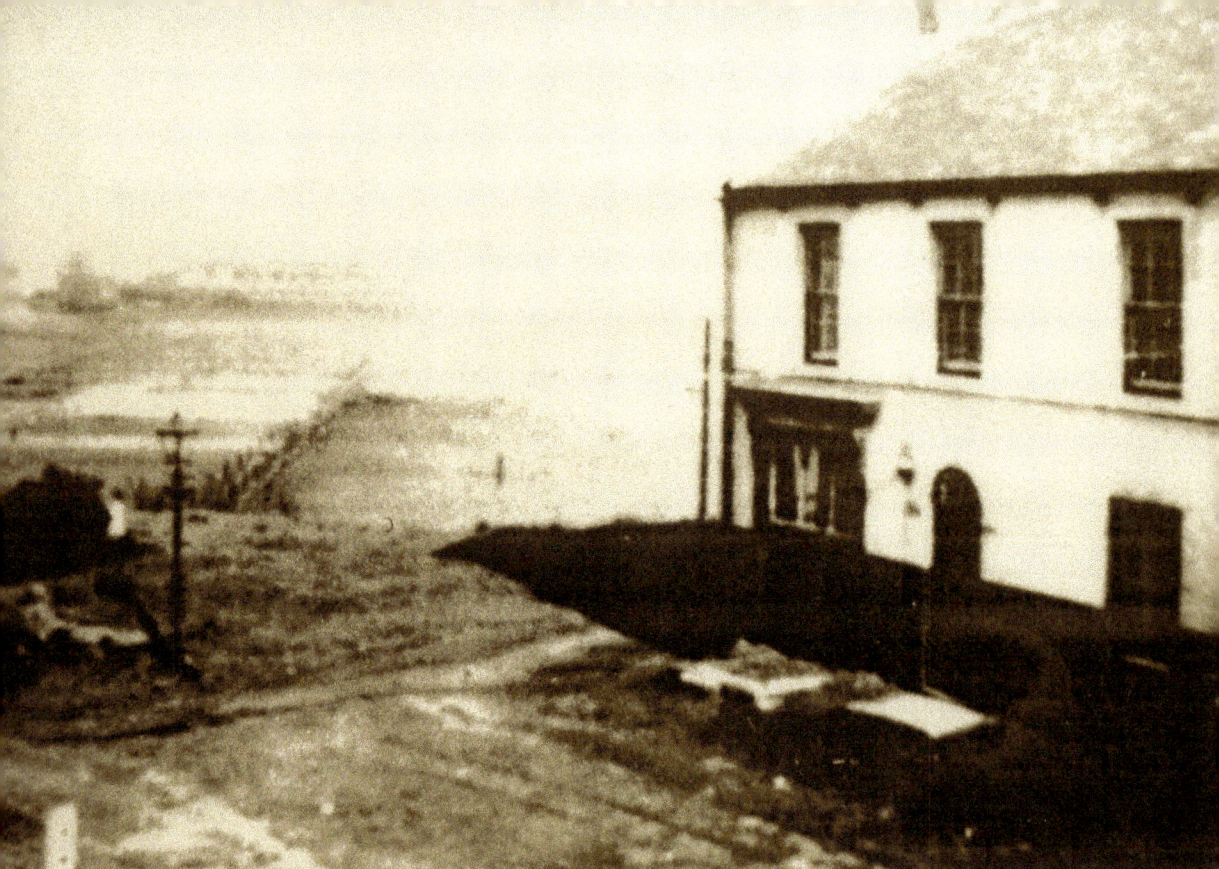

East Ferry Inn, Jarrow Quay.

when he saw William Russell push a schooner off the quayside with a hand hook. Unfortunately the hook slipped and he heard a splash; William had fallen between the schooner and the quay. Captain McKenzie, from the ship the *Gezzell of Dundee*, managed to get the deceased out from under the schooner, but not until around an hour after he had fallen. A verdict of 'accidental drowning' was given by the jury. In 1873 Elizabeth Williamson became the licensee, keeping the inn until 1885 when Robert Sutherland Moffett took over. The inn's address was East Quay Corner at that time. In 1890 Robert Samuel Moffett, possibly a son, became the licensee, running the inn for eight years. On 24 November 1898 Mr J. P. Williamson, of No. 128 Bede Burn Road, held a complimentary dinner for a few officials of Palmer's and friends at the inn, which was at the time managed by James Forsyth. Later it became known as 'Spike's', but was pulled down for the building of the Tyne Tunnel.

The Bridge Inn

The Bridge Inn (to the far left of the image) stood facing the River Don with St Paul's Church behind it. First advertised by Cornelius McConnell in 1850, the address was Jarrow Church. In 1865 Ann McConnell had taken over the licence but only stayed a few years before Thomas Black became the licensee in 1871. In April 1877 Dr Huntley from the Sanitary Committee reported that the rows of houses facing the River Don

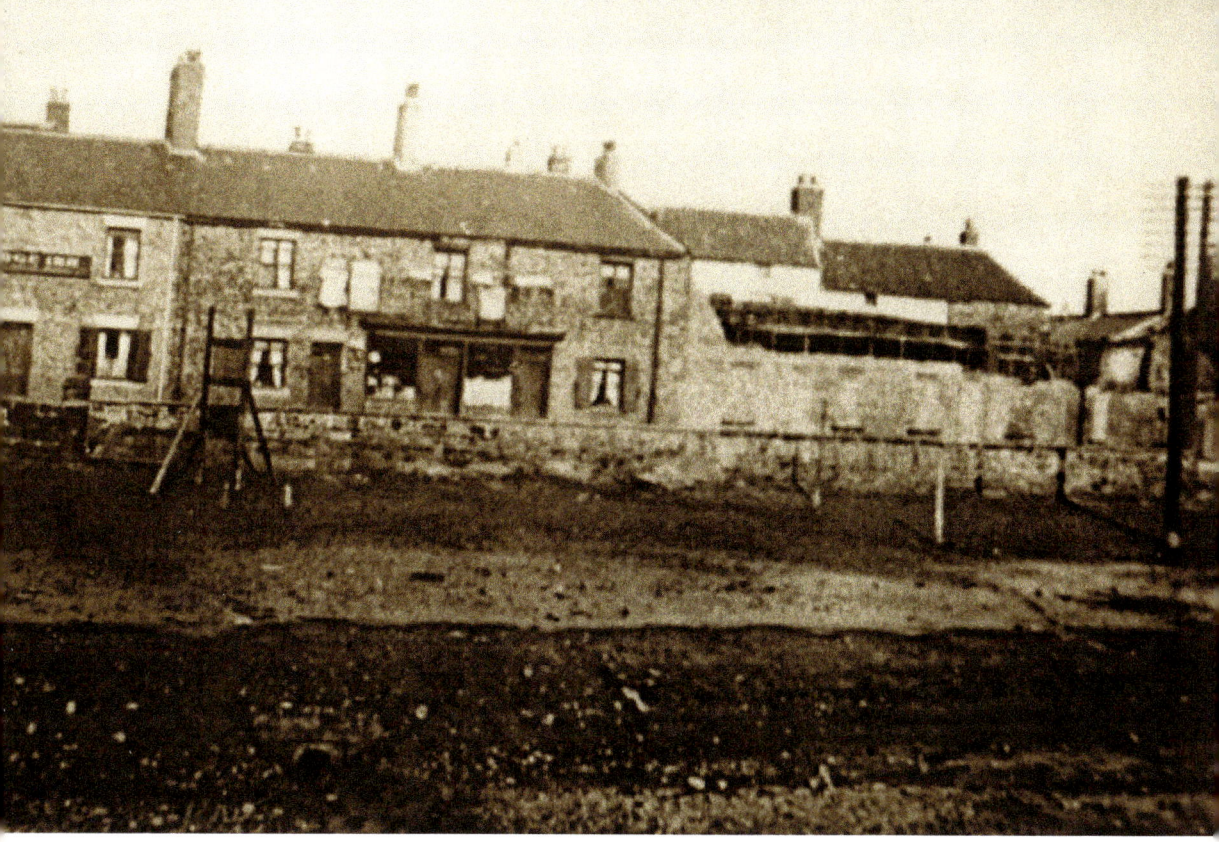

Bridge Inn, Jarrow Church, East Jarrow.

and the Bridge Inn had been certified by the medical officer of health as unfit for human habitation. Recommendations were made to serve notice on the owners to make the properties fit for human habitation. Arthur McKegney took over the tenancy of the Bridge Inn in 1881, staying as licensee until his death in March 1916, although it was not always plain sailing. In February 1884, only two weeks after being find 10s and costs for a breach of the Licensing Act, Arthur McKegney was once again in front of the Jarrow Police Court. On Sunday morning, 24 February, William Fawcett was seen knocking on the back door of the inn, which was opened a short time later by Mrs McKegney. After a short conversation, Mrs McKengey returned to the house, coming back shortly afterwards with a bottle, which she gave to Fawcett, who handed over a silver coin. Several witnesses reported this, although Fawcett and Mr McKegney denied it. The case was proven and a fine of 10s and costs or fourteen days' imprisonment was imposed. On Sunday 5 March 1916 Arthur McKegney died at the age of seventy-eight after a short illness. He was at the time the oldest licensee in the borough.

The Allison Arms

The Allison Arms was originally called the Chain & Anchor Inn, Straker Street, Jarrow, when Peter Mitford, the licensee, advertised it in 1848, the name possibly coming from the Hive Iron Works situated close by in Swinburne Street. In 1856 Jane Mitford took over the licence of the Chain & Anchor. By 1859 Richard Backhouse Close had become

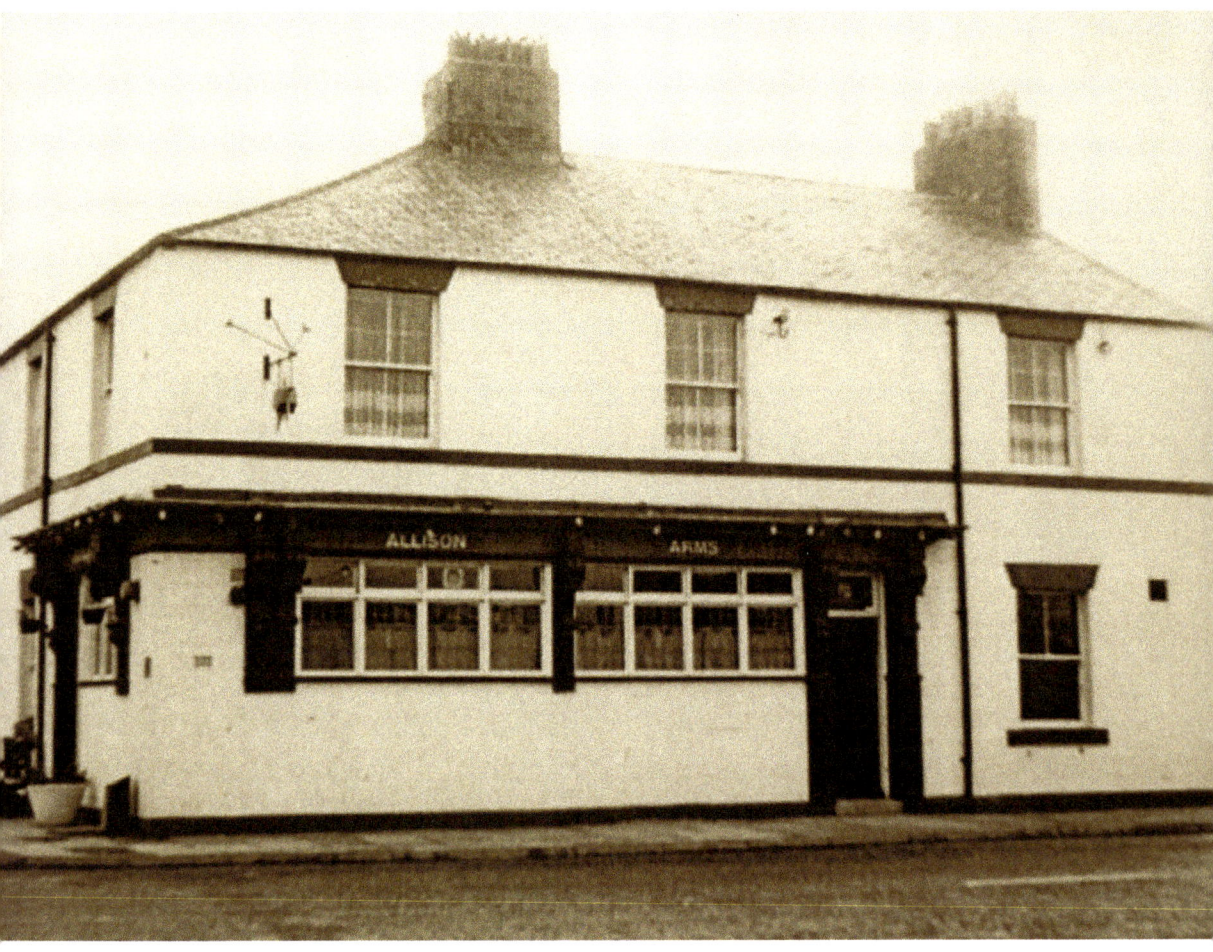

Allison Arms (originally the Chain and Anchor Inn), Straker Terrace, East Jarrow.

the licensee, renaming the public house the Anchor Inn, and by 1861 it had become the Ship & Anchor Inn. In 1871 Henry Barrasford reverted back to calling it the Chain & Anchor Inn, but in 1875 James Atkin gave it the name the Allison Arms. In January 1886 James Atkin was up before the bench for an alleged breach of the Licensing Act and was charged with selling liquor on Sunday 3rd during prohibited hours. A young girl was seen by a policeman in plain cloths coming out of the public house with a bottle in her hand, which was found to contain whiskey. At first she had said it was bought on the Saturday night, then said it was bought on the Sunday morning. Mr C. W. Newland for the defence told the court that the girl was a servant to Mr Aitkin and had paid for the whiskey on the Saturday night, which she was to take home to her mother, but having forgotten it she had returned on the Sunday to collect it. The case was dismissed. On 26 May 1887 James Atkin died, leaving a wife, Margaret. Henry Jackson took over the Allison Arms around 1890, and it was not advertised again. Pulled down around 2012, a garage now stands on the site.

Alkali Hotel

This photograph of the Alkali Hotel, Swinburne Street, East Jarrow, taken early 1920s, shows the landlord with some of the regulars – charabanc trips were common at this time. The Alkali was originally called the Straker Arms when John Lamb was the licensee in 1839. John White became the licensee in 1848 but only stayed until Hugh Moore had taken over the public house in 1850. Jane Moore then changed the name to the Alkali Hotel in 1854, possibly after the Don Alkali Works that were close by. Rebuilt in 1899, this Grade II-listed building has had quite a chequered life, having had its name changed several times over the years. Made famous by Catherine Cookson as the pub her grandfather would send her to get his jug of beer, it later became the Zenith. On Saturday 23 June 1990, having been taken over by Norman and Corinne Pinnock, there was a grand renaming, changing it back to the Alkali. This two-roomed pub was described at the time as, 'old fashioned with bar and cosy lounge, small but friendly', with not a spirit measure in the place; the customers drank double spirit measures in the form of miniature bottles. In 1994 a report of a friendly spirit had once again been spotted in the cellar and the lounge where stairs had once been. Apparently it had been seen by previous tenants but as it was friendly and a good talking point, landlord Mick Donnelly did not mind. Unfortunately the Alkali lost its battle to stay a public house and is now a children's nursery.

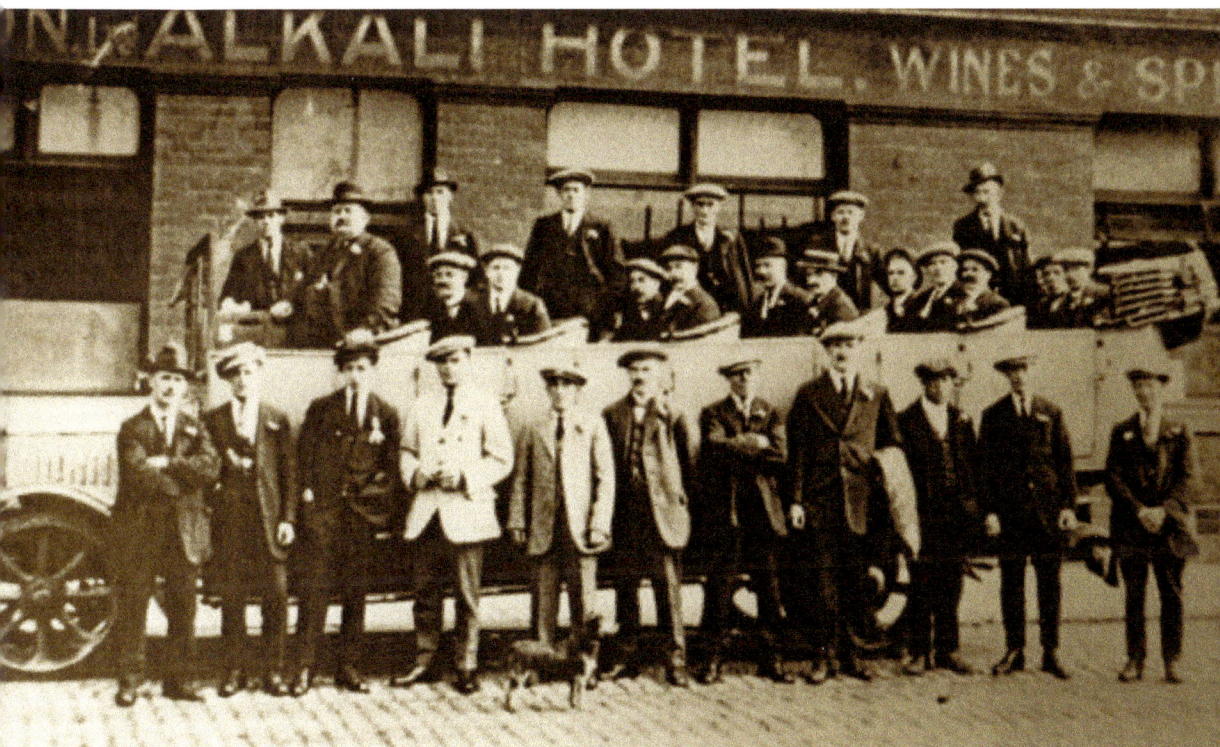

Alkali Hotel, Swinburne Street, East Jarrow.

Acknowledgements

I would like to thank Richard Purvis for the advice he gave me while I was writing this book. I would like to thank Catrin Galt of The Word, South Tyneside Library, for giving permission to use photographs from their collections donated by unknown photographers. Also thanks to Julian Harrop of Beamish Open Air Museum of the North for giving me access and permission to use photographs from their collection; to Winnie Curry and members of Jarrow and Hebburn local History Group for their help and permission to use their photographs; and to Jenifer Bell of Gateshead Library for her permission to use photographs from their collection.

I am also grateful to a number of landlords for allowing internal photographs to be taken of their establishments and being so helpful.

Photographs from South Tyneside Library: Argyle Hotel, Station Hotel, and Ellison Arms Hotel in Hebburn; Rolling Mill Hotel, Queen's Hotel, North Eastern Hotel, Station Hotel, Ellison Arms, Bell Rock Hotel, The Cottage, Borough Arms, County Hotel, Golden Fleece, Ferry Street, Commercial Hotel, Staith House, The Queen's Head, Bridge Inn, Allison Arms, the Alkali in Jarrow; and the Alexander Hotel in East Jarrow.

Photographs courtesy of Beamish, the Living Museum of the North: The Highlander, Whitburn; the Railway Tavern, West Boldon; the Colliery Tavern, Boldon Colliery; the Lord Nelson, Monkton village; and the Halfway House, Felling.

Photographs courtesy of Jarrow and Hebburn Local History Group: The Ship Inn, Cleadon village, and Alnwick Castle Hotel, Royal Hotel, Royal Engineer Hotel, Lord Nelson, Prince of Wales Hotel, Golden Fleece, Pit Heap, Globe Hotel, Royal Oak, Duke of Wellington, and the East Ferry Inn in Jarrow.

Photographs courtesy of Gateshead Library: Blink Bonny and Mulberry Tree Inn, Felling, Felling Shore; and the Albion, Bill Quay.